About the author

Award-winning foreign correspondent Irris Makler has been based in the Middle East for nine years. She has filed stories from Jerusalem, Baghdad and Cairo for radio, television and online news services around the world. Previously based in Moscow and London, Irris reported extensively from Afghanistan as one of the first journalists on the scene after 9/11. She wrote about these experiences in the highly acclaimed *Our Woman In Kabul*.

Irris has always been interested in the stories women can tell, and what affects their day-to-day lives. Before becoming a journalist, she was a lawyer. She has a good ear for languages and a cast-iron stomach – two out of three requirements for doing her job. Unfortunately, she has no sense of direction.

Hope Street, Jerusalem

IRRIS MAKLER

HarperCollins*Publishers*

HarperCollins*Publishers*
First published in Australia in 2012
by HarperCollins*Publishers* Australia Pty Limited
ABN 36 009 913 517
harpercollins.com.au

Copyright © Irris Makler 2012

The right of Irris Makler to be identified as the author of this work has been asserted by her in
accordance with the Copyright Amendment (Moral Rights) Act 2000.

HarperCollins*Publishers*
Level 13, 201 Elizabeth Street, Sydney NSW 2000, Australia
31 View Road, Glenfield, Auckland 0627, New Zealand
A 53, Sector 57, Noida, UP, India
77–85 Fulham Palace Road, London W6 8JB, United Kingdom
2 Bloor Street East, 20th floor, Toronto, Ontario M4W 1A8, Canada
10 East 53rd Street, New York NY 10022, USA

National Library of Australia Cataloguing-in-Publication data:

Makler, Irris.
   Hope Street, Jerusalem / Irris Makler.
   ISBN 978 0 7322 9416 8 (pbk)
   Women journalists – Israel – Biography.
   Women journalists – Australia – Biography.
   Jerusalem – Biography – Anecdotes.
070.92

Cover design by Matt Stanton, HarperCollins Design Studio
Cover image by Kevin Dutton / Getty Images
Typeset in Baskerville by Kirby Jones
Printed and bound in Australia by Griffin Press
The papers used by HarperCollins in the manufacture of this book are a natural, recyclable product
made from wood grown in sustainable plantation forests. The fibre source and manufacturing
processes meet recognised international environmental standards, and carry certification.

5 4 3 2 1   12 13 14 15

For Rami

1

25 October 2009, Jerusalem

Nothing was out of the ordinary on the day that trouble hit me, or picked me, or I got in its way, depending how you see it. It was a warm, sleepy Sunday morning in autumn, and I was on my way to the Old City, a 3,000-year-old walled town in the centre of modern-day Jerusalem. There were reports of rioting, and I was heading towards the danger, but that's part of the strange reality of being a journalist, running towards locations most people are running away from. I'd been covering protests in Jerusalem for months, so why should this morning be any different? I had no premonition that something was about to smash into me and mark me for life.

I parked in my regular spot outside the Old City walls, grabbed my recording equipment and raced down the street, in a hurry to keep my appointment with fate.

Palestinian women in dark dresses and white headscarves were sitting on the pavement, home-grown vine leaves, herbs and olives laid out on plastic sheets in front of them. I swerved to avoid them. Arabic music blared out of watch-repair stores. The sun was warm on my skin, and one of Oum Kalthoum's passionate, pain-filled songs followed me along the pavement. *I thought it was a greeting, but it was only a glance* ... A cafe was grinding coffee beans with cardamon, a scent to match the song. Autumn was the kindest season in Jerusalem, the air dry, the sun gentle. I was on my way to a riot but I couldn't help smiling.

The walls of the Old City loomed ahead of me. They enclosed an area of 2.5 kilometres square. Until 1860, this had been the entire city. Its gates were locked at night to keep out brigands, and to protect the inhabitants and the holy sites sacred to three religions. As I walked through the thick sandstone walls, via the grand Herod's Gate, I felt I'd been transported hundreds of years back in time, or further back, to the time of legend.

Modern-day Jerusalem disappeared, and was replaced by a bustling Middle Eastern souk nestled in amongst churches, synagogues and mosques. Stalls overflowed with jewellery, silver, gold, precious stones, lengths of glittering material, embroidered cloth, clothes, shoes, baskets of spices, beads, candles, perfumed oils, incense and crucifixes; the profusion part of the pleasure.

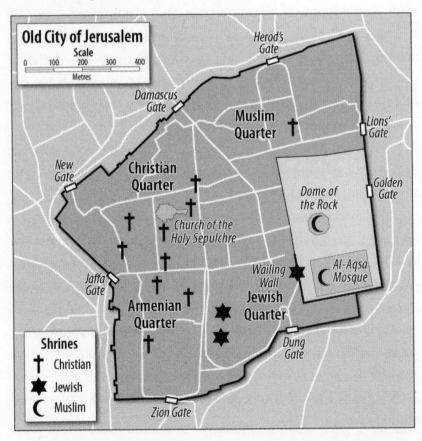

Muslims, Christians and Jews live in houses above the market, higgledy-piggedly apartments shared by many generations of each family, just as they have since the time of Jesus. They have lived side by side, and fought each other, bloody upheavals followed by periods of wary coexistence, an unchanging pattern over two thousand years. In this tiny area, Jews believe the Jewish Temple once stood, Christians believe that Christ was crucified and resurrected, and Muslims believe that the Prophet Mohammed ascended to heaven. You could sit where King David played his harp; you could walk in Christ's footsteps, along the Via Dolorosa; you could pray at the Rock where the Prophet Mohammed had stood before he rode to heaven on a horse travelling on a beam of light. No wonder they ended up fighting.

I pushed down a narrow cobbled path, inhaling the scents of rosewater and frankincense, rotting vegetables and animal dung. Donkeys trudged by, pulling wooden carts, forcing me to flatten myself against a wall. A Palestinian boy was perched on a tyre behind each cart, a small human ballast to stop it sliding too quickly down the stones, worn smooth by centuries of pilgrims.

People were drawn here from all over the world. That morning I pressed my way through a group of tourists from India. As the carts passed by, women wearing red and pink saris pushed themselves against the opposite wall, which was strung with gold crucifixes and brass discs. The angle and the colours made them appear like part of the display, beautiful dark-skinned Russian icons. We smiled at each other over the donkeys' ears. Shopkeepers yelled a phrase they knew in six or seven languages, 'For you my friend, a very special price!' Their voices harmonised with the tapping of the donkey's hooves, the pealing of church bells and the mesmerising staccato cry of the Muslim call to prayer, the pauses as important as the song. After the carts passed, I reminded myself I had a riot to get to and forced my way down the path, juggling my equipment.

My destination was the Al-Aqsa Mosque, the third holiest site in Islam. It is set on a raised square, a grand, beautiful, spare space which in fact housed two mosques, Al-Aqsa itself and the golden Dome of the Rock, built above the boulder where the Prophet Mohammed had stood. Some worshippers believe you can see the mark left by his shoe. The elegant eight-sided building is covered in blue and turquoise tiles, echoing the colour of the sky. Its golden dome reflects the sun, and it is still the defining image of Jerusalem more than thirteen centuries after it was built.

At the other end of the compound sits the holiest site in Judaism. The Western Wall is the last remaining structure to mark the spot where the Jewish Temple had once stood. In Jerusalem, each new conqueror triumphantly took over or – better yet – destroyed his rival's house of worship and erected his own in its place. The Muslims had built their mosque on the ruins of the Jewish Temple. It's why everything was so entwined, and peace was so elusive here in the City of Peace.

I reached the large wooden gate at the entrance to the Al-Aqsa compound to find it shut – walls within walls. Israeli border police and Muslim worshippers were milling outside the gate. They were not engaging with each other. There were also dozens of journalists and TV crews. The atmosphere was tense but not threatening. I heard stun grenades, apparently from inside the closed compound. There was no tear gas. Only one cameraman was wearing a helmet.

I recorded interviews with the Muslim men who arrived for midday prayers but had been prevented from going in to worship. Israeli authorities, in control of the city since 1967, had shut the compound because they anticipated violence. As often happened here, expecting trouble created trouble. I filed a radio story on the spot, back into breakfast news programs in Canada, as I was working for the Canadian public broadcaster, CBC, that morning.

Narrow alleyways radiated off from the square, where the crowd of angry worshippers stood. In one of the alleys, between flat-roofed sandstone buildings leading to the Lions' Gate, about a dozen young Palestinians were running and shouting. Their faces were covered, some with black-and-white checked keffiyehs, others with balaclavas. Israeli police in black uniforms with riot gear were only fifty metres away but they still weren't engaging with the demonstrators. The young men in the alley began burning rubbish and throwing stones. A cynic might say that they were performing for the media. Performance or not, it was now news. I went closer to record some sound.

Shopkeepers hastily pulled down their roller doors, one after another, bam, bam, bam, as they watched the situation develop. I hugged the wall in front of one of the closed shops, and stood under a balcony for added protection. The youths burning rubbish were forty metres ahead of me. Halfway up the alley, about twenty metres ahead, there was a group of journalists. Small stones skimmed the ground. A Palestinian photographer picked up a plastic chair and put it over his head as he ran forward. He gestured to a friend to do the same. Since I was working for radio that day and didn't need pictures, I stayed where I was. It was safer. Cameramen and photographers don't have the option of staying back, that's why so many of them get killed.

The Israeli police were standing behind me, gossiping. I stood in my protected spot recording the stones clattering past my microphone. After less than a minute, I became aware that the rhythm was changing. The stones were getting more frequent, louder and larger, and turning into fist-sized rocks. It was time to go.

As I turned, the rock with my name on it finally struck. I was still under the balcony when it caught me – in the face. It was a head-snapping blow and I reeled from the force of it. Everything went black for a moment. The rock hadn't bounced up from below, like the small stones I'd been recording. It had come in from above. I put my hand up to my face and felt blood. There was a large gash and my lower jaw felt wobbly. I was spitting blood in a stream.

I looked up and saw young Palestinians running along the roof opposite, hurling rocks down into the alley. Thousands of years ago it was these flat roofs that gave birth to the expression 'Shout it from the rooftops', areas good for communicating, or for attacking the people beneath. Fighting over this small city has a long history. I had just become part of it.

It's easy to forget that life can change in an instant, that you can fall in love or discover you have cancer in the space of a morning, and that after that morning you are never the same. It was such a close-run thing. I could have walked on unscathed, back to my life as it was before, back to my car and to my office, grumbling about the traffic as I rushed to meet my next deadline. And if I hadn't turned my head at that precise moment, the rock could have caught me front on, in the skull, or in my nose or eyes, instead of my jaw. I was wearing sunglasses. Doctors could have been picking glass and plastic out of my eyes for months to come. I saw all the possibilities clearly, like a film unwinding in my head. I didn't want to say to myself that I could have been brain-damaged, or that I could have been killed.

I felt relief as I put one foot in front of the other and was able to walk by myself. I was aware of shock rather than pain as I ticked off the good points. *I haven't lost consciousness and I don't feel nauseous.* When I reached the crowd of police, journalists and worshippers ten metres away, a small distance that seemed vast, I sat down heavily on a step and felt my jaw lurch sideways, as if it were no longer connected to my skull. A TV cameraman was filming me when paramedics appeared from nowhere. Their ambulance was nearby, waiting to help people wounded in the riots. Was that really me? I insisted on walking without assistance and only remembered to turn off my recording equipment when we reached the vehicle. I was rolling the whole time. Perhaps one day I will have the nerve to listen to it.

The ambulance was old and shabby. It belonged to the Red Crescent, the Muslim affiliate of the Red Cross. The crew were

Palestinian, a male paramedic and a female medical student. They strapped me onto a trolley with a short, dirty sheet and told me to lie down so they could drive me to the nearest Israeli hospital. We sped off, siren wailing, but I was afraid to lie flat for it felt as if I were drowning – was that blood going down my throat? I half lay, half sat, as the ambulance bounced and jolted to the hospital at Mount Scopus.

I thought about my mother in Australia and how worried she would be. My boyfriend in Tel Aviv, and my pretty, patient dog waiting at home for her walk. I felt the sting of tears for the first time. A job like this takes a terrible toll on the people who love you. The dog was the only one I wouldn't have to explain myself to.

In the past I had flirted with danger, dancing around her. She had appeared indifferent. Today she had finally taken a step towards me. She hadn't picked me for all time, I wasn't *the* one, but now I knew what it would be like when she desired me too. I'd always felt lucky, sometimes superstitiously so, when other journalists were kidnapped and killed and nothing happened to me. I had returned safely from Iraq, Afghanistan, and Gaza, but here in this familiar location my luck had finally run out.

The ambulance rounded a corner and I clung to the trolley to stay upright, but another lurch of the vehicle nearly threw me off altogether. It took five minutes of wild driving to reach the hospital. We then spent a further ten minutes at the gate while the Israeli guard reviewed the ID of the Palestinian ambulance staff, taking his time over each one. The driver was furious.

'This is bullshit. It wouldn't happen to an Israeli crew.'

When we were finally allowed in, they wheeled my trolley into the Emergency unit. The Israeli charge nurse was a plump woman in her sixties, whose brown hair was streaked with grey. She was wearing theatre greens, as if she had just come out of surgery. She had kind eyes and a tired face, and spoke to the Palestinian paramedics in the tone you generally reserve for a child with learning difficulties.

'Why did you bring her here? What's wrong with her?'

She paused and looked at them, answering her own question.

'It's her jaw isn't it?'

She paused again.

'And do we have a Mouth and Jaw department here? Do we? No, we don't. So where should you have taken her?'

The paramedics, stung by her tone, and the interrogation at the gate, responded angrily.

'We were obeying the rules! We have to take a wounded person to the nearest hospital.'

The Israeli nurse resumed speaking even more slowly.

'Let's try again. What's wrong with her? It's her jaw. And do we have a Mouth and Jaw department here? No, we don't. So where should you have taken her?'

'We did what we have been instructed to do, and we won't take her anywhere else!' The Palestinian ambulance driver folded his arms across his chest. 'And while we're at it, what was with that reception at the front gate? Do you think this is Gaza or what?'

They had all momentarily forgotten me as they pursued their conflict right over the top of my bleeding body. I struggled to sit upright, to tell them that I wanted to go to the right hospital as soon as possible. I was frightened and now also in pain, but that seemed to be irrelevant. The staff responsible for treating me couldn't resist the old antagonisms, a form of communication some people here could slip into in an instant. No one listened to me.

I closed my eyes for a moment and swallowed the blood coursing down my throat, fighting against tears. I felt lonely and vulnerable and wasn't sure I had the strength for this struggle. I gave in to a tug of self-pity. What was I doing here?

2

There are many positions of greater authority and renown within and without the British Empire, but in a sense I cannot explain, there is no promotion after Jerusalem.

Sir Ronald Storrs, British Governor of Jerusalem, *Orientations*, 1937

The air was humid and gritty and alternately hot and cold when I flew into Tel Aviv, on a grey spring evening in 2002. At the airport, an Israeli taxi driver in his sixties shepherded me towards his cab, talking non-stop, as if he'd found a long-lost sister. I wheeled my bags tiredly behind him.

Too many drivers, not enough friends. That was my verdict on my life, as I slung my suitcases into the boot of yet another cab, in yet another dangerous location.

'This weather is strange,' said the driver, surveying the sultry sky. 'Like the politics.'

He wanted to be my new best friend, he wanted to rip me off, and he couldn't see why one should contradict the other.

He began cross-examining me before I'd shut the door.

I guess I shouldn't have been surprised that catching a cab in Israel involved an interrogation session, but it had been a long flight and I was tired. I was also too flustered to answer his questions, since I wasn't sure of the exact address of the friend I was on my way to. Alright, I confess: I am as disorganised as the next journalist. I emptied my backpack onto the back seat beside me. As I hunted for the piece of paper with the address scribbled on it, I admitted that I was a reporter. Revealing your name, rank and serial number was permissible. The driver asked if I'd been to Afghanistan and barely waited for me to reply that I had before moving directly to the crucial issue that raised.

'Are you married?'

I looked up from my search. His eyes met mine in the rear-view mirror and he answered his own question.

'No, of course you're not. You couldn't have a husband. No one would put up with you being away so much.'

He stared at me pityingly over his shoulder.

I looked at him closely for the first time. He had a florid complexion and was heavy-set. He was wearing a tight shirt with too many buttons undone exposing grey chest hair. Chunky gold jewellery nestled there, and he wore matching gold-framed sunglasses with graded lenses. Even seated, he seemed to have a swagger. I gave up searching for the address and told him that male correspondents went away from home just as much and they didn't have trouble getting married.

'Men even have women lining up to marry them when they are in prison. Murderers get married in jail!'

'Yes, but who would marry you?' he retorted. 'You're never home!'

Obviously being a busy woman was worse than being a murderer.

The cab sped up the highway to Jerusalem and I looked out the window. That was enough conversation for now. The brightly coloured bougainvillea near the airport had given way to fields farmed in neat green patches. The road climbed into the mountains and the air became cooler. The fields were replaced by groves of grey-green olive trees. From that first encounter, I sensed that living in Israel had the potential to be exhausting, but I had no notion of how consuming, cruel and dangerous it would turn out to be.

When we reached Jerusalem, I heaved my suitcases out of the trunk – apparently women no one will marry don't need help with their bags – paid the driver and headed indoors to see my old friend, seething and laughing at once.

Jerusalem, the city sacred to both sides, and claimed by both as their capital, was home to around half a million Jews, a quarter of a million Muslims, and a sprinkling of everyone else. My first impression was that it was too small to be this famous – like meeting a supermodel whose face you know from magazines and billboards and finding that she's the size of a skinny twelve-year-old. The Jerusalem I saw was a sleepy mountain town, small and poor. Its sacred core was mysterious and beautiful, but overall there was somehow less to it than you expected. *Could they really be fighting over this?*

It was also very tribal. People in an array of costumes crossed my path. The ultra-Orthodox Jews were a study in black. The men wore black silk coats and dark, furry round hats over closely shaven heads. The only hair allowed to grow long was their side curls. Their costume and their beards were reminiscent of the Amish, another people who lived guided by the past. Their wives also wore black – long outfits covering everything except their face and hands, their hair concealed by scarves or wigs. They had large numbers of children, whose clothes were dark too, and their small faces pale.

The ultra-Orthodox lived in their own suburbs and chased out anyone who didn't obey their strict religious rules. On the other side of town, where the Palestinians lived, some older men still wore the traditional garb of long pale cotton smocks, very practical in the heat, with a black-and-white checked keffiyeh on their heads. Younger Palestinian men, though, had gone Western, and many were sharp dressers. Their hair was gelled, their shoes pointy and their jeans tight. Religiously observant Palestinian women wore dark coat-dresses and white headscarves, but many younger women matched their headscarves with jeans and figure-hugging tops. They were modest but head-turning.

Secular people on both sides wore whatever they wanted, in all the colours of the rainbow. In the everlasting summer, Israeli women wore very little, showing off curvy figures, long hair and longer legs. Hair was a sensual subset all its own; it seemed that everywhere there were heavy dark manes of curls, tumbling down over shoulders, or pinned up seductively and threatening to fall under their weight, a temporarily leashed allure. It was such a voluptuous presence that fearful rabbis and imams insisted on covering it up. In fact, Israelis and Palestinians were both attractive; heartbreakers actually. They looked similar, like cousins, dark-haired, good-looking cousins who detested each other.

Everything seemed intense. The sun. The heat. The flavours of the food. People raised their voices and grabbed your arm when they spoke. They cried openly. Feelings were fierce. Love of land, love of tribe, and hatred all went deep. Sometimes the hatred was a force field.

Both Israeli and Palestinian poets refer to this as a burning land, and my first impression was that the two sides were going up in flames. 'Israelis and Palestinians are going to hell – together,' a Palestinian politician sombrely explained to me. Not long after I arrived, a suicide bombing took place near Jerusalem's main fruit and vegetable market. Six people died and dozens more were injured when a Palestinian woman blew herself up at a bus stop outside the market. There was pulp everywhere, blood and flesh mingling with strawberries and tomatoes. It was horrible. An Israeli doctor who had been doing his shopping stopped to help the wounded. When the rescue services arrived and freed him to return to his ordinary life, he told me a story from the Old Testament.

'Before the Children of Israel entered the Promised Land, Moses sent twelve emissaries, one from each tribe, as scouts, to look around the Land of Canaan. Ten of the twelve came back and advised against entering, describing it as "a land that devours its inhabitants". That's what this is …' he said despairingly, gesturing at our surroundings.

It was a strong description but I recall it also because he was the first person to present a story from his Holy Book to help explain what was happening today. It was to become a common experience, underscoring how crucial religion is here. Jerusalem was its wellspring and everything circled and came back to that.

It didn't matter that most historians agreed that the Via Dolorosa, where Christ had walked carrying His cross, was probably somewhere else, or that despite determined digging, there was no archaeological evidence of King David here in David's city. Nor that in the early accounts, Al-Aqsa – 'the far mosque' – hadn't been very significant in Muslim history. It was what people believed, and that was more powerful than any other force.

In the spring of 2002, the Old City souk was almost empty. Tourists had been frightened away by the bloodshed, and many stalls were shut. The few that were open did no business. Their morose owners sat and drank coffee, pretending they had a job so they had a reason to get up in the morning. I walked unknowingly along the same path where I would one day be injured. Strolling behind priests wearing black robes, their long hair tied up in buns beneath black square hats, carrying silver containers of smouldering incense, I felt it could have been one hundred years ago – or it could have been one thousand. It was easy to imagine turning a corner and seeing Jesus. Or the Prophet Mohammed on his winged horse. Or King Solomon, who was so wise they say he understood the conversations of animals.

Sometimes the bright light bouncing off the white stones caused visitors to believe they really could see all these historical and religious figures. When they started talking to them, they were diagnosed with a psychosis called 'Jerusalem syndrome' and whisked off to a specially assigned ward in a psychiatric hospital, where they could rest till they got over it.

I found that phenomenon so remarkable I went to do a story. I was brought up in a Jewish family but I had been an atheist for as long as I

13

could remember, and I found the psychiatric hospital, and Jerusalem, fundamentally mystifying. My time in the Middle East would be about learning to see through a new lens, to hear in a different register.

At the psych ward, doctors explained that Jerusalem syndrome awakened in ordinary tourists the belief that they were the Messiah. In fact, the hospital frequently had more than one Messiah in at a time. The men – and it was most often men – coped magnificently. They banded together without conflict, recognising One amongst them as the Alpha Messiah, the Top God, and fell in behind him, to help with his vital work in Jerusalem.

'It's a fine line, isn't it? When you talk to God you're religious. But when God talks to you, you're crazy,' the psychiatrist in charge said cheerily. 'Most of them get better with time; some of them are very intelligent people. I am still in contact with one of them more than twenty years later, after he returned to Europe.'

The psychiatrist, a large, clever, good-natured man, spoke at a breakneck pace, barely drawing breath. After a while I started wondering whether the lengthy exposure to messiahs hadn't begun to affect him too.

Maybe he was right and it was a short-lived physiological response, or maybe the air here was different. The water in the nearby Dead Sea, the lowest spot on earth, was not like ordinary water. It was hot and oily and so full of minerals and salts that no fish survived and no person could swim in it. On it, well, that was a different matter. Tourists brought newspapers and lay back reading, testing that strange H_2O that allowed you only to float on top. Perhaps the air above Jerusalem was not ordinary air, and like the Dead Sea water it had its own combination of currents and perfumes.

Jerusalem always had the power to make men mad.

Nothing's changed.

* * *

It wasn't an obvious straight line that led me here. The road to Jerusalem had started in Moscow and curled around Kabul and Baghdad. No foreign correspondent led a normal life after 9/11, it was the pivot point for us all. I was in Moscow during the Al-Qaeda attacks in 2001 and two weeks later I was one of the first journalists into Afghanistan. I stayed for three long, hard months and returned to Moscow exhausted.

It had been a warm Indian summer when I'd left in September. Now Moscow was covered in snow. In the morning when I walked across the courtyard of my apartment building, mine were the first footprints in the fresh snow. A cat hurried lightly by, his paw prints a small neat track near mine. Snowflakes fell into the coffee cup I was carrying. Russian pleasures. But after the demands of Afghanistan, I experienced an overwhelming desire for sunshine, and love. For Home. I put my things in storage, left freezing Moscow and flew to Sydney.

At last I was back, hugging my mother, inhaling the familiar scent of gum trees, salt water and traffic, and holding my face up to the sun. I saw family and friends, ate good food, and took my small nephew to the beach. We swam in rock pools, counted seagulls and built sand castles which the tide swept away. In Afghanistan I had worn long loose clothes and covered my hair, and no one could stop staring, simply because they could see my face. Here on the beach, no one looked particularly, and the normality revived me. I wished that golden summer could last forever, but once the days began to shorten, I had to decide where to go next.

Like all freelancers, I was always chasing work. A slow story, one that had gone off the boil, meant there was no way to pay the bills. Volume dictated your destination, and you had to be flexible and nimble. It helped to be 'unencumbered', without a husband or children or pets to consider. If Moscow was now quiet, it made sense to go to where the story was hot. I had a visa for Tehran, but in 2002 Jerusalem was the story. The city was literally exploding.

The Palestinian uprising known as the Second Intifada was at its height. There were suicide attacks across Israeli cities, with bombs going off in buses and restaurants. Israel began its largest military operation since the 1967 war, re-occupying the main Palestinian towns in the West Bank. Tourists cancelled their holidays. Christians abandoned their pilgrimages. The only people fighting to get in were journalists.

A friend from Moscow, Orla Guerin, was working there as a correspondent for the BBC. She invited me to come and stay and promised to show me the ropes. I decided to go where the doors were opening. Why not try sunny, newsy Israel for a short spell? It might work out and it might not, but it was worth giving it a go for a month or two and seeing how I fared. A life-changing decision made unknowingly, almost on a whim.

It was Orla's address I'd been searching for in the taxi on my first evening. A slender, brilliant Irishwoman, she had tawny curls framing a narrow face – a 1940s face, I used to think when I watched her on television before I'd met her. Orla possessed razor-sharp political acumen and great humanity, a rare double in TV news and, along with her Irish lilt, it set her reporting apart. She was one of the finest war reporters of her generation, and also called it like she saw it, which gave her stories great force. There was nothing cautious or mealy-mouthed about her work. It was out on the edge. You either loved it or you hated it, but you never forgot it.

Her apartment was on the top floor of a beautifully restored nineteenth-century Ottoman-style house, with high ceilings and exposed sandstone walls. It was very different to the shabby Soviet-era apartments we'd rented in Moscow, but I found Orla unchanged, apart from an even larger collection of frothy scarves and spangly flat sandals.

'They are all airport purchases,' she said. 'I never have time to shop anywhere else.'

And then, noticing that I couldn't take my eyes off a pair of sky-blue rhinestone sandals shimmering invitingly, she said, like an American cop, 'Step away from the shoes.'

We'd first met on a plane flying from Moscow to the Arctic city of Murmansk in August 2000, after a Russian nuclear submarine sank in the Barents Sea. One hundred and eighteen Russian sailors were trapped on the seabed in an aging sub. Some were believed to be still alive. The passengers on our Aeroflot flight smoked furiously. The stewardess was wearing a fur coat, matched with kitten-heeled stilettos as a concession to the summer. The woman sitting in the seat in front of us sobbed the whole way to Murmansk. She turned out to be the girlfriend of one of the sailors, and she was right to cry. No one saved those men.

A letter recovered weeks later, after the sub was finally raised, confirmed the relatives' worst fears. Twenty-three men had survived and waited for rescue. Dimitri Kolesnikov, the son of a submariner, wrote entries in his journal. He penned his last one in the dark. 'I am writing this blind,' he said, and they were still waiting, blind, while their government dithered and their air ran out. I shuddered imagining that terrible end. The fear, the bitter, black cold, the last painful breath.

Though we met on such a harrowing story, Orla and I quickly became firm friends. On screen, she appeared serious, but in real life, as I soon discovered, she was mischievous and quicksilver fast, possessing that Irish talent for 'the craic'. A year later, when she left Moscow for her next posting to Jerusalem, I understood my job in a new way. You finally made a real friend in a new city and they left. The Correspondent's Lament.

Now two years later, I had the odd feeling that I was following Orla, drawn by an invisible cord behind her, as much as by the pull of the story. I worked from her airy sandstone apartment and hired a car to travel around Israel and the West Bank. I stuck the letters

'TV' in silver gaffer tape on my windows, hoping this would protect me from Israeli and Palestinian bullets alike. I didn't know then that the car was basically uninsured in the Palestinian areas and blithely drove it everywhere – down the main West Bank highway, Route 60, a good road through wild, rocky terrain; down small, dusty gravel tracks when the main road was blocked by Israeli tanks and military vehicles.

The West Bank is still largely rural and to someone with an Australian eye, it is tiny. It seemed that as soon as you put your foot on the gas you hit a border. Like both sides said, there was too much history here, not enough geography. The one thing there was in abundance was fascinating, passionate people.

Everywhere I met intelligent, wilful, gruff, kind, opinionated, dynamic people, and I could have sat for hours with each of them. Italian author Italo Calvino observed that the end of World War II unlocked a stream of storytelling across Europe. Talking became a compulsion as people met and babbled to each other, unable to stop describing what they had just lived through. 'We circulated,' he said, 'in a multi-coloured universe of stories.'

That's how I felt it was here.

It was harder to be lonely in Jerusalem than in the two big cities where I'd lived, Moscow and London. It wasn't just size, it was also because in Jerusalem everyone was minding your business in every language in the world. In my second week, I was about to park my car, grappling with driving on the 'wrong' side of the road again, when an older Israeli man with white hair and a paunch came up as if he knew me and indicated that I should wind down my window. He said excitedly, 'No, don't park there!'

I wondered what mistake I was making.

'I'm about to leave and there's still an hour on my metre, you have to take my spot,' he insisted.

I did as I was told and walked away from my car, which I'd parked for free, smiling at this funny place. It was a warm spring day. The sky was a deep blue. Crimson bougainvillea threaded its way up a honey-coloured sandstone building, dark green fir trees swaying nearby. The colours were so vivid it was as if they'd been tweaked in Photoshop. A young Israeli woman, with a biblical face and long dark curls, walked by and said, as if intoning a blessing, 'May you smile like that all the rest of your life.'

The other impressive thing about Israel is its attitude to the media. There's respect for the public's right to know. Israeli authorities imposed restrictions on reporting military actions during Operation Defensive Shield, but we were still able to report as events were unfolding. My journalist's card gave me access to the West Bank and to the Gaza Strip, and I could go about unaccompanied. That was very different to my experience reporting in Chechnya, for example, where if you came in from the Russian side, the Russian military spokesman set your itinerary and never left your side.

The Israeli media was fizzing. There was news in Hebrew, news in Russian, news in Arabic and news in English. It was vibrant and raucous, every shade of opinion represented. People loved to talk, to argue, to shout at each other, and they did it in print, on radio, on TV and on each new online format, as soon as it was invented. The most searing exposes of Israeli political and military blunders were inevitably in the Israeli media. Their satirical TV comedy program was compulsory viewing. Daring and hilarious, it wouldn't have survived a month in any Arab capital. Israel was creative, noisy and exciting, though I barely had time to appreciate that as I rushed off to report on the cancer in its body politic, its war with the Palestinians.

Ramallah sat in the West Bank, fifteen minutes from Jerusalem. It was the Palestinians' de facto capital and yet their leader, Yasser Arafat, was a prisoner there, besieged by the IDF, the Israeli Defence Forces. He was a symbol of resilience and hopelessness, tenacity and thwarted dreams, and the town's 50,000 residents could only enter and leave the city where they were born via an Israeli checkpoint, patrolled by Israeli soldiers.

When I went to Ramallah for the first time, I parked on the Israeli side of the main checkpoint at Qalandia and crossed over on foot. Taking my cue from Orla, I didn't cover my hair. Hundreds of people stood like cattle in two lines, going in and out, separated by concrete and wire barriers, with rolls of barbed wire on top. Some people were desperate, some angry, others resigned as they crushed up against one another.

'I have to remember that this is not normal life,' said an older Palestinian man in a three-piece pinstriped suit, after he'd shown his ID papers to an Israeli soldier less than half his age. It was a difficult way to arrive in a town.

Once across, I had to battle the chaos on the Palestinian side, the minibuses and fruit-sellers, dusty from the white gravel they were crowded onto, in between cars lined up in a permanent traffic jam at the checkpoint's vehicle exit. There were such large crowds because the Israeli military had lifted the week-long closure it had imposed on the West Bank town when its tanks had rumbled in on 29 March. People were now rushing to get provisions, to visit each other, and to bury their dead. They didn't know when they would be locked into their homes again.

One woman caught my eye. She was sitting in the garden of a four-storey apartment building, looking incongruously peaceful. I went up to ask why she wasn't busy scurrying about getting food like everyone else.

'When the curfew was lifted for a few hours on 2 April, I saw an Israeli soldier shoot a Palestinian boy. He looked about fourteen years old.' The woman paused. 'I don't want to die for a piece of bread.'

After Ramallah, I went to Nablus, the largest town in the West Bank and its main commercial centre. Israeli troops attacked the town over five days from 3 April, and enforced a curfew for another four days after that. The first opportunity for journalists to enter was in the middle of the month. We followed the route taken by the Israeli military. Fighting had centred on the historic Kasbah in the centre of town. We saw where Israeli bulldozers had demolished old buildings and damaged churches, mosques and traditional bath houses, to clear a path for their tanks.

It was IDF practice to give warnings to families to leave houses that were about to be demolished. Usually there was not enough time to take much of value, just enough time to get out with their lives. In the Kasbah on 4 April the residents said there had been no warning. The Shuabi family was still inside when bulldozers brought their home down on top of them, burying them alive.

There was one lucky Shuabi brother. Mahmoud had been away from the house when it was demolished. On 11 April, when the Israeli military curfew was lifted, he organised friends and neighbours to start digging. They found a small opening under the rubble, and discovered that Mahmoud's uncle and aunt were alive under a mass of stone and dirt, in what had been their living room. Abdullah and Shams, both in their sixties, had given up hope and believed they were about to die. They were saying goodbye to each other when they heard the rescuers calling down to them. They had survived for eight days, with only one bottle of mineral water and two slices of pita bread.

The rescuers continued digging through the night. They found the rest of the family huddled in a circle in one small room: Mahmoud's brother Samir, his pregnant wife Nabila and their little boys. Also there were Mahmoud's two older sisters and his 85-year-old father. They were all dead. Eight people, three generations of one family, snuffed out.

I called the IDF spokesman in Jerusalem. He said he had no information yet about the Shuabi family, but that generally houses slated for demolition were evacuated beforehand. In fact, he added, the army had engineers on hand when homes were demolished to prevent damage to neighbouring buildings. Plainly, something had gone wrong. The neighbours said they believed the Israeli troops had begun to demolish one part of the building, when the second half collapsed on its own.

I stood looking at the eight bodies wrapped in cloth near the destroyed house and remembered the six people, torn to shreds, in the Jewish market in Jerusalem. In the twenty-first century, in this ancient land, the concept of warfare had been turned on its head. It was no longer young men marching off to fight, to keep the people waiting back home safe. It was ordinary people, in their homes, or catching buses, who were the new shock troops.

I returned to Ramallah at the start of May, on the day the Israeli troops were due to end their siege and withdraw from the Mukata, the former British military compound which Yasser Arafat had made his headquarters. I crossed the Qalandia checkpoint, the same way I had before, on foot, and found a taxi to take me to the Mukata.

My driver was a tubby, jolly man with a gold tooth, who spoke good English. Worry beads dangled from his mirror. When I told him my destination, he asked if I didn't have anywhere better to go, adding laughingly, 'Why are you wasting your time with those bastards?'

He spent the rest of the journey alternating between showing me photos of his children and complaining about Arafat's corruption. The Mukata sat on the top of a hill in the centre of town. When we reached it, I could see that the Israeli troops had departed. They left behind destroyed buildings and crushed vehicles, all covered in fine white dust. Journalists and locals were wandering around, looking at the mess. A flattened silver Maserati sat near a pile of rubble, and nearby a red BMW convertible and a powder-blue Mercedes lay in a pile like crushed children's toys.

'Someone here drove some very fancy cars,' an Italian journalist said dryly.

Most of the buildings in the compound were still standing, and inside the rooms the Israeli soldiers had used as their base it was complete chaos, as if flood waters had thrown everything around before receding. It also stank. Furniture was pushed into corners, and there was rubbish everywhere, boxes, food scraps and bottles full of urine. The knowledgeable Italian journalist explained that Israeli soldiers weren't allowed to go outside to pee, for fear of snipers. Okay, I get the bottle thing – but why leave them behind? So much of war is about humiliating the enemy.

Back outside, a crowd formed, and I turned to see Yasser Arafat being driven up in an open-topped sports car, waving and throwing kisses. He came so suddenly and at such speed we barely had time to jump out of the way. The car braked as abruptly as it had appeared. Arafat said a few words condemning 'Israel's acts of terror', before he was hustled inside. The locals around me cheered but this return to power seemed to have a pitiful air. Arafat ruled over so little. I did some final interviews and returned to Jerusalem to file.

Before I knew it, my six weeks were up. Orla and I were meeting for a farewell drink at the American Colony Hotel in East Jerusalem. It was one of the most beautiful hotels in the world and a step up from the usual journalists' watering holes. The building was serene. Rooms with high-domed white ceilings radiated off a lush courtyard garden, where a fountain tinkled. Oak tables adorned with bowls of roses, or Bedouin carpets, sat beside exquisite dark wooden chests, inlaid with enamel, in the Syrian style. Its history was diverse. The hotel had been the estate of a rich local *effendi*, or nobleman, as well as a commune for messianic Christians from the US.

In the 1880s Horatio and Anna Spafford, a God-fearing American doctor and his wife, had been members of a messianic church in

Chicago. The church expelled them after they suffered a series of tragedies, including the deaths of their children, because so much bad luck was clearly a sign they must be sinners. The Spaffords took refuge in Jerusalem and set up a commune. When it prospered and they needed more space, they bought up the Arab *effendi*'s estate and turned part of it into a hotel. Their descendants were still there more than 100 years later, when I arrived.

Through four turbulent changes of government – Ottoman, British, Jordanian, Israeli – the hotel was known as a neutral oasis where enemies could meet. Lawrence of Arabia, Winston Churchill, Lauren Bacall, Peter O'Toole, Marc Chagall, Bob Dylan, Graham Greene and John le Carré had all stayed there, as did lucky reporters today, whose bosses were footing the bill. For the rest of us, drinking at the American Colony bar was the next best thing.

In the warm months, they placed tables in the garden among rose and lavender bushes. The lighting was discreet and Ibrahim the bartender knew everyone's drink. One of the best Arab inventions for a warm day is lemonade made with fresh mint – cool, refreshing and sour-sweet. Ibrahim improved it, making a special version for me by whizzing up whole lemons, including the peel, with ice, mint leaves, sugar and vodka. On a balmy evening, when there were no bombings or incursions, it was unbeatable.

I sat with Orla at an outdoor table. She was drinking mint lemonade, and I drank my alcoholic version as we planned my future. The call to prayer floated in from the nearest mosque. A cameraman came up to say hello and threw at us cheekily over his shoulder: 'This is the Islamic paradise, with alcohol.'

After he'd left, Orla said there was more work in the Middle East than there was in Russia and that I should relocate to Jerusalem permanently. I confessed that I was fearful of how distressing the story here was. You needed great personal strength to chronicle so much suffering. We were suddenly serious, leaning in towards each other and talking in low tones amid the shouts of laughter and the buzz from the bar. Orla reminded me that we would also have other stories to report. The US was poised to invade Iraq.

'Baghdad will be our next big story. You can't do Baghdad from Moscow; well, you can but it's much more difficult and expensive. It will be easy to cover it from here. And the weather is better than in Russia.' She smiled as she delivered this clincher.

We clinked glasses.

'To your safe return! And remember, you can always stay at my place again while you look for a house.'

My feet were now firmly on this path.

3

It proved surprisingly difficult to leave Russia. I had been there nearly three years all up and didn't realise how attached I had become to Moscow's snowy grandeur, to the complex, heartbreaking Russian language, and to the thrill of achievement I felt at surviving each difficult day. My eye had adjusted to churches with golden onion domes outlined against a brooding sky; to marble statues of Lenin looming over gridlocked traffic; and to people dressed in fur coats and hats descending long wooden escalators into splendid subway stations. Though the city was not welcoming to outsiders, I had begun to feel at home.

It was hard to say goodbye to Irina, my kind, precise Russian teacher, and to my journalist friends. I was sorry to leave the dazzling commentators I had interviewed, and also the Uzbek and Chechen women who sold me vegetables and home-made yoghurt and honey at my local farmers' market. Theirs were the best tomatoes I'd ever tasted. *'Tashkentsky!'* the Uzbek women stated proudly, for everyone wanted produce from the capital of Uzbekistan, Tashkent. Who knew you had to come to Russia for the perfect tomato?

I was even sad to leave my gym, certain that I would never find such exacting, pitiless instructors anywhere else in the world

Suddenly, I was chalking up a list of 'lasts'. Last goodbye to the babushka who worked at the concert hall near my home and always let me in, even when I was late; last look at Saint Basil's Cathedral on Red Square; last visit to Sandunovsky, Moscow's famous steam bath.

The attendants had been so stern at first, until I became a regular, and now their faces lit up when they saw me.

During my final week, I stumbled across a performance by world-class violinists busking in a subway station under Red Square. They were moonlighting from the Russian State Orchestra, and played to a hushed grateful crowd of Moscow music lovers, who stayed till the final note. It was like a farewell concert.

This is a demanding job in many ways. Moving from city to city you feel as if you are enduring the first day at a new school over and over, only each time they're speaking a different language. As soon as you do finally make a friend, they leave for the next location – or you do. You miss your family and old friends, and you don't know the things insiders know, like where to find the best cafes, pubs, gyms or farmers' markets; or the best doctors, physiotherapists or computer technicians. It's a process of discovery, and it seems that as soon as you finally understand a place and get comfortable, it's time to go again.

Russia had changed me, making me tougher, as well as more fatalistic, and leaving was a wrench. Then at Sheremetyevo airport, I was shaken down by a corrupt official before he would let me take my things out of the country, although I'd already paid the requisite bribes to the tax department back at head office. Departures were obviously a fruitful area of revenue raising. I inhaled the odour of pickles, vodka, smoke and sweat. *Last bribe.* I smiled to myself. *Won't miss that.*

I arrived in Jerusalem in time for Christmas. The holiday season has a different character in each place I've lived. In Australia, it's a winter festival transplanted to summer. The fake snow and tinsel on shops along the beachfront at Bondi had been mysterious to me when I was growing up and had never yet seen real snow. The butcher had Bing Crosby's slow, syrupy 'White Christmas' on loop on a loudspeaker.

It seemed a visitation from another world, as we made our way past his window, where cuts of meat lay separated by sprigs of parsley, and down to the surf, the sun pounding down on our heads, the sand burning our feet.

In Russia, Christmas falls in January and is always white. The haunting choral singing in the Russian Orthodox mass would ring in my ears as I walked along the frozen Moscow River and crossed the bridge back to my apartment building. It sat opposite one of the city's seven grand Art Deco skyscrapers, and its Soviet star, gleaming on top, guided me home.

In Jerusalem it was different again, so close to the source and so far from peace. The churches in Jerusalem and Bethlehem were usually thronged with pilgrims and tourists at this time of year, but now, in the Christmas of 2002, there was almost no one.

I walked through the Old City to the Church of the Holy Sepulchre, built by Crusaders on the hill of Calvary, the site where, according to tradition, Christ was crucified. It was a grand ninth-century sandstone building in a small square set back from the street. Tour guides were gathered outside and pounced when they saw me. Desperate for work, they became angry when they learned I was a journalist, not a tourist. After shaking them off, I stepped through an immense wooden door into the church.

At the entrance, there was a large vestibule built around the stone where it's believed Christ's body was anointed after He was taken down from the Cross. A brightly hued mosaic charting His life filled the wall behind the stone. Oil lamps of coloured glass edged with gold hung over it. The beauty made me catch my breath. A woman in black robes threw herself down on the stone, arms outstretched, sobbing. It wasn't the original, but that didn't matter to her. The spiritual power here was palpable.

The church beyond was vast, dark and cavernous. Hooded monks disappeared around corners. The walls were covered in tiny crosses,

28

carved by centuries of worshippers. Six denominations shared the church, often conducting services at the same time. Searching for a Catholic priest whom I was here to interview, I went to the small, freezing vestry where Franciscan monks were holding mass.

'Pater Noster!' a brown-robed monk sang, and the others responded. The repetitive Latin phrases had an almost narcotic effect, though it was far too cold to fall asleep. Around the corner, Armenian monks began their service. Their deep-voiced chants seemed to come from down inside the earth, more like a drum roll than a human voice. Smoke and aroma from two sets of incense were dispersing in the air, catching at my throat like tear gas last did. Both groups seemed to be using their prayers to drown each other out. It was like listening to competing operas side by side at full volume.

When the services ended, I found Father Fergus Clarke, an Irish priest who had been living inside the church for five years. He glowed with pleasure when I told him how moving it was to be here in this intensely spiritual place.

'Like yourself, I'm hypnotised by this place and I can't explain it. And I'm happy not being able to explain it. Willy-nilly it touches us and moves us, whatever our belief system.'

Our breath materialised in clouds, and our shoes echoed on the smooth flagstones as we walked around the church and I recorded an interview about the meaning of Christmas. This year the facts were grim. There was an Israeli military curfew in the West Bank, including in the town of Bethlehem, where it's believed that Jesus was born. Israeli troops had re-occupied Bethlehem in November, after a Palestinian teenager from there had blown himself up on a Jerusalem bus, killing eleven people. Bethlehem's mayor declared there could be no Christmas tree in Manger Square while Israeli troops were on his streets. The only symbol that remained unchanged from the Bible story was the star shining in the sky above the town. In the cold, empty church in Jerusalem, I walked where Christ had walked and found myself confessing to the priest that it was impossible not to despair. Naturally, Father Fergus disagreed.

'We still have hope in our hearts,' he said. 'That's also unchanged. The day will come when all three religions will cherish what they have here. We are all sons of Abraham, and this will be a model for the rest of humanity.'

I looked at him in disbelief. Outside the church, the sons of Abraham were trying to kill each other, and even the monks inside couldn't be stopped from fighting. I opened my mouth and then closed it again, for he was telling me that external reality didn't matter. This was the message of hope and love that Jesus came here – literally here – to bring.

After Christmas it was time to set up a permanent base. I found a pretty basement flat on the Jewish side of town, within walking distance of Orla's. When I told her my street address, we both smiled. Here at the ideological heart of the Middle East conflict, I'd found a home in Hope Street, Jerusalem.

It was good to come to rest after perpetual motion. For the past year, my things had been in storage and I had been living out of a suitcase, dependent on the kindness of strangers and friends in Afghanistan, Sydney, Moscow, and Jerusalem. That was something I'd never done before. My few clothes had become frayed, and I hadn't dared to buy anything other than the smallest tube of toothpaste or hand cream. Now I went to the supermarket and bought two of everything I wanted and actually burst into tears when I put them in a cupboard, *my* cupboard, where they could stay, waiting for me, without me having to carry them to my next location.

A year spent with only what I could fit into a rucksack had made me aware of how much we are defined by what is familiar to us – books, music, furniture, even pots and pans. After so long without your things around you – who are you? Even a nomad needs some kind of base. Or maybe I was learning that I was not a real nomad …

As I waited for my boxes to arrive from Russia, I discovered that my new apartment was in a great location. The Old City was a kilometre from my front door, and I could gaze out on its imposing stone walls, changing from pale cream to butterscotch and back again as the sun moved across the sky. For nineteen years, from 1948 until 1967, when Jerusalem had been a divided city controlled by Jordan on one side and Israel on the other, my apartment had sat overlooking no-man's-land in the valley below. Soldiers from both sides shot across at random.

After the 1967 War, this area suddenly became the new centre of town and prime real estate. Like the derelict land in the centre of Berlin after the Wall there fell, it also became extremely valuable. The houses were refurbished and the sandstone paths were mended. Gardens were planted and the streets closed to traffic, turning it into a village in the centre of town.

Before I'd arrived, I'd harboured a secret hope that Jerusalem might work some of its magic on me. Being an atheist didn't stop me from wondering – inconsistently – if I might perhaps see an angel folding its wings and floating above the Old City walls, or even guiding me around the ancient stone streets. Without me having to go mad, of course. I reasoned that surely if angels were going to appear anywhere in your reporting career, it would be here. But despite my optimistic street address, in reality Jerusalem was moody and divided. Innocents were dead everywhere. It was my job to head straight to the scenes of carnage.

I went from one suicide bombing to another. They occurred throughout Israel, but were most common here in Jerusalem. During that first autumn, I didn't even have to drive to the story. Five bombings in a row were within walking distance of my home. I would hear the unmistakable BOOM – a huge crack of sound – grab my recording gear and race out the door before the news beeper began sending out alerts.

At each road side, I'd pass the gawkers, show my press card and join the swarm of journalists, police and rescue services at the charred skeleton of a bus, or the smoking ruins of a bus stop or cafe. The air was heavy with the stench of cordite and burnt flesh. The main targets of the bus attacks were working-class Israelis who couldn't afford any other means of transport. Ironically, the other people forced to catch buses, despite the danger, were the city's Arab population and they were also victims.

We crunched over broken glass and blood – *am I really walking in someone's blood?* There were body parts everywhere, a dismembered hand on the path, a head, usually the bomber's, in a tree. Medics were treating the wounded and body bags would be piled up nearby. Sirens wailed urgently, while police and doctors barked into phones and beepers. The people lucky enough to be alive would be crying, scrabbling for their mobile phones if they could, lying moaning if they couldn't. We talked to people who hadn't made it onto the bus because it was too crowded, or had simply been late to lunch at a restaurant. They had been saved, while the punctual friends they were due to meet were not so lucky.

'What would have happened if I'd been on time? I would be dead now too. It's incomprehensible,' cried an Israeli woman in her fifties. She had survived a suicide attack at Maxim's, a popular Haifa restaurant which served Arabic food, and was jointly owned by Arabs and Jews. She sat in the street, rocking back and forth, her clothes blackened and torn, her beautiful face crumpled. Her friends' bodies were somewhere behind her, in the ruins of the restaurant. Her life, which had been spared, would never be the same.

'What would have happened if the bus hadn't been full? I had my foot on the step …' A woman, an immigrant from the former Soviet Union, stood in front of me on a main street in Jerusalem, in shock. 'I was on my way to the doctor,' she said, explaining herself like a small child. She lifted her foot, re-enacting climbing onto the bus, and then collapsed to the ground in a dead faint. I didn't even have a chance to get her name.

It was a series of 'what if's', as people puzzled over their miraculous survival, ascribing it to inexplicable good fortune, or God's grace, depending on their world view. These stories made me even more fatalistic, suggesting that our fortunes were 'written', for good or ill, and that we couldn't avoid them, no matter how hard we tried. If there was a purpose to this suffering, I couldn't see it.

In a Palestinian town after an Israeli military raid, the smell was the same: cordite, blood and panic, a sour stench all its own. There was chaos as people ran screaming, carrying the dead and injured in their arms. In Gaza, death often came from the air, part of a policy of 'targeted killings' carried out by the Israeli military. Only, the pilots didn't always hit their targets.

At the scene of a missile strike on a car near Gaza City, I saw a black depression in the road and two burnt-out vehicles. The targets were the Palestinian militants driving in the first car. The passengers in the taxi van behind it were 'collateral damage'. That chilling American phrase was often in use here too, to shield politicians and spokesmen from having to refer directly to the innocent victims of a military operation.

A young woman crawled out of the wreckage and was standing stunned on the road. She appeared forlorn and isolated in the middle of the crowd, cut off from them by a force field of distress and grief. She had been travelling with her mother and sisters, on their way into Gaza City to do some shopping. They were discussing what they would buy when the missile struck.

Her mother shielded her from the blast with her body, protecting her to the end. But she couldn't protect all her daughters, and she couldn't protect herself. Now this young woman was the only female from her family left alive. She kept moving her hands in front of her in a helpless repetitive motion, a precursor to shock setting in. When her father arrived, she fainted in his arms.

In northern Gaza, which was a rural area, many Palestinian farmers were also the unintended targets of Israeli missiles. One farmer was ploughing his field when an Israeli missile struck. His farm supplied fruit and flowers – carnations, cherry tomatoes, strawberries and watermelons – to an Israeli export company. In the morning the produce was in Gaza, two hours later it was in Tel Aviv, and in the afternoon in London or Paris.

On the day of the air strike, the farmer's crop was ready for harvest and he was on the phone, reminding his cousin that they still had to pay the final instalment for a two-year agricultural training course. The course was run by a Jerusalem peace-building group, founded by a Palestinian and an Israeli. Its aim was to ensure that Palestinian farming methods met stringent new European standards, so that produce from Gaza would be accepted for sale in the EU. The farmer said goodbye to his cousin, shut his mobile phone, turned back to his work and was vaporised by an incoming missile. Another mistaken target, another innocent casualty. When I went to the farm three days later, his blood still stained the earth in the watermelon field. His son told me sadly that if he took over his father's farm, he would have to start all over again with the training course before he could export their fruit and vegetables to the EU. That knowledge had died with his father too.

The futility of such deaths made it hard not to despair.

Funerals. I had never attended so many funerals. I came to know the order of service for both Muslim and Jewish burials. The sound of a mother weeping was the same everywhere. It is not a sound you ever forget.

'Take me, God! Why didn't you take me?'

The emotionally draining work often seemed intensified by the heat. I really understand the connection between sweat and tears now. After a long hot day, I'd eat late, alone. Or I'd try to catch Orla, if we both finished in time. One Saturday night, we planned to have dinner and watch an episode of the BBC's *Pride and Prejudice*, which she'd brought over from London. We watched all six episodes back to back, two tough reporters swooning over Jane Austen, unable to resist the tug of that happy-ever-after ending.

I began questioning why I was doing this job. I'd been a journalist for more than fifteen years, exciting, demanding, fun years, which hadn't left much time for anything else. I recalled the exchange with that taxi driver on my first visit and found it niggling at me. *Who would marry you?* Perhaps it was his gloomy certainty, or perhaps he had touched on a fear I hadn't been prepared to put into words. Had I spent too long married to the job?

I hadn't been seeing anyone in a long time. I'm not sure why. Our own lives are often mysterious to us. I can't explain why I hadn't settled down, surrounded by a happy brood of children in a house in Sydney, not too far from my mother's. I can imagine me and those children, carrying towels down to the beach on a summer morning, swimming till we were hungry and then going up to my mother's in the afternoon, still covered in sand, everyone squabbling as they climbed the hot, rocky stairs into my mother's garden, continuing to bicker till it was time for dinner, a replay of my own life growing up, ideally minus the angry father.

No, wait, re-wind. That's too soft and dreamy. It captures the regret, but not the reality. If I am more exacting with myself, looking back I see that I did make choices, even if I wasn't conscious of them. I was unable to resist the addictive adrenaline of TV journalism. It gave me purpose, meaning and excitement, and I succumbed – in fact I dived right in and made my career my priority.

Journalism is a vocation, we were told as new recruits. One of my friends put it another way. She described herself as a news nun, wedded to the job, with no time for anything else. I didn't mind that, because I came to journalism after trying and failing at another career. I'd put myself through law school and had spent years studying something I wasn't really suited to, sitting in classes filled with people born to be lawyers – and me.

When I graduated, I was one of the lucky ones who landed a job. They stuck me all on my own in a high-rise office, updating shopping-centre leases. Not much scope for us curious, dreamy types there. Dry, dull words were soon swimming before my eyes. 'The party of the first part [hereinafter known as the Lessor] warrants that …' Surely an hour had passed since I last looked at my watch? No, only two minutes and nineteen seconds. I was twenty-three years old and certain that I'd gone to hell. Sartre was wrong. Hell isn't other people; it's other people's property leases.

I knew in my heart that was no place for me, so I fled on the well-worn Australian path to London and wangled a job as a researcher at BBC-TV. I felt it was 'meant', when such a sought-after job fell into the lap of a non-English non-journalist on a tourist visa like me. So did the guy who gave me the job. 'I get a hundred letters like yours every week,' he told me months later. 'But on the morning I had a program that was a legal minefield, I got a letter from a lawyer … And you're still here!'

The boss called and said, 'You're going to Liverpool to do a story on the health service. It has to air in two weeks,' and our small production team picked up and didn't go home or snatch more than a few hours sleep between that phone call and the night of transmission. As I tripped from one of these assignments to the next – 'You're going to Ireland …', 'You're going to South Africa …' – I learned to keep my passport and vaccinations up to date, and believed I was the luckiest person in the world. It wasn't well paid and there was no job security, but I'd found the job I was born to do. What the net nerds called 'RL' – real life – couldn't compare.

On a visit back to Sydney, my mother said that when I was three years old, I used to come home from kindergarten full of stories about the other children's doings. I knew everything – who'd eaten, who'd

36

slept, who'd cried and who'd been naughty and forced to stand in the corner.

'You've been a reporter from the start,' she said, smiling.

That was very kind of her, since she would have preferred me to be a well-paid lawyer safely at home near her, rather than a poorly paid journalist at the end of God's earth. She's generous, my mum, and with her encouragement I went on my way.

I hadn't thought about much else when I'd rushed headlong into the arms of this new career A relationship could come later. Only, now it was later, and it hadn't. I didn't have a family, a boyfriend or even a dog. I was living in a rented apartment and spending yet another birthday filing on a breaking story.

But forget my own birthday – that was my choice. How had I missed so many milestones in the lives of the people I loved? Their birthdays and weddings, and the births of their children. I had always been somewhere else, doing something 'more important'. In Jerusalem I began to fear I was documenting other people's lives rather than living my own. Returning to an empty flat after a day immersed in blood and sorrow and working into the night was becoming harder to do alone.

I was ready to fall in love.

4

May 2002

SCENE ONE: *A busy, noisy cafe in central Jerusalem*

On my first visit, when I was staying at Orla's, I stopped at one of Jerusalem's few happening cafes between interviews. Cafe Aroma had a definite buzz, with hip young wait staff serving good coffee and a TV screening MTV, which was switched to the news if there was a suicide bombing. Bread and croissants were made on the premises, the scent of baking mingled with the smell and pneumatic clatter of the coffee machine – is there a more glorious combination? – and people's names being called over an intercom to pick up their orders. Elaborate triple-decker sandwiches were prepared and served by a multi-lingual crew of Palestinians from East Jerusalem, blond Russian-speaking teenagers, and striking dark-skinned Ethiopian immigrants.

The cafe that day was filled with office workers and students, and Israeli soldiers in olive-green uniforms, black M16s on their hips. No one seemed to pay much attention to the machine guns jostling so close as we queued for coffee, except me, unused to this highly militarised society. Many people were getting take-away, and no one was staying for long, as Jerusalem cafes were a prime target for suicide bombers.

I decided to sit in, despite Israeli police warnings. Possible bombings were reported on the morning news, like the weather. 'It's thirty-two degrees in Jerusalem and there are ten "hot warnings" for bombings today.' When every day and every warning was 'hot' it became hard to treat it as unusual. I did my customary bargaining with fate. I wouldn't sit for long, I'd be gone within fifteen minutes, so could I stay safe? I couldn't believe how quickly I was adapting to local habits.

If Orla had known, she would have stopped me. At that stage, we only went for dinner to the same three restaurants, all on the east side of the city, where most of the patrons were Palestinians and she reckoned we were safe from suicide bombers. I was just deciding that I wouldn't tell Orla about this little adventure when a young Israeli in his twenties, wearing jeans and a brown leather jacket, came up. His hair was in a ponytail, and he inclined his head as he indicated my table, checking if he could sit down. I didn't want to share, since I had work to do, but I didn't have any reason to say no. Note to self: when a handsome man wants to share your table and all you can think of is your next interview, it's no wonder you are still single.

Many Israeli men are aggressive but the first thing that struck me about this stranger was his direct, gentle gaze. We shared a cup of coffee and then another. His name was Raphael, a name I've always liked, and he was a musician and actor. I stayed longer than I meant to and in the end we exchanged smiles and phone numbers. We did speak again, but Israel's military operation was at its height and I was so busy reporting that we lost touch.

In fact, I was only visiting Jerusalem for six weeks and romance wasn't on my mind back then, especially not with a local who might drag me too far into the story I was meant to be reporting on, not becoming part of. The assignment was dangerous enough as it was and it was complicated just surviving. That's all I can say in my defence. It must have been convincing, because I was given a second chance.

August 2004

SCENE TWO: *A busy, noisy cafe in central Jerusalem*

Two years later, after I'd packed up my life in Moscow and was now living in Jerusalem, I went back to the same cafe. It was a bright summer's day. I'd spent the morning in a west Jerusalem beauty salon interviewing Israeli women, while they had their nails done and their legs waxed, about how they experienced the conflict. The location induced candour. The answers were different to what they would have been if they were in a TV studio or at their offices. The next day I was going to a beauty salon on the Palestinian side of town to ask the same questions.

I ran across the road from Rikki's salon to Cafe Aroma and waited in the queue for take-away. Thinking about the remarkable stories the women had told me, I was absent-mindedly listening to the coffee machine and admiring the ponytail of the guy in front of me when he turned round. It was Raphael.

'Hey!' he exclaimed happily. 'Where have you been? It's so great to see you!'

I was flattered that he remembered me. He was more handsome than I recalled, with glossy dark hair framing delicate features. His smile was bewitching. We chatted happily – 'What are you up to? Are you living here now?' – with a slightly giddy undertone.

'You're so shiny,' he said.

The compliment made me blush. I actually felt more dull than shiny, since I was wearing no makeup and having a bad hair day. By the time I returned to the beauty salon, the coffee I was carrying was cold and two women looked up and said in unison, 'You were gone a long time.'

They knew without me saying a word. You can't fool women in a beauty salon. No, strike that, you can't fool women anywhere about anything romantic. They sniff out the truth quicker than you can think up a lie. I blushed again and said I'd run into an old friend. At that moment, as if to discredit me, my phone buzzed. It was a text from Raphael. *So happy to find you again.* I went back to my interviews and my cold coffee, glowing.

One chance meeting is an accident, twice is starting to look like it's been planned – or someone up there likes you and won't take no for an answer. Maybe I've been reporting from the Middle East for too long, for I now see the possibility of a divine plan, or at the very least a guiding nudge, in the smallest of coincidences. The larger tragedies still seem mysterious – what divine plan could they be part of? Living and working in this region, with its surfeit of wars, dictatorships and political miscalculations, as well as its revolutions and lucky escapes, hasn't helped me to resolve the most basic of questions: are our fates 'written' or do we write them ourselves? Are we actors or pawns? Has it all been foreseen or can we change the script?

Raphael and I met the next evening and once again it was his beauty which struck me. The dark eyes with their gentle expression, and the cloud of soft, thick hair that most women would envy. His smile was captivating, a thing apart from his beauty. A 'conquering' smile, as they say in Hebrew. Raphael didn't seem to be aware he was handsome, or if he was he didn't play on it. When we'd finished our coffee and were getting ready to leave, he looked slightly anxious and said he didn't want to lose me again. I put my hand flat against his chest and told him it would be alright. I don't know what gave me the confidence to do that. My hand tingled.

Later that evening the phone rang and I felt anticipation – was it him? As I pulled my mobile out of my bag I realised it had been a long time since I'd experienced this excitement. Romance is so lovely when it comes along and mugs you.

Autumn turned out to be a good season for falling in love. The sun had lost its sting, leaving behind bright warm days. The trees were a dusty end-of-year green, and the air in the parks was heavy with the scent of dying herbs. Bougainvillea petals lay in pink and red swirls on the kerb, like spent paper streamers. There was a sense of loss, as the days shortened, but we still wore summer clothes and the breeze was a warm caress, known by the lovely name *Nasiim* in Arabic. It blew the faded papery petals gently around our feet. The nights were cool and darkness fell suddenly, as if someone had turned off a switch.

There were no long twilights so close to the equator. The weather, like the people, was direct.

The seasons in the northern hemisphere also seemed more distinct than I remembered from Australia, and Jerusalem became very cold, colder than any city back home. As winter drew near, with its short days, a spike of light before the long night, I huddled close with Raphael over endless cups of coffee. We went to the cafe where we'd met, a sentimental favourite, as well as to others nearby.

'Why are you so far away?' he asked, if we were seated across from each other, reaching out to me, dark eyes smiling. It didn't matter what they served us, as we were still at that stage where you hold hands and don't eat much. If only someone could figure out how to bottle that …

Raphael performed in a bar in the centre of town, a smoky sandstone beer cellar, sometimes with his band and sometimes alone. When he was solo, he sat spot-lit, hair and guitar both gleaming, and dedicated songs to me. We wandered from there to our favourite cafe and back again. I threaded my arm through his and put my hand in the pocket of his leather jacket. He kissed off my lip gloss and complained when it wasn't the flavour he liked.

Perhaps best of all he wasn't interested in my work. If that sounds strange, it was astonishing how much I craved an 'off' button sometimes, just some respite from the awful things I saw and heard, and Raphael provided it. He was writing a film script based on his life growing up in Jerusalem. Unlike my day-to-day experiences, it was a comedy. Thinking of the checkpoints, curfews, suicide bombings, home demolitions and military incursions that I saw, and the funerals I attended, people's faces contorted with grief and loathing, I was hard put to imagine anything funny enough to fill a single scene. If I were writing a film, it would be a tragedy.

Memory is very slippery. Some details are as sharp and clear as if you are looking at a photograph; others are fuzzy, like grasping at smoke, and all you can remember is an overall feeling. In *A Child's Christmas in Wales*, Dylan Thomas looks back to his childhood in years 'around the sea-town corner now', and can't remember whether it snowed for six days and six nights when he was twelve, or for twelve days and twelve nights when he was six. Exactly. Recollection also often depends on mood; whether you are looking back in anger or with love, whether your memories remain golden or have tarnished.

The beginning with Raphael is not so far away that it is around a sea-town corner, but he and I are both different now. The times are different too, those times that contributed so much to our getting together, so I hope I describe both accurately. I am trying to reach back to the people we were then, before we met and melded.

I was studying an intensive Arabic course, taught by a wonderful teacher. Professor Omar Othman had been born in Jerusalem in the 1930s, during the time when the British controlled Palestine. Though he was from a Muslim family, his parents sent him to the city's best school, which at that time was run by Christian nuns. He learned French and English from them and became a linguist. I don't know that I ever learned enough Arabic to do Professor Othman justice, but that was my fault, not his.

Raphael and I spent our first night together at this time. I had to leave him early the next morning to run to Arabic class. I was clutching the homework that I'd finished – luckily – the previous afternoon, but was too exhausted to remember any of it. I slipped into my seat in a tired, happy haze just in time to say 'present' – *mawjude* – when Professor Othman called my name. He looked up sternly then grinned. I opened my book and tried to focus. Who had conjugated these verbs? Surely not me, not one seemed familiar. Sometimes I felt I could no longer speak English properly, with all the new languages battling inside my head, Arabic mingling with Russian and Hebrew, and words in the wrong language inevitably coming out at the wrong times. When I did speak English, it was in strange pidgin sentences. 'Did you walk by foot or by car?' 'Is there dead?' 'Where bomb?'

The first word we learned in Arabic class that morning was *jild* – 'skin'. Hyper-aware of my own skin, I texted Raphael to tell him. But the moment I'd pressed send, I felt uncertain. We'd said goodbye only four hours earlier. Was this too much too soon? Shouldn't I be more cool and wait for him to contact me?

He replied instantly. It was fine. I breathed a sigh of relief.

Things very quickly became very tender. In this difficult place, Raphael's combination of confidence, sweetness and humour were irresistible. One of those rare people who is comfortable inside his own skin, he seemed to inhabit himself completely. This appealing quality was partly innate and partly the result of his childhood. He was the accidental fifth child, born well after his siblings and adored by them all.

'We used to fight over you!' his oldest sister laughed one Friday night, as we sat around the dinner table at their parents' house.

'We'd wait for you to wake up each afternoon. It was the highlight of our day,' she said, looking at Raphael fondly.

'I hardly walked till I was three,' he admitted, smiling lazily.

There was always someone to carry him. And in that family there always will be. That wave of love made Raphael very self-assured, and it was soothing to be with someone like that. It meant I could be the one with the issues.

Raphael bore me along on the tide of his feelings. Taking a deep breath, I decided to ignore the age gap. But that meant first telling him about it. I resisted for as long as I could, because how could this relationship last? Our birth dates were ten days and many years apart. So many that I can hardly bear to write it down, even now. If I don't look at the screen while I type, or better still shut my eyes … Sixteen. There, I've done it.

I couldn't imagine any older man saying to his friends that a beautiful woman was falling in love with him but he was in a bit of a fix because she was sixteen years younger ... I can't see that thought being born in a male mind. But it was how I felt. Like the tinny recording on the London underground, I did mind the gap.

I tried to tell myself that I was swimming in the mainstream. Somehow I was reading about 'toy boys' in almost every women's magazine and men's magazine too, come to think of it. And Hollywood star Demi Moore was getting very serious with her boyfriend Ashton Kutcher, who was sixteen years her junior. But we don't all look like Demi Moore and I wasn't comfortable; I felt that mainstream tide pulling me out of my depth.

When, after a few weeks of spending most of his time at my place, Raphael looked up and said, affectionately, 'We haven't talked about our ages,' I replied in a weak voice, 'No, we haven't.'

'I'm twenty-four and you're – thirty-two?' he hazarded a guess.

I intended to tell him the truth. Twenty-four plus sixteen equals forty, however you do your sums, but instead I opened my mouth and out came: 'I'm thirty-five.'

I looked around to see who had told him that lie. Had someone else spoken? That wasn't like me. And why had I bothered? Was eleven years so different from sixteen years? We'd have to wait and see.

Raphael didn't seem to care. I have never figured out why it didn't bother him. It simply didn't. His last serious girlfriend had been five years his junior, and she used to ask him if he didn't mind that she was younger than all his friends. Now I was sixteen years older, which he thought was eleven years, and he didn't mind about that either, while I was obsessed about numbers and differences, adding and subtracting feverishly, as if I were preparing for a maths quiz.

'I wouldn't care if you were twenty years older,' Raphael said.

'Why not?' I asked him suspiciously.

'I don't know – I just wouldn't.'

How could it not bother him? I wanted to shake him to see if it was true, as if I could turn him upside down and the real answer would tumble out. Why didn't it matter to him when it mattered so much to me?

And why *did* it matter so much to me? I couldn't answer that either, but I didn't seem able to accept that Raphael didn't care because he just liked me for myself. While I was busy doing more sums – *He thinks I'm eleven years older than him, which would make me sixteen years older than his last girlfriend, but since I lied to him about that, I'm actually twenty-one years older than she was, and that is way too extreme* – I was reading a newspaper that a BBC friend had brought over from London.

It was a British tabloid with a special section devoted to my current obsession, aging. What this meant was that it pounced mercilessly on every sign of deterioration in luminously beautiful supermodels. They were fair game. They'd turned thirty. There were pictures of each model's perfect face, with a close-up of the areas under the eyes and near the mouth, so that you could see the damage for yourself, as if she had a disease. The caption asked in horror, *'What happened!?!'*

I looked away from the paper and back at Raphael. Why wasn't he with some stunning girl his own age? There seemed to be an overabundance of them here, with their long legs and flawless skin, no cellulite or wrinkles in sight. The British tabloid hacks and I had no answer for that one.

While these doubts overshadowed our relationship, I didn't share them with Raphael. Instead I burdened my girlfriends. The brunt of it fell on Orla. When we weren't out reporting, we sat talking on her long sandstone balcony, the tips of nearby cedar trees swaying in the cool air, as if they were taking part in the conversation. I loved listening to Orla talk, it didn't actually matter what about. She could make a laundry list interesting. But once I started dating Raphael she barely got a word in edgewise.

We were in our usual spots on her outdoor sofa, our legs curled up beneath us while Orla listened to my worries. Her gaze was serious and sympathetic, the one she usually reserved for people she was interviewing.

'I don't think of myself as a rigidly conventional person, but this has shown me where I am very conventional,' I said. 'I don't know if I can do this.'

'He's not an age, he's a person. He obviously cares about you, you look good together. Just relax.' This was Orla's practical, kind advice. She knew and liked Raphael but there was another factor. She had recently fallen in love herself, and saw every relationship with that optimistic glow.

'But a relationship like this is against nature. It can't last!' I wailed. 'So what am I doing?'

Orla pointed out that we all did lots of unnatural things, like living in tall apartment blocks where the windows were never opened and the air was pumped in, and scuttling to work each day in trains that moved under the ground, and buying food that someone in another country had cooked, then frozen and shipped out to us, and pouring wax onto our skin so we could yank our hair out by the roots, and that not much of that was pleasurable.

'Raphael brings you a great deal of joy. He's loving and kind, and God knows that's rare enough amongst the single men we meet.' Orla paused meaningfully for a moment to let that sink in, as we reviewed the sorry lot of commitment-phobes, no-hopers and married men pretending to be single that we both knew. Orla was so happy that she wanted everyone else to be happy too.

'It doesn't matter if it doesn't last, just enjoy it while it does. You never know what will happen next. None of us do,' she added sombrely.

She went quiet, remembering two friends, journalists who had recently been killed on a story in Africa. 'I'd always thought Miguel was indestructible,' she had said sadly when we learned of their deaths.

She didn't have to add that this could happen to us too. I knew she was right. Life is short and you should grab happiness when it comes along.

I'd never had a 'rock star' boyfriend in my teens, when you actually want one. I was the studious, plump girl back then. This was out of its right place and time but that was another reason to kick back and enjoy it. I might be crying later but at least I wouldn't miss out on driving through Paris with the warm wind in my hair. No mournful 'Ballad of Lucy Jordan' for me.

After listening to Orla, I vowed to shut off the censorious voice inside my head and to try to live in the moment, as the Buddhists tell you to. Perhaps I would learn to savour love and not to be complacent, taking it for granted, or poisoning it with unrealistic expectations. Perhaps I would come to see that it's sweeter when it can't last.

Raphael and I were both born in October. Ten days and yes, yes, all those years apart. (It's hard to turn that voice off ...) When we celebrated our birthdays together for the first time, our different perspectives emerged.

'It's amazing, this is so intense after such a short time, it's only been a month,' I said.

'It's such a long time, it's been more than a month!' was how Raphael saw it.

We agreed to meet at a cafe in Jerusalem's German Colony for dinner. I decided to walk, since it was only fifteen minutes from my home, down a lovely wide Jerusalem street with ornately carved sandstone buildings and large shady trees. The area had been founded by German Templers, a breakaway Protestant sect who settled in the Holy Land in the mid 1800s. The Templers arrived before the new Jewish movement called Zionism, and in some ways they were an inspiration for it. In the 1860s, one of their leaders predicted that Christ would return to earth and the Templers settled in the hills near

Haifa to wait. Although they were disappointed, they stayed on in expectation until the 1940s.

By then the Turks had left, after their 600-year-old empire collapsed, and it was the British who controlled Palestine. The Brits were at war with Germany, and they regarded the Templers not as a small kooky Christian sect, but as Germans, first and foremost, and therefore as enemy aliens. In fact, they were right; some of the Templers were Nazi sympathisers, holding rallies where they displayed Nazi swastikas in Haifa and Jerusalem. But the Brits didn't distinguish. They deported them all – mostly to Australia.

What the Templers left behind them after their eighty years in the Holy Land, waiting for the Second Coming, was construction. They had built orderly, well-spaced suburbs in a number of large towns. Design was not a high priority in the new Jewish state, where the main aim was to put up as many functional apartment blocks as quickly as possible, and move Jewish immigrants out of the tent cities where they had been dumped during the 1940s and 1950s. The state of Israel built fast, cheap and ugly. But design had been important to the Templers. Their charming, well laid out stone houses, easily the most beautiful in every city in Israel, seemed only to improve with age, and not only in comparison with the awful high-rise that followed.

I was walking by a cluster of their buildings, soothed by the perfect proportions and clean lines, when I spotted Raphael. He was wearing his leather jacket and smoking a cigarette as he waited for me, leaning against a wall on the pavement opposite the cafe. My heart skipped a beat. An Israeli police car was parked nearby, blocking the pavement, lights flashing, in order to deter Palestinian suicide attackers. Raphael was lit up by the on-off blue glow of the car's lights. Like everyone else on the pavement, people on their way home, or to dinner, I had to walk around the police car. It was strange to live 'on guard' like this all the time. Raphael hugged me close, the strobe lighting changing the colour of his jacket from brown to a metallic hue and back again. I shut my eyes and, lit by a blue flickering light myself, wondered if this might go part of the way to explaining why this was such an aggressive society.

We went into the cafe and sat near the window, something Orla would never do. She had been working here for three years by this time and had the dubious honour of having been to the scene of almost every suicide bombing in Jerusalem.

'It's too dangerous. The injuries from glass shards are terrible,' she warned.

Despite reporting fearlessly from every front line, including the former Yugoslavia and Iraq, Orla didn't believe in taking unnecessary risks. She even worried when I began going out with Raphael.

'Please be careful! We don't know his family!'

Cautious and brave, a nice mix.

The next evening, there was a double suicide bombing in Egypt, in the Sinai resort town of Taba. Palestinian militants drove trucks laden with explosives into the Hilton Hotel, killing thirty-four people, including the two bombers, and wounding more than one hundred and seventy others. Their targets were the Israeli holiday-makers who flocked to the Sinai each year, drawn by its stunning desert beaches and relaxed attitude. The Israeli government had published warnings about possible attacks, but the holiday-makers ignored them. Israel had returned the Sinai Peninsula to Egypt more than twenty years earlier, but they joked that Israeli tourists would never leave. As it turned out, this double bombing killed more locals than Israelis. Suicide bombs are an imprecise weapon.

I called Raphael to tell him I wouldn't be able to meet him later that evening as we'd planned. It looked like I'd be going down to Egypt.

'Oh man! Really? *Really?* You have to come by before you go so that I can give you one more kiss first.'

Now, that's what every reporter wants to hear on her way to a suicide bombing …

It was part of the miracle of Raphael, whose light-hearted radiance, like a balm, tempered the sorrows and difficulties of working here.

5

The conflict between Israel and the Palestinians had been going for more than five decades when I arrived, ever since the state of Israel was established in 1948. The names said everything. The Israelis celebrated 15 May as Independence Day, the Palestinians mourned it as Nakba Day, or Catastrophe Day.

Was it theft of Palestinian land or the reclaiming of Jewish land? Or was it both? The answer seemed to depend on where you stood. The establishment of the state of Israel created two competing narratives: that of the return of the Jews to their historic homeland, and that of the dispossession of Arabs from their ancestral farms and villages. For Israelis it was a story of pride and achievement. The Jews back in the land of their forefathers for the first time in two thousand years, returning from the four corners of the earth to which they had been exiled, forging a new society, reviving the long-dead Hebrew language and creating a nation.

For Palestinians it was a story of loss, of people who turned from proud landowners into stateless refugees, their villages emptied and then destroyed, nursing an ache which never healed. In a sense this dispossession also created a nation, forging a Palestinian identity for the local tribes who had lived under various Ottoman overlords before the British took power in 1917.

In November 1947, the UN voted to create a Jewish state by dividing British Mandatory Palestine in two, giving one half to the Arabs and the other to the Jews. Neither side was really satisfied –

no one ever is when asked to divide a baby. Jews accepted the UN partition plan, because it was better than nothing. Arabs did not, for they were losing part of their territories. When Jewish leaders announced the establishment of their state in May 1948, five Arab countries attacked: Egypt, Iraq, Jordan, Syria and Saudi Arabia. The war was bitter and long. Israel lost more than six thousand people, about one per cent of its population. Arab casualties were estimated at between eight and fifteen thousand.

By the time the armistice agreements were signed in 1949, between three hundred and fifty and five hundred Palestinian villages had been emptied, and hundreds of thousands of Palestinians had fled. Israel bulldozed most of the Palestinian villages and built new ones for its citizens in their place, or planted trees over them, which have now grown into forests, so that no one could return. In the few empty Palestinian villages that had not been destroyed, the houses were handed over to new Jewish residents. The Palestinians who didn't flee became citizens of the Jewish state. Today they make up one-fifth of its population, known in Israel as Israeli Arabs, and to Palestinians as 'the Arabs of 1948'.

Israeli authorities claimed that the Palestinian villagers who fled did so at the instigation of the invading Arab armies. They hadn't wanted to kill their own, and had therefore instructed the Palestinians to run and leave everything behind, assuring the villagers they would soon be back. They needed only to take their house keys. Some Israeli historians now join Palestinians in arguing that expelling the villagers from their homes was a deliberate Israeli policy, to ensure a Jewish homeland free of Arabs.

From today's vantage point it seems clear that Palestinians were pushed to leave, for very different reasons, by both Israeli and Arab troops. More than 700,000 people fled, between fifty and eighty per cent of the Palestinian population. They were housed in refugee camps in Gaza, Jordan, Lebanon and Syria. Their number has now swollen to nearly five million, for their children and grandchildren also regard themselves as refugees. I have interviewed young people in Palestinian refugee camps in the West Bank and Gaza, and also in Jordan and Lebanon, who said they were from Jaffa or from Haifa, although these are towns which they have never even visited. Their grandparents were the last to have been there, in the 1940s. But their ID cards stated they were born there, and they felt as if that were true.

Their families still have the keys to their grandparents' homes, beautiful, large, old-fashioned keys, made from wrought iron, a cold, heavy weight in the hand. They are kept in pride of place on barren shelves in the concrete slums the UN built for the refugees and which it is still maintaining more than half a century later. Although most of the exiles' original homes no longer exist, and the keys are all that remain of that other historic rural Palestine, with its low stone houses and fragrant orange groves, the longing and the memories burn fiercely.

Both sides have a deep desire to see the other simply disappear, feelings I have not identified in other national struggles. Many Palestinians believe that the 'Zionist entity' (unable to bring themselves to utter the word 'Israel') will fade away over time. All the Jews will 'go back to Europe', even those who were born in Israel, and the Palestinians will return to their old homes, even though these no longer exist.

'A land without a people for a people without a land,' was one of the early Zionist slogans. This was patently false, for Palestine had not been a land without people, but a number of Israelis hope, like small children, that if they simply close their eyes the Palestinians will vanish. It's as if neither believe in the physical reality of the other, convinced that if they just hold fast to their own position it will be enough to bring about their opponent's defeat.

My job involved trying to get to grips with this history of hostility and hatred. Difficult days were lightened by text messages from

Raphael saying he missed me or simply 'kisses'. He played his guitar or downloaded clips from his favourite sixties bands, so he could explain seminal moments in rock and roll history to me. I was there for Robert Plant and Jimmy Page, it took me longer to come round to Raphael's favourite, Ozzy Osbourne. It was the mad intensity of 'I Just Want You' that finally swung me. Staying in period, I played him Eric Clapton's 'Layla' (the acoustic version) while he told me stories about growing up in Jerusalem. They reminded me of Garrison Keillor's *Lake Wobegon* tales, which always began, 'Nothing much happened in Lake Wobegon this week ...'

The characters had names like Dido and Chupchik. The stories started with lost keys and pesky dogs, and involved Raphael having to sneak back home at 5.00am without waking his parents, and somehow always ended up with everyone eating in Raphael's kitchen, where his mother, a legendary cook, whipped up spectacular spreads. I suggested that Raphael should write a book with these stories and put his mother's recipes in between. He said that if he included the recipes the publisher would have to pay double.

When we knew each other better, he started bringing over pots of his mother's famous Iraqi kubbe soup, coloured ruby red by a beetroot broth, and her garlicky eggplant dip and green beans in tomato sauce. I could see what he meant. This raised home cooking to another level.

After eating take-away from his mother's kitchen, we lay on the couch and watched Raphael's favourite Israeli movies. He had his arms around me, explaining the plot and translating the best bits. We laughed a lot. In fact, looking back through the haze of memory, I remember only laughter from this time – surely a good sign? Sometimes we talked about moving in together or getting a dog. But I didn't think either was a real possibility, just a lovers' fantasy. The attraction of opposites was strong. My world was mysterious and irrelevant to Raphael. Perhaps that carried the seeds of problems later, but it was very appealing right then.

When I told him about my last trip to Iraq, he simply asked in horror, 'Iraq? Why would you go to Iraq?'

Raphael's mother's family was from Mosul in northern Iraq, but that made no difference to him. Sitting on the sandstone step outside my house on a cool autumn evening, looking out over the walls of the Old City, he was honestly mystified. A fat yellow moon had been hanging low over the ramparts since twilight, as if it were too lazy to climb any higher into the sky, and leaning against Raphael I didn't know how any of those overworked Jerusalem angels could resist coming down to enjoy such a magical aspect.

'Iraq is so dangerous,' Raphael said lighting a cigarette, 'and it's not as if you're doing something useful, like being a doctor. You're just a journalist ...'

I burst out laughing. That was one way of looking at it! And it was very different from the way we correspondents viewed ourselves and our 'mission'. Raphael provided me with a cold, hard dose of perspective.

That night he woke and pulled me close saying, 'I dreamed I was in a war, that's what happens when you sleep with a journalist. Why didn't you come and visit me in my dreams?'

The central political question I was reporting on focused less on the grievances from 1948, when the Jewish state was founded, and more on the fallout from the war nineteen years later in 1967, when Israel captured the West Bank. How much of this land should Israel give to the Palestinians, for their new state? All? None? Some? Could the two peoples divide and share this tiny patch of rocky ground? Outsiders thought they obviously should. The locals were less certain. After decades of conflict, the majority on both sides agreed that they could divide some of it, though they didn't always agree on which bits. But few on either side were willing to compromise on Jerusalem.

Orla described it as 'a fight about real estate', but religion was the additional complicating factor in the story. Even more than in most wars, everyone who was fighting here had God on their side. Since the time of Jesus, power changed hands among Jews, Christians and Muslims in Jerusalem like a relay race baton. The handover was never peaceful. The city was conquered, sacked, rebuilt and then re-conquered and destroyed again. Each new ruler exhibited a desire not only to occupy Jerusalem but to possess it.

For the majority of the last two thousand years, the city has been under Muslim control. When the Christian Crusaders came in the eleventh century, they saw their mission as reclaiming Jerusalem for Christ and cleansing it of Infidels. There were no pilot-less planes back then, and no clinical targeting of unseen victims from a computer screen. The Crusaders killed every man, woman and child inside the walled city – Muslims and Jews, on the same side then – in a brutal frenzy of face-to-face butchery. Contemporary chronicles record the victorious holy warriors wading through Jerusalem's narrow stone alleys, in blood up to their knees, shouting *'Deus Vult!'*, God wills it!

This image is horrifying – even some of the Christian historians couldn't hide their revulsion – and the memory of the cruelty of the Crusades affects Muslims to this day. But what most troubled me when I read that description was that it didn't feel foreign. It seemed that people were only a whisker away from that now. The quality in Jerusalem that inspires faith to the edge of madness was in the very stones, and it hadn't diminished during the years of renewed Jewish sovereignty. Everyone still wanted to occupy Jerusalem and also to possess it.

Conscription is compulsory in Israel. At age eighteen, men are drafted for three years, women for two years, though many women receive exemptions. Despite his military service, I felt Raphael was softer than me. It wasn't just because after the first twelve weeks of punishing basic training, Raphael's service had been in the IDF film unit, where he'd interviewed old generals and made documentaries about them. (When she heard that, Orla was pleased. 'At least you know he hasn't killed anyone. That would change a man,' she said.) It was because there was something sensitive in Raphael's spirit.

After we'd been seeing each other for about three months, Raphael confessed that he was upset by a poster of Saddam Hussein which was hanging on my bathroom door. I was attached to that poster. I had looted it myself from an abandoned government office in Baghdad, just after American forces had taken over the city.

Baghdad then was in utter chaos. I like chaos before it turns dangerous. It's a journalist's paradise. Everything's wide open, you can go anywhere, see anything and talk to anyone, before the next regime imposes limitations – zones, passes, press officers, appointments. Like most government buildings, the Iraqi Health Ministry was a tip when I turned up there on a hot morning in May 2003. Furniture was overturned and broken, with parts of desks and chairs lying on top of each other at odd angles. The glass in the windows was cracked and wires were hanging from the ceiling where light fittings had been pulled out. Everything was covered in dust, as if this were a Mesopotamian ruin that had been destroyed hundreds of years, and not just days, earlier.

There, on the back wall in the midst of all that mess, in pristine condition hung a photograph of Saddam Hussein. It was black and white, the official face of the Handsome Young Dictator, which had loomed neat and orderly, over every government office. Like the photos of Soviet leaders in Russia, it made him appear exactly what he wasn't – moderate and trustworthy. My translator pointed it out and asked if I wanted it. I decided that I did and that I would do what the locals were doing and help myself.

I scraped the rubble off a desk, clambered up onto it and pulled the picture down. Taking this kind of memorabilia out of Iraq was forbidden at that time, so I removed the photo from its frame, rolled it up and smuggled it out of the country wrapped up in a carpet. Back in Jerusalem, I stuck it up on my bathroom door, where it gave me a small feeling of achievement each time I passed it, symbolising my safe return as well as my success as a smuggler. But for Raphael it was different. He said he couldn't bear to look at that evil man every morning when he woke up. I told him to lighten up. He said he was serious. I was confused.

A friend in Sydney advised me gently that Raphael might be right, and that she wouldn't want to look at Saddam Hussein every morning either. There was a danger that my job was making me lose awareness of what things meant to people, especially if they were sensitive, but even if they weren't. After that, I reluctantly agreed to remove the poster. I pulled it off the bathroom door and stood there, debating whether to roll it up or simply to shift it and hang it inside the electricity cupboard where it wouldn't bother Raphael.

After a moment's indecision, I opted for the cupboard. I found some tape and wondered why it was that I didn't mind seeing this monster every day before breakfast. Maybe living in Moscow had toughened me up. If there was ever a place where only the strong survive, it's Russia. As I stuck Saddam up in his new dark home, where he would disturb only the electricity meter and the occasional shocked technician who came to read it, I remembered returning to Sydney after my first year in Moscow and looking around in surprise at the easy, civilised place where I'd been born and grown up. Australians seemed spoiled, too soft and happy, too lucky. Wintry Russia, with its bleakness, and its injustice and suffering, was seeping into my bones.

In contrast, Raphael was someone who wanted things easy. The perfect cup of coffee, the perfect new trainers and the perfect parking spot right outside the restaurant.

'What do you mean I've parked too far away?' I asked in disbelief one evening after dinner, as he complained about what I'd thought was a brilliant spot, barely five minutes from our destination.

It turned out Raphael didn't want to walk that far.

'How did you ever do your army service?' I asked.

'Like a man,' he replied, giving me a wide, cheeky grin.

I loved shopping at farmers' markets in every city I visited, but in Jerusalem I didn't dare. There had been a number of suicide bombings at Mahane Yehuda, the farmers' market in West Jerusalem, and under Orla's firm guidance her friends never ventured there. In fact, other than covering the bombings as a journalist, I'd never set foot in the place, not even using it as a cut-through in the evenings when it was empty. But this was where Raphael was braver than me.

One day he had an urge to try the tamarind juice his dad used to buy him in the markets when he was a kid. I started to say that I wasn't sure it was safe, but he wasn't having that.

'What, you'll go to Afghanistan and you won't go with me to the markets?'

I had no answer so I took a deep breath and off we went. The market consisted of a series of covered stalls in the centre of town. It was an exciting venue, noisy, sprawling and colourful. The lanes between the stalls selling fruit, vegetables, nuts, cheeses, meat, breads and spices were crowded with shoppers. Other people obviously weren't as frightened as me. The stallholders set up competing calls to attract them.

'Two shekels, two shekels, two shekels!' or 'Grapes, grapes, grapes!' they yelled over and over, like a chant or a prayer. But I remained anxious. I couldn't shake the fear that the gleaming rows of fruit would explode at any moment. An active imagination is often a liability. Trailing behind Raphael, keeping his leather jacket in view, I found myself asking uncertainly, 'Are you sure this is safe?'

I didn't know if I could rely on his answer, since he caught buses in Jerusalem, a manifestly unsafe activity and something I would never do. Wandering along beautifully laid out rows of produce, red tomatoes, green cucumbers and asparagus, purply green artichokes, purply black eggplants, we found the stall that sold tamarind juice. Raphael was thrilled it was still there. The dark-purple tamarind drink was icy cold and sour-sweet, but diluted, so that it reminded me of children's cordial. As we drank, we inhaled the scents of Middle Eastern spices and baking bread. Something about Raphael's delight at this taste from his past, and the ordinariness of going shopping for food, enabled me to finally relax enough to enjoy myself.

Wandering further, we passed an eye-catching health food stall. It was run by Uri Azrieli, a crotchety Yemeni naturalist with greying curly hair and mahogany-coloured skin, as smooth as a teenage girl's. He sold a variety of juices and face creams, all of which he made himself, most from citrus oils and ingredients used by traditional healers in Yemen. He claimed his know-how went back to the Jewish sages, including Maimonides.

Rabbi Moses Maimonides was a towering Jewish figure from the twelfth century. As well as being the most brilliant rabbi of his generation, Maimonides was also a physician. In fact he was court physician to the Egyptian sultan, the famous Salahaddin, who went on to liberate Jerusalem from the Christian Crusaders. Above the stall, Azrieli had placed a pencil drawing of Maimonides from the 1100s, next to glossy publicity shots of himself, taken for his radio show, *Health with Azrieli*. I asked what he'd been talking about on the radio that week and he replied, 'Pomegranates,' as if that explained everything.

As soon as any woman stopped by, Azrieli barked at her to close her eyes and sprayed her face with his latest citrus-based oil. When his hapless victim cried that she was wearing makeup he ignored her, instructing gruffly, 'Rub it in, rub it in!' Everyone always ended up doing what they were told – including me that first time.

'Now you buy it and you will look like me!' he'd say, proffering his own impossibly smooth cheek to clinch the sale.

Raphael wasn't much into health food or face cream. He preferred more mind-altering substances and was immediately interested in the juice Azrieli sold as a 'pick me up'. It was pressed from two ingredients, citron, which was basically a large lemon, and *qat*, a leaf they chew in Yemen and other parts of Africa to get high. It was cold, bright green and so sweet and sour that it made your teeth ache. One small glass was very zippy, like drinking five cups of coffee at once.

Raphael bought us some green juice as well as a bunch of the narcotic *qat* leaves. He chewed some on the way home, and the rest lived in the vegetable tray in my fridge until they wilted, forgotten. Later I read that *qat* led men to have sexual fantasies and also to become impotent – a cruel combination. Still, from then on Raphael had me hooked. Not on the *qat* but on the markets. Once I overcame my fear I felt at home there.

In the modern world of supermarkets and snap frozen vegetables where everything – albeit tasteless – is available all year round, I'd almost forgotten what it meant when produce was seasonal. Here if you asked for plums or cherries in spring, the stallholders simply said, 'No, sorry, there aren't any yet,' and you had to wait till the summer.

'And don't ask for persimmons. They're finished!'

Once I adjusted, I enjoyed this very much, and looked forward to the fruit and vegetables in their season. As in Shakespearean times, ripeness was all, and the anticipation was half the pleasure. In a world of instant gratification, it was good to be taught the delights of waiting.

6

ack in Jerusalem I was developing this hunger that sometimes
comes over a girl born by the beach who's living in a mountain
town – I had to see the sea. Raphael said he'd come and we could have
our first holiday. We'd been together for a little over three months,
and I admit I was nervous. It was only for a weekend and it was
inside the country, so no airport stress. Entering and leaving Israel
invariably involved hours of questioning and detailed luggage checks
for journalists, and often included body searches ... that wouldn't put
you in the mood for a romantic weekend away, would it? But what
if we fought or got on each other's nerves? Raphael, in his laid-back
way, was simply excited.

We decided on a secluded beach up near Nahariya, in the north
of Israel. It was as far north as you could go, any further and you'd
be in Lebanon, which meant it was about four hours' drive away. The
tiny distances here always shocked me. In Australia, you'd barely
be setting out. We agreed on a date and found a seaside camp site
with wooden cabins. I booked the one with the jacuzzi. Neither of
us is very punctual, and at one point I began to doubt that we were
actually going to manage to leave that day. But finally, an hour before
sunset, we had everything packed and loaded in the car. By the time
we drove into Nahariya it was dark.

'Doesn't matter, we can see the sea tomorrow.'

It was warmer up there. The night was balmy. When we went to
dinner, Raphael was wearing jeans and a blue T-shirt. He liked blue,

it suited him. I was in a gauzy summer dress, perhaps for the last time that year. We walked to the restaurant holding hands. I confessed that I was feeling guilty about being here on holiday while one of my friends was in Iraq. American journalist Meg Coker was going house to house with US forces in search of militants in Fallujah. Raphael thought I was crazy.

'Would you rather be in Fallujah than here with me? *Fallujah???*'

His indignation made me smile. Before he met me, would Raphael have even known there was an American military operation to clean out insurgents in Fallujah? We decided on pasta. The first call came while we were still eating.

'Yasser Arafat is dying.'

Colleagues rang from Jerusalem and then broadcasters began calling from overseas. I put them off and looked helplessly at Raphael. This wasn't the romantic holiday we'd planned. He responded with his easy, happy smile. The death of any leader after forty years in power is a story. The death of Yasser Arafat – an international figure and in many ways the symbol of the Palestinian struggle for statehood – was a huge story.

'There is only one other story I would think of going back for, and that would be if Israel's Prime Minister, Ariel Sharon, was dying,' I said, thinking out loud. Raphael said we should get an ice-cream to help me decide.

Arafat had always been a controversial figure. He'd begun as a guerrilla leader, in olive-green fatigues and a black-and-white keffiyeh, when the West Bank was still under Jordanian rule and Jerusalem was a divided city, controlled by Israel in one half and Jordan in the other. Some Israelis alleged he had never stopped being a guerrilla, nor abandoned the policy of attacking Israeli civilians, even during the time he was supposed to be negotiating a peace accord.

Palestinians saw him differently. Many revered him, calling him by his nom de guerre, Abu Amar. They regarded him as the father of the nation, the man who had pulled this collection of disparate clans together and given them an identity, and a national project. But increasing numbers were disillusioned, seeing his political organisation, Fatah, as corrupt, and his personal legacy as one of failure. If he were judged strictly on results, forty years after Fatah had been founded, Arafat had not achieved his fundamental aim. There was no Palestinian state. Whether the blame was his, or Israel's, or both, that was the fact that Palestinians had to live with.

Channel 9 in Sydney wanted to know if I could talk to them live from Jerusalem that night, and TVNZ wanted me to be in Ramallah live at 7.00am the next morning. Channel 9 was easy. Tonight was out of the question. It was already midnight and the drive back would take at least four hours. As for the Kiwis, I said that I wasn't even sure if the morning was do-able, since I would have to drive through the night. I still might not reach Ramallah in time, as I needed go via Jerusalem first. They weren't put off.

'Jerusalem will be fine.'

In order for me to talk live from Jerusalem to the southern hemisphere, the broadcasters booked slivers of time on a satellite that linked up to a series of other satellites orbiting the earth and beamed the reporter overseas into the studio back home. They could see and hear me but I didn't see them; I only heard them via an earpiece. I knew that spots on the satellite would be booked up fast on a big story like this, so I asked TVNZ to make sure there was time available. I didn't want to leave my holiday and drive all night if it wasn't absolutely necessary. After they hung up, I told Raphael it was up to him. We wouldn't go if he didn't want to. He was very gracious.

'Whatever suits you. I don't mind,' he said.

An American friend called and said to stay but I still wasn't sure. In a gap between phone calls, Raphael said he loved me. It's magical to hear those words for the first time. I felt all tingly and I'll always know the exact date and time, because at that moment, 2.00am, on

27 October 2004, which was 1.00pm that afternoon in Wellington, TVNZ rang back to confirm they had a satellite booking for their evening show, now five hours away. We'd have to go back. I was all smiles, nothing to do with TVNZ or working on a big story. Raphael and I packed the few things we'd managed to unpack and left twenty minutes later.

We never did see the sea.

We drove through the night, racing down Route 6, Israel's main toll road. The pink dawn lit up the West Bank and the delicate minarets of the mosques rising above the homes in village after village. It had a calm beauty, at odds with how tense I felt. *Raphael says he loves me!* Smiles were chasing frowns across my face. *Will we make it in time?* We drove back into Jerusalem just before 6.00am, which left enough time to get home, grab some TV clothes and get to the studio. But it would still be a close call, which may be why I burst a tyre on a rock as I reached my own driveway.

I parked the car as well as I could, snatched some clothes, kissed Raphael and ran up to the nearest hotel to look for an early-morning taxi. I was so tired that I left my wallet behind. I couldn't believe that I would have to try and catch a taxi without any money, but the deadline was looming and I didn't have time to do anything else. To show that bad luck doesn't always come in threes, the first taxi I hailed was driven by Abu Samir, a Palestinian from East Jerusalem, who agreed to take me, even without payment.

'You pay me afterwards, as you like.'

Now that's something that wouldn't happen in Sydney or New York! I walked into the studio with ten minutes to spare, heart pounding, eyes burning. The makeup woman said, with Israeli directness, 'You look terrible!'

She had five minutes to do what she could to fix that.

They have a number of cameras stationed at various points around these studios and naturally, because time was so tight, they directed me to the wrong one. The man at the downstairs spot said, 'No, you're not here, you're upstairs!'

That was three minutes away. With the deadline bearing down, the lift took its own sweet time. When the doors finally opened – *Come on, come on!* – I ran up another flight of stairs and climbed a ladder onto the roof. I was still putting in eyedrops when the satellite connected to Wellington.

After all that, I babbled for four minutes and it was over. It hardly seemed worth it, especially since Arafat lingered for another two weeks. That's why most correspondents left the country when they took holidays. It wasn't so easy to be called back. I'd been running on adrenaline, and now that the job was done I slumped. I headed back home, exhausted. My throat was dry, my eyes scratchy, my shoulders tense and I owed Abu Samir for two taxi rides. I felt like a rag. *Rag. Ragged. Ragged hag. Hag rag.* My feet beat out a rhythm on the stone stairs back down to my apartment. When I let myself through my front door, Raphael was awake and in a much better mood than me. He looked at me and smiled.

'Why have they put so much makeup on your beautiful skin?'

That's when I realised that age didn't matter. I loved him too.

Rumours were flying around about Arafat's condition. Sick. Very sick. Dead. The Fatah leadership decided that he needed to be sent to a hospital in Paris for specialised treatment he couldn't receive in the West Bank. It would be the first time Arafat had voluntarily left the Palestinian territories since he had returned from exile more than a decade earlier.

Arafat roused himself to farewell his people. The cameras filmed him wearing blue trackies and a woollen cap, instead of his trademark black-and-white keffiyeh, and patting various aides on the head, smiling gormlessly. *So he's not dead*, Orla and I said to each other, sitting in her office watching the TV feed. Arafat no longer looked like a leader; he looked like a sick Alzheimer's-ridden old man, the ancient uncle everyone avoids at family parties. Simply being able to sit up was a remarkable achievement, given how ill he was, but for Palestinians the sight of their weakened leader was also embarrassing. As it turned out, it was the last time they would see him alive.

On the morning Arafat was to be flown to Paris, Channel 9 in Sydney wanted me to be in Ramallah at 6.00am for a liveshot. Filing to different time zones is exhausting. They didn't know and didn't care that I'd been working till after midnight for a broadcaster in Europe. I stumbled out sleepily and left another 'Gone to Ramallah' note on the kitchen table for Raphael.

Almost on autopilot, I passed through the Israeli military checkpoint at the entrance to Ramallah and caught a taxi to the Mukata, Arafat's compound. The streets were quiet and, as we zipped through them, I asked the taxi driver what his feelings were on this day when Arafat would leave Palestinian soil, perhaps forever.

'Zay ay yo'om (It's like any day),' he answered phlegmatically in Arabic.

As if to confirm this assessment, Arafat's compound was almost empty, apart from journalists and Fatah diehards. Arafat was being farewelled by his party faction, not his people. They stayed home. It was an anti-climactic departure. I did my satellite interview as Arafat's helicopter lifted off and flew slowly over the West Bank, heralding the end of an era in Palestinian politics.

Afterwards, I looked up and followed the chopper in the sky, wondering what was going through Arafat's mind. Was he awake, asleep – or already in a coma? Was he looking out over the land he failed to divide, the state he failed to build? The helicopter was now only a small dot and I kept my head tilted back, looking till I couldn't see it any more.

After it had disappeared from sight, the skies opened. I'd never seen a downpour like it. The water fell in sheets, and then in one vast torrent as if a container as wide as the sky was being emptied out. In

Shakespearean times they believed that when kings died, the elements reflected the tragedy – graves opened, lions walked, the weather became extreme. Here the weather provided the missing drama.

I was waiting at an outdoor taxi stand for one of the little yellow minibuses that travel the back roads between Ramallah and East Jerusalem. Within seconds everyone was drenched and the road had turned to mud, its potholes filled with water and small stones. One driver parked his minibus and said, 'I'm not going anywhere.' But he kindly let me in, to wait till the rain eased. The windscreen misted up, water trickled down my neck and in my socks, and the vehicle smelt of cumin and wet denim. I wanted to talk about Arafat, but the driver was more interested in why I didn't have children.

When the rain subsided and the taxis started moving again, I hopped out to wait in the mud. Men with improvised raincoats, black plastic garbage bags pulled over their clothes, called out destinations: 'Shuafat!' 'Nablus!' People were slip-sliding through the grey-brown clay to the right taxi. When they sang out my destination, 'Bab el-Amoud, Damascus Gate,' the small yellow bus filled up quickly.

The floor was scuffed with muddy footprints and the driver was playing a tape of fiery sermons in Arabic. We drove to Jerusalem from the east, past outcroppings of barren grey and green rocks jutting into the sky, and long stretches without any cultivation – not even olive trees. It was windswept and wild that day, and the city outskirts appeared suddenly: donkeys and carts, stone houses, rows of peach, almond and olive trees. Civilisation.

The minibus dropped us at the grand Damascus Gate. Its stones were shiny with rain, black at the bottom, fawn at the top. Stalls nearby were opening, and I went to a bread cart. A Palestinian teenager was busy putting out soft, sweet rolls, oval-shaped and covered with sesame seeds, warm from the oven and slightly damp from the rain. I bought some for Raphael, along with two bunches of fragrant coriander, and walked home along the Old City walls, inhaling the smell of newly washed earth as I trudged up the hill. Palestinians streamed past me, heading in the opposite direction, down to the Al-Aqsa Mosque for prayers.

At the next corner, near the Jaffa Gate, I passed two ultra-Orthodox Jews, wearing black from head to foot. Their long, curly earlocks reached to their shoulders. Furry hats like boats were perched on their heads. One was wearing a shower cap over his fur hat, the other a plastic shopping bag.

After them an apparition appeared, a man dressed in flowing white robes, wearing a golden crown and carrying a golden harp. He was soaked to the skin but happy, even exuberant. No plastic bags for him. He looked like he was about to burst into song – *Raindrops keep falling on my harp!* – but what was strangest about him was that he didn't look out of place. Standing near the Old City walls, as the sun was struggling out from behind rain clouds, his clothes plastered to him, his crown gleaming, he appeared to fit in seamlessly. Was he crazy, or was he perhaps one of the angels I'd been waiting for? They say you don't always recognise them ... I'll never know because I avoided him and headed for home and breakfast with that other angel, Raphael.

Arafat had fallen ill halfway through the holy month of Ramadan, when Muslims fast from dawn to dusk each day. The fast is one of the five pillars of Islam, along with giving charity to the poor and going on a pilgrimage to Mecca. It's widely observed in Palestinian society, even among secular Muslims.

In Jerusalem, a cannon was fired twice every day, at sunrise and sunset, to herald the start and end of the fast. The same family, the Sandoukas, had been doing the job for generations. I could hear the BOOM! from my house and thought it was a bomb each time.

Watching me jump, Raphael said, 'How do you go to Afghanistan and Iraq? You jump at the slightest thing, you must turn into a different person there!'

Maybe he was right, maybe I did.

Yasser Arafat died in Paris on 11 November 2004, two days before the end of Ramadan. He was seventy-five years old. Afterwards, his body was brought back for burial in Ramallah. For journalists covering the funeral, it turned out to be fraught as well as dangerous.

I drove to Ramallah with two other reporters, my friend from Moscow the American journalist Craig Nelson and a tall adventurous Dane called Allan Sorensen, whose height and fair colouring made him stand out in any crowd here. He possessed a flair for languages and an impish sense of humour, and I could easily imagine him as a Viking, vanquishing one nation after another and quickly learning to talk to them all. Craig and Allan were possibly my two favourite colleagues to go out with on a story, but I was in a bad mood that morning after having had a fight with Raphael.

I felt he kept me waiting too often. It was wonderful when he got here, but I had so little time in my deadline-driven life and didn't want to spend my free evenings at home, not going out because Raphael was due any minute. One night I texted, but then didn't send, 'Waiting for you is like waiting for Arafat to die.' When he finally arrived, late, on the night before the funeral, we quarrelled. It's not good to go out on a big story in a bad mood; you are distracted just when you need to have your wits about you, so I was very happy when he rang to make up.

'Just remember that I love you,' he said. It wasn't an easy conversation to have with two male colleagues listening in.

'Me too,' I replied, trying to hide my smile.

It was a perfect autumn day, the sky clear, the sun shining warmly. We arrived early at the Mukata, located on a hill in the north of the city. Many journalists were already ensconced in surrounding buildings, having paid huge sums to rent them for the day so they could look over the high grey concrete walls and see what was happening inside Arafat's compound. The BBC was one of those broadcasters with a prime spot, naturally, but its building was barely there. It was still a shell, with no doors or windows and no railings on the unfinished concrete stairs. The enterprising owner of this unsafe structure was charging the Beeb thousands of pounds, and Orla was running up and down the incomplete steps as carefully as she could. Craig and Allan and I couldn't afford those prices, and we didn't need a top shot, since we weren't filing for TV that day, so we decided that we would be better off on the ground.

In contrast to the morning of Arafat's departure for Paris three weeks ago, this time Palestinians did turn out. Tens of thousands came from all across the West Bank, men and women of all ages and all walks of life. They perched on surrounding buildings and walls, and even climbed up trees. Journalists were allowed into the VIP area where Arafat's chopper would land, but there was no real crowd control, and within a short time large numbers of people were pouring into the compound. Inside the VIP area, the police linked arms to try to hold back the mourners but, as I watched, their arms gave way and the rest of the crowd poured through. I lost sight of Craig and Allan. I am slightly claustrophobic and didn't feel safe in that press of humanity. I breathed in deeply, held my possessions tight and, like everyone, looked up at the sky.

We waited a long time, squashed close together. More than two hours passed and then a swirl of dust heralded the arrival of two helicopters. As they hovered in the air, I realised that I was directly beneath them. I was trying to calculate exactly where they would land – hoping it wouldn't be on top of us – when the crowd suddenly gave way to clear a space. It seemed to be an organic process, like an amoeba dividing.

I was lifted up and carried along. My feet weren't touching the ground. If any of us had fallen, we'd have been trampled. The lack of control made me feel seasick. I fought feelings of panic, but my feet still weren't on the ground when I saw a wall coming towards me. The noise of the chopper blades was deafening and I had visions of the Hillsborough disaster in the UK in 1989, where a crowd at a football match surged forward and squashed dozens of fans to their deaths against the stadium fence. I can't remember smell or touch, just the sound of the choppers and the sight of the bricks drawing nearer. The crowd finally deposited me back on earth, just short of the wall. I could see that the two choppers had landed safely very close by, but there was too much adrenaline coursing through me for me to speak into my microphone. I could only stand there trembling.

I had barely gathered my breath when the crowd re-formed, a living creature once more, and picked me up again. It was a bizarre sensation, and maybe the Zen approach would have been to give in and enjoy landing wherever you were dropped, like surfing a wave. But I was way too frightened for that. I was panicking again, fighting tears and willing myself to breathe deeply. This time the crowd surged and carried me with it over to the second helicopter, where Arafat's body was being unloaded. The afternoon sun shone down on its blue steel doors. The Fatah leaders were trapped inside, and plans for a stately walk past with the coffin had to be abandoned. The crowd took over. They bore Arafat's body to the grave on their shoulders, surging this way and that, as each person tried to touch him. He was already in the process of turning from a human being into a magical relic. In the end, the Palestinian people buried their controversial prophet, forgiving him and taking him back into their hearts.

Afterwards, mourners pulled out weapons and shot into the air, an Arab funeral ritual. There was so much gunfire it sounded like a battlefield. I'd recovered enough to start working, and the gunfire became an extra character in every interview I did. When Irish radio called, the producer could hardly hear me.

'Surely that's not *live* fire???'

It was remarkable that no one was killed. When I had enough material, and had located Craig and Allan, we raced back to Jerusalem to file. We felt like ants among the crowds leaving Ramallah, even though we were in a car and not on foot like most of the others. Time was tight and I barely made my first deadline. The Irish got their story with seconds to spare.

'Thanks for that! Really appreciate it. We did a program on stress last week and I think we probably just took three months off your life,' the producer said cheerfully.

I wanted to reply – 'Ha, more like six months!' – but I didn't have the time. It was a no jokes day as the next deadline loomed. I worked down to the wire on that story, and two more afterwards. Raphael and I had planned to meet and I was running very late. He was already at the cafe when I rang to say I wouldn't be there for at least another hour. And only yesterday we'd been quarrelling because he kept me waiting. When I arrived, Raphael didn't say anything. I announced that in certain Arctic societies, being late was regarded as the highest sign of love. We looked at one another, stern gaze meeting hopeful one, then both burst out laughing.

The cupboard was bare. The laundry basket was full. The electricity was about to be cut off, and so was the phone. That was the problem with big news stories, your ordinary life fell by the wayside. Like the iconic 1970s American feminist article, I wanted a wife to take care of all this for me. Or perhaps I would update it to 'I want a producer' who, in addition to doing shopping, washing, cooking, ironing, mending and paying bills, would pitch stories for me and stay across technical issues, telling me when to upgrade recorders and cameras and computers, as well as phone and internet packages. Since there was no one like that on hand, I fought with the power company, which it turned out I had paid, and apologised to the phone company, which it turned out I hadn't, and then went shopping to stock up.

Once Raphael had shown me the way, I had quickly become a regular at Mahane Yehuda. Like the locals, I had my favourites – a cheese man, a fish man, the place with the best olives, the best fresh herbs, the best dry spices, the best plums in summer, and the best fennel in winter. The passion for food there was all-consuming, and regulars loved nothing more than to find other habitués, and compare notes. The tone was always competitive, accompanied by lots of dismissive hand wavings and head shakings.

'You go where for cheese? No, no, the best cheeses are two lanes away at the Georgian's.'

'Those chickens that you're buying simply aren't as fresh as at Nissim's at the corner. No, you can't compare! And he always organises a discount for me. But then he has known me for a long time ...'

You weren't even safe at the hairdresser. One morning, while I was getting a haircut, I casually mentioned that I was on my way to the markets afterwards. I was just making conversation, but Meir, the Israeli hairdresser, suddenly perked up, his eyes gleaming.

'You go to the markets? What are you buying? Fish? Who do you go to? You have to go to my fish man. He's the best.'

I told him that I liked my own fish man and happened to think he was the best. Meir had groovy glasses and short, spiky hair which was a different colour at each visit. He was relaxed and softly spoken, but now he was looking at me fiercely. He'd turned into Market Guy.

'I've been going to the markets for twenty-five years,' he said, pulling rank, holding his scissors up in the air as if he were taking a pledge. '*My* fish man is the best. Give him a try, you won't be sorry. I'll tell you how to get there.'

So with heavy footsteps and feeling like a traitor, I followed Meir's instructions. I walked into the market from the main entrance, past two Israeli soldiers, beautiful, bored eighteen-year-old girls, one ash blond, the other a dark-skinned Ethiopian with long curls. Both were wearing sunglasses and chewing gum. Following the repeat suicide attacks here, their army duty was spent guarding that entrance all day. I took a right turn, passing stalls with bread and cakes piled high, turned in at the pickle store, with its vats of shiny olives and mounds of different-sized dried red chillis, walked past the butcher's … and ended up standing in front of my very own fish man!

Anyone who wasn't afflicted with my poor sense of direction would have realised earlier that my hairdresser was sending me to the stall I already knew myself. But I was so happy to have arrived there by this new roundabout route that I told Haim the fish man the story too.

Haim was a small, stocky man with a big presence. Loud and brusque, I could tell from the way he pursed his lips and pushed his round glasses up his nose that he was touched, though he pretended not to be.

'Why didn't you know the way? You should have known by the corner at least!' was all he said.

Like many market stallholders, Haim was a philosopher with plenty to say, about life as well as fish. He also always remembered what his customers had bought the last time and was interested in how they'd cooked it.

'Hmm, Asian spices? Soy, ginger, what else?'

Haim's stall was clean, with different varieties of fish lying in piles on ice, no personality left in the one cold eye they turned up to you. At the Jewish New Year, when it was traditional to cook fish patties called *gefilte* fish, there was also a sight I couldn't bear – huge carp, gold and black, lying on their sides, still alive, breathing heavily, opening their gills and sucking in the air that was poisoning them. Haim dismissed my sensitivity.

'You're too soft. That's how people have always bought carp here. They have to be fresh!'

There were always queues at Haim's, but when he had time, he taught me about local fish.

'This is *musht*, I can't remember its name in English – you know *MUSHT*,' he said, repeating the name more loudly, as if the problem was that I hadn't heard him the first time. He pointed at a shiny striped grey fish, lying neatly among a pile of its brothers on the ice. 'It's a freshwater fish, delicate and delicious.'

'And this one?' I pointed to a beautifully patterned orange fish nearby.

'That's also *musht*. Yes, I know they're different colours, this one is orange and that one is grey, but they are the same fish,' he said shortly. 'What do you think – that I don't know my fish?'

Realising that he was losing patience, I decided on the orange one, attracted by its bright colour and the coral-shaped patterns on its skin. Haim held up two orange fish, balancing one in each hand, inspecting them closely.

'I think this one is better, what do you think?'

'Whatever you say,' I replied, deferring to his experience.

This made him irritable.

'What's wrong with you? You have to pay more attention when you choose a fish,' he said severely. 'It's important.'

'It's only fish, it's not a husband!' I said jokingly and he didn't miss a beat.

'You know, if you could only have a husband like one of these, you'd be happy.' He paused, drawing out the next word. '*Qui-iiii-et*. Not a word out of him. Why do you think I work with fish? Twenty-five years and they don't answer back.'

Then he took the fish he'd picked for me instead of a husband, and sent it off to be cleaned. At home, I steamed it for Raphael with coriander, fresh chilli and green beans and my favourite soy and sesame sauce.

Following Arafat's death, there was a news lull as the Palestinians went through a re-assessment. In early 2005, Palestinian militant groups signed up to a *tahdiya*, a 'period of quiet', in which they would not carry out suicide attacks against Israeli civilians. Israel for its part declared a moratorium on targeted killings in the Palestinian territories. Israel and Hamas didn't have diplomatic relations or even speak to one another, so that was as close to a formal ceasefire as it got.

There was also a personal re-arrangement. Raphael moved to Tel Aviv to do a postgraduate music course. It was a prestigious school, and he was lucky to get in, so he explained that it was simply more practical that he should live there. The catch was that the course ran for two years. When I said in a small voice that two years seemed like a very long time, Raphael looked sad.

'I hope it won't change things between us,' he said seriously.

Something about his concern made me bury my own anxiety and switch into reassuring mode.

'It only takes an hour to drive from Tel Aviv to Jerusalem. In Australia you have to live at least eight hours apart to qualify as "Geographically Impossible",' I said airily.

I told him that Orla had never yet lived in the same city as her new husband, who was a reporter based in Baghdad. If they could survive between Israel and Iraq, surely we could survive between Jerusalem and Tel Aviv? Raphael looked relieved but not convinced.

Once he moved, I was surprised to find that he was right; things were different. I hadn't appreciated how much time we'd spent together, or how much I would miss him. In a short time, he'd become a huge part of my life. He tried to arrange it so that he came up twice a week, but it was hard to be spontaneous, or to meet by accident, when you weren't in the same city. One Sunday night when he was back in Tel Aviv, he called to persuade me to come down to see him. I let him convince me that my work could wait, but I took my laptop in case there was breaking news and I had to file in the morning.

When I arrived, Raphael was all smiles. On the balcony of his small house there was an ancient sofa, which had originally been beige and was now brown from spilt coffee and alcohol and God knew what else. It was low slung and once you sank down into it, you felt you could never climb out. Raphael pulled me down onto the sofa and held me close against his chest. He couldn't stop smiling, and kept repeating, 'It's Sunday and you're here, it's Sunday and you're here.'

I don't think I've ever made anyone so happy before just by turning up. Life with Raphael was a series of small delicious pleasures.

'I love you, I love you, I love you, I love you …'

Natasha Bedingfield woke me with her rap ballad 'These Words', my favourite song of the winter. It had a catchy, sexy sound and spoke straight to me, since it was about a woman, waste-bin full of paper, struggling to write a classic. I snuggled up to Raphael's warm back to listen to the English news bulletin.

'You tried to get away during the night, but I pulled you back,' he said drowsily.

Luckily, there was no news I needed to report, so we didn't have to get up immediately.

'Isn't it amazing that you can meet someone by chance in a cafe and be happy?' I asked, lying with my head on Raphael's shoulder, feeling the pleasurable weight of his arm on my hip. I was always brooding on fate. The way I saw it, you could meet a bastard by chance – we've all done that – but a nice guy? That's what they call in the newspaper business a Man Bites Dog story.

Raphael looked down at me. 'You've got that author's look in your eye. Do you want me to describe everything I remember about our first meeting?'

'No, I mean it … isn't it strange that meeting someone important can be just a matter of luck? What if one of us hadn't been in the cafe that day – or had come an hour later?'

Raphael was less impressed.

'But we didn't. That's how it goes. My parents met on a zebra crossing, you know. My dad was walking behind my mum and then they both stopped and they got talking while they waited for the lights to change, and by the time they walked across, he'd asked her out.'

I liked this story about Raphael's enterprising dad – a fast worker and a pre-iPod romance. Raphael's parents, Avi and Hannah, had always been very welcoming to me, never making me feel that I was too old for their son. Since Raphael didn't seem to care how old I was either, that left me as the only person worried about the age gap.

As we lay talking, I realised we'd been together for six months and we were still happy. To me, it seemed like a miracle. But Raphael was about to change that.

7

Tel Aviv, April 2005

It was a warm spring evening. My beeper was sitting quietly in my pocket – a sign that there was no news – and I was walking with Raphael in Tel Aviv. Actually, walking is too definite a word, too earthbound. I was floating along that day, happy for no real reason, which is another way of saying in love, I guess. My best friend in Sydney poses a trick question: how does it feel when everything's going right and there's love in your life? The answer is that it just feels natural. The alternatives, such as rubbing along with someone you no longer care about or jogging along completely alone, are the ones that feel unnatural.

I thought of that as we strolled along the sunny, dusty Tel Aviv street, holding hands. Palm trees were planted at intervals in front of 1960s apartment buildings showing their age, a ramshackle street in a Mediterranean port town. Raphael's dark hair was back in a ponytail and his guitar case was slung over his shoulder. When he turned his head and smiled, I caught my breath. I wondered if his smile would always do that or if I'd get used to it one day.

Usually I gave myself lectures when I became too floaty, reminding myself that this relationship was unlikely to last. I ran through the familiar arguments – the differences in culture and age, as well as my demanding job, which would ultimately see me settle somewhere else. But that afternoon I let those gossamer strands of happiness ensnare me and put off thinking about the future until 'tomorrow'. Surely sometimes you could follow your heart, even if you were a journalist?

We passed a Russian language book shop and a bakery, emitting a delicious gust of cinnamon and sugar. Next door was a pet shop, with rabbits and guinea pigs in the window and a canary trilling away in a cage hanging on the door. You could be trapped and happy, it seemed. There were signs in Russian for lawyers and agents, which I decided most likely meant prostitutes, as we headed towards a cafe.

Tel Aviv has always been a city of cafes. Jewish immigrants founded 'the first Hebrew city in more than one thousand years' in the early twentieth century here on the Mediterranean coast, just up from the Arab port town of Jaffa. They wanted their new city modern and secular, as different from Jerusalem as they could make it. So they built broad paved roads, instead of winding alleys, a water and sewerage system instead of wells, and electric street lights and high-rise. (Well, three floors was considered high-rise here then.) Since the immigrants were mostly from Europe, they set up those other European necessities: cafes and bakeries. They prepared buttery poppy-seed rolls, yeast buns swirling with nuts and spices, and light-as-air strudels filled with apples, sour cherries and cream cheese. And what would go better with those than a cup of coffee? The cakes were outstanding from the start – with one strudel so delectable that it was reputed to end quarrels between lovers – but the coffee wasn't up to much. Today, it's caught up, and everything's irresistible.

Still, the chemistry has to be right. There could be six cafes in a row along a stretch of pavement, and you'd turn up your nose at five of them before settling on the sixth.

'This one's just right!' you'd declare, in your best Goldilocks voice, and that was it, you always went back there.

Raphael and I were heading for our local favourite, which had an outside patio shaded by an overhanging willow tree. The owners, immigrants from Argentina, said hello. Their coffee was strong and caramelly, and Hebrew, English and Spanish newspapers lay invitingly on long wooden tables. We sat inside. Our table looked out at the willow in its pale-green spring dress. Raphael put down his guitar, pulled back his ponytail and ordered croissants.

'Isn't it amazing how you suddenly crave yeast when you know you won't be able to have it?'

We wouldn't be able to have yeast because the Jewish festival of Passover began the next day. In modern-day Israel, it is Old Testament festivals that set the rhythm of the year. Christmas is an ordinary working day, but the country comes to a halt at Passover, when Jews retell the story of the exodus from Egypt.

Passover isn't one big festive meal like Christmas dinner, over and done with in an evening. It is a week of strict observance, when no beer, bread, cakes or anything baked with yeast is available in any Israeli food store. The aim of the ban is to re-create the experience of the biblical children of Israel when they fled Egypt.

According to the Old Testament, they ran so fast, one step ahead of Pharaoh and his army, that they had no time to bake bread. The story ended well: God performed a hugely satisfying miracle, parting the Red Sea so His people could cross, then re-joining the waters so that the Egyptian soldiers drowned. It was a rollicking tale that also spawned stirring gospel songs – *Tell old Pharaoh, to let my people go!* But if you were living in modern-day Israel, it wasn't an easy week. Yeast-free crackers become monotonous when they are all you eat. And pretty heavy. Israelis complain of seven days of constipation, an unexpected consequence of life in the Jewish state.

A waitress brought us flaky croissants and cappuccinos with leaf-shaped patterns in the froth. She smiled and turned to leave and almost fell over a straw-coloured puppy trailing at her heels. It looked like a small, fluffy blond fox. It had white socks, a tail curling into a spring, and dark eyes with a saucy look. Its tongue was poking out of the side of its mouth. It seemed to be grinning at us over its shoulder as it ran, not watching where it was going, past the waitress back towards the kitchen. There was something of American cartoonist

Gary Larson's wild-eyed dogs about that naughty gaze. This was a puppy not entirely in control, and all the more appealing for that.

'Raphael, look …' I pointed at the tiny dog scurrying out of sight. (That's the good thing about being the storyteller. You can describe things as you remember them. If Raphael were writing this, he'd say he saw the puppy first and showed it to me.) We tried to call it over, but it was still so young that it didn't respond and just ricocheted around excitedly, like a pinball, wherever its nose led. It wasn't much more than a blond blur, but Raphael said it was love at first sight.

'It was that silly look, with its tongue out the side of its mouth, as if it was concentrating very hard. I knew we were going to have something with that dog,' he later said, as if you can explain love.

The puppy ran back through the cafe, from table to table, first out the front, then back inside, following some inner puppy GPS, incomprehensible to any other creature. It was wearing a collar, so it belonged to someone, and we watched as it headed out to the patio, where a mother was sitting with two small children and a large blue pram. When the puppy's unreliable nose led it past the willow tree and towards the road, we became worried. We told the woman that her dog was in danger. She looked up blankly from wiping chocolate off her toddlers' hands, and replied, like Inspector Clouseau, 'That's not my dog.'

Raphael and I followed the puppy outside. It was running towards a three-lane road, with cars driving in both directions. Raphael was ahead of me. I was looking around for someone who could be a possible dog owner when I heard Raphael shout '*No, no, no!*' followed by a squeal of brakes.

The sounds seemed fused in that moment, so I'm not actually certain which came first, the car braking or Raphael shouting. I turned my head in time to see Raphael running into the traffic and was aware of flashes of colour, a silver car door, the green of the willow tree, his blue T-shirt. I watched him bend down to scoop the puppy up from under the wheels of a four-wheel-drive, which had stopped just in time, and saw the driver's face, pale and angry through the windscreen.

It happened in an instant but seemed to take a very long while, as if time had stretched and I was watching events unfold in slow motion. Once Raphael and the puppy were both safely back on the kerb, time contracted back to normal, and I realised that I had also been holding my breath. I exhaled and ran over to them. The puppy was a ball of fur against Raphael's chest and I swear I heard their mingled heartbeats. Relief flooded through me.

Raphael announced, his face intent: 'If we don't find its owners, it's mine.'

That slowed the relief down, like an anaesthetic. Did he mean 'mine' or 'ours'? And would it end up being ours, whatever he meant? The puppy clutched to his chest looked quite pleased with itself. It didn't seem to sense that it had just narrowly avoided being killed. They're so silly when they're small. Instead, it settled back against Raphael – *This one will protect me* – and looked up at me confidently.

'We'll leave a note at the cafe with our numbers and take it home,' Raphael said, striding purposefully back to our table, the puppy still in his arms.

Home? Not to the police? I found myself wondering, but I could see there was no point in saying anything. Some animals, like some people, are just born lucky. We left our details with the waitress and headed for the car, Raphael clutching the puppy all the while. It stayed snuggled against him as we drove. On the way, we discovered that it was a she, and with her alert curiosity about the world outside the car window she seemed to know intuitively that she was better off with us than she would have been in a Tel Aviv police station over Passover.

Raphael had one last class before the spring break so we drove to the conservatorium. It was housed in a sprawling, dusty campus north of Tel Aviv. Shabby low-slung buildings were dotted between large old trees, European imports like oaks and beeches in amongst the local palm trees. Students with dreadlocks and nose rings walked by, carrying their musical instruments, laughing with each other. It felt relaxed, and different from the law school I'd attended in Australia. No one seemed to mind Raphael bringing a dog along to learn what she could about modern musical history. I worked on my laptop, while the great bands of the sixties played again.

The lecturer liked The Doors and so did I. When Raphael put the puppy down, she was friendly to everyone and very jaunty. If we couldn't see her for a while, it was simply because she was behind one of the loudspeakers, with some students fawning over her. Raphael says now that it was this early exposure to rock 'n' roll that made her the dog she was. Yes, we loved her madly … For her part, she didn't appear to be missing her owners at all. That should have made us wary but it didn't. Instead, we congratulated ourselves that she was so good natured.

On the drive out of Tel Aviv, cars were crawling, almost at a standstill. The first Hebrew city wasn't immune to that twentieth-century blight, traffic. Flocks of cranes flew in formation overhead. They were heading from Africa to Europe for the summer, but at this rate we suspected they'd reach their destination long before we reached ours. We put the puppy in the back seat, where she vomited, before creeping back onto Raphael's lap and lying there quietly for the rest of the journey. When we reached home, he carried her inside.

Like all small new creatures, she was beguiling. She had a clever, wild gaze, and fur like lambswool. She wriggled like an eel and smelt like a puppy, a scent, like that of a baby, that is so singular you don't know you've missed it until you smell it again. Her tail was gorgeous and silly at once, curling up in a loop and then falling. Raphael and I were enchanted.

'A curly tail isn't something I'm used to. I think Australian dogs have straight tails,' I told her, holding one end of an old sock while she tugged at the other end.

I was still certain that we were only minding her until we found her owners, hopefully soon so they wouldn't spend the Passover holiday worrying about her. When the sock game palled, she pulled her cutest trick, rolling over on her back, covering her eyes with her paws and then peeking out at us over the top of them.

Raphael and I burst out laughing. That trick was a winner. There was something so human, enticing, almost coy about it, as if she was saying, 'Go ahead, have your way with me … I won't look. I'll just lie here and think of England.' Or wherever it was local dogs directed their thoughts to – Mecca? The Temple Mount? We responded by doing what she wanted, which was to scratch her tummy.

After we fed her and scratched her tummy some more, we took her outside, praising her lavishly when she peed on the grass. 'See, that was easy,' we said to each other with pleasure. We decided she would sleep on a carpet in the corner of the bedroom, where she'd already shown an interest in curling up. She obliged by running straight there and turning around in slow circles before settling happily. Raphael and I looked down at her proudly. So far, it was going very well. The puppy fitted into my apartment as if she had always lived there.

But just as I was thinking about going to sleep too, CBC, the Canadian broadcaster, phoned to request one more story. Late-night calls are an occupational hazard, and I left Raphael and the puppy and went to write a report on the death of former Israeli President Ezer Weizman. He'd been a World War II flying ace, taking part in the Battle of Britain, and then setting up the Israeli air force. He also lived large, so the piece wrote itself.

For the first time since I'd met him, on this of all nights, Raphael fell asleep before dawn. When I came to bed, there was no room for me. He was sleeping on one side, and the puppy was curled up at his back on the other. They were like two musical notes, or two question marks, facing away from each other. I burst out laughing – she didn't waste any time! – and grabbed my camera.

The puppy had only been with us a few hours and I was already laughing a lot. After I'd taken one picture, she moved to make herself more comfortable, shifting her head up further onto my pillow. I snapped a few more shots and then pushed her off. Raphael protested sleepily, but I'm not crazy about dogs in bed, and anyhow there wasn't enough room. The puppy snuggled up uncomplainingly on her carpet on the floor. Then she opened one eye and gave me a very direct look. She'd deal with *me* later.

And that's how the dog made her splashy entrance, beginning as she meant to go on – self-confident, adventurous, and with a strong need to be protected from herself. The following morning, before the entire city shut down for the Passover holiday, we rushed to the vet to see if she had an identifying microchip.

She didn't.

The vet looked at her teeth, as sharp as needles, and pronounced her three months old and healthy. Those teeth! The puppy gnawed on my finger and almost severed it while the vet searched for the chip that wasn't there. From the vet's we called the Jerusalem Society for the Prevention of Cruelty to Animals but no one had contacted them about a lost blond dog. We rang around to other vets. We rang the cafe. Nothing. Now what?

I was enchanted but also nervous. If Raphael took the dog in, it would spend at least half its time with me. How could I ever fit in looking after a dog with doing this job? Did I have the energy to look after a dog, even fifty per cent of the time?

8

It was our second morning together.

Like most three-month-old creatures, the puppy didn't know how to walk tethered to a human on a leash. She and I left the house and immediately twirled around each other and almost fell over. I unwound us and started again. After a couple more false tries, she pretended to understand the general idea that she was attached to me and the two of us would be walking together, and we set out.

She broke into a run, a pace she intended to keep up the entire time. Trying to teach her to slow down was a frustrating experience. Once she did reluctantly stop running, she wound herself and the leash around me, and we started all over again. As we did this stop-start walking, I became aware that I lived in dog heaven. I had always felt lucky to live in this beautiful place, with its sandstone homes and cobbled streets, but I hadn't noticed how practical it was for pets. Familiar things often look different when your circumstances change.

The puppy scampered along at a breakneck pace, dragging me behind her. We passed rose bushes standing in proud bright rows, like soldiers, flaunting their flowers. Palm trees towered above. I held the leash tight and said, 'Slow!' but we were still at a trot as we continued past gnarled grey olive trees set between aromatic beds of lavender and rosemary. The air was fragrant with their scent as we jogged down the shallow sandstone stairs, past gardens filled with low desert shrubs and pomegranate and lemon trees.

If only it wasn't quite so early it would be wonderful, I thought, squinting down at my watch. It said 5.50am. No wonder I had to squint. The world did look different, but I was too tired to figure out how. I yawned and held the leash tight. The puppy screeched to a halt, stopping suddenly to sniff at an unremarkable-looking section of fence. I almost tripped as I jerked to a stop behind her, but there was only a moment's rest before she set off again.

Who were we running away from, I wondered, as she yanked me along like the Hopeless Owner from a before-and-after ad for dog training. I tried to yank her back, and after thirty minutes of this we turned around and headed for home. I needed coffee – or maybe to crawl back into bed. It was still an hour and a half before the time I usually woke up.

I made my first mistake on our evening walk two days later. Our suburb was built on a hill, and in a lovely park one street below our house, I let go of the leash. I did it because it was a safe area, with no cars, and I believed that a dog has to be free sometimes, to run with other dogs, or simply to sniff the grass. The puppy rewarded me by running away, just like she did from her first owners.

She zipped back up the stairs to the street above, leash bouncing behind her, and disappeared around a corner like the white rabbit in *Alice in Wonderland*. When I arrived, panting, the sandstone street was empty and I counted six possible exits. I didn't know which one she'd taken so I climbed endless stairs, calling out to this small dog, which didn't even have a name yet. I repeated directionless little prayers, *Please let me find her, Please let me find her*, almost in tears. There is something about the idea of a puppy, alone and lost, that makes you anxious, even if *she* actually ran away from *you*, and is apparently a survivor who always lands on her paws.

After half an hour, I glimpsed her perky blond tail among the red and orange blooms in a rose garden. When I finally caught her trailing leash – 'Come here, sweet little thing, come on!' – relief instantly turned to anger. I held on tightly all the way home.

'Bad dog! You mustn't run away! I was so worried about you!'

Not that she seemed to notice. She trotted happily in the warm afternoon sunlight, still intent on discovering this new world, and as I observed her alert enthusiastic wildness – a puppy is an unmistakable state of being, quite different from a dog – a story from my childhood flashed into my head. I don't remember it exactly, because I was only two years old at the time, but it has been retold so often in my family that it *feels* as if I do. In fact it has been retold so often, it feels like a family fairytale.

Once upon a time, my mother and I visited my grandmother in her house in Bondi, an area that is now very trendy, with international celebs falling over themselves to pay high prices for poky apartments. Then it was modest and sleepy. My grandmother's house was a small semi, which seemed very large to me, far away from the beach, and set back from the road. You climbed up eight steps dividing a neatly mown patch of grass to reach the house. Inside it had parquet floors and tidy rooms, where my glamorous grandmother, Lea, baked cakes when she wasn't gossiping with her neighbours across the fence. She smoked cigarettes in a long holder and wore high-heeled stilettos. When she dressed up to go out, she looked like Ava Gardner.

'Our family was never wealthy, but from the start, I've only been able to wear the best,' my grandmother used to tell me and my wide-eyed sisters. 'So I only buy one pair of shoes, where other women would buy three, but mine will be good ones.'

We nodded gravely, absorbing this important lesson. I don't know at what age I noticed how much more attractive she was than other grandmothers – probably when I was quite a bit older.

On the sunny morning when my mother brought me to visit, and beauty was a headache still waiting far in the future, Grandma Lea was doing the spring cleaning. Her stilettos stowed safely in the cupboard, her cigarette holder on her dressing table near a crystal perfume bottle with a rubber spray atomiser, this was a job my grandmother tackled in her slippers. She had hung all her rugs out over a rail on the veranda so that she could beat the dust out of them. When her back was turned, 'for just one moment', as she always told the story later, I opened the gate, toddled from the veranda down all eight stairs as fast as my little legs could carry me, and ran out into the middle of the road.

Patterson Street in Bondi is quiet now, and it was even quieter then, but my grandmother was terrified. She raced down the stairs, as fast as her slippers could carry her, scooped me up off the road, brought me back and spanked me so hard that my mother was convinced that she was still beating the carpets. That was always my mother's contribution at this point when the story was being retold. Unlike Raphael, I was brought up with tough love.

But I understood my grandmother now. It was exactly what I wanted to do with this puppy. I paused, suddenly aware that the past had muscled the present out of the way, and that these half-buried memories had resurfaced, miles away from Australia and light years away from my childhood. How surprising that a puppy had led me back there.

I had had a hard time growing up, and not from my kind, down-to-earth Grandma Lea, actually; I loved her like crazy and miss her to this day. The grief came from my dad, her son. He was handsome, charming, in fact charismatic, but also erratic, aggressive and often violent. Later I learned words like narcissist and sociopath, but when I was young all I knew was that he was unpredictable and I was frightened.

He was barely twenty when I was born. My mother was ranged with us, on the receiving end of his sudden, explosive rages, and his becoming a father too young was one explanation she offered years later, as we tried to account for his destructive effect on her life and ours. He'd also longed for a son, a chip off the old block, and instead his wife had produced three daughters. That was another explanation, which blamed us for his inability to love us. It was our innate failure. We were *girls*.

Both explanations are partly true but still not enough. They don't account for his violence, or his cruelty, if you were his terrified daughter, heart pounding when you heard his key turn in the front door. *Oh no, what kind of night are we in for?* These days the rotten childhood has become almost a fashion accessory. Survivors write harrowing books, claiming that in the end it made them, or that they climbed out from underneath and succeeded in spite of everything. Some even argue that you need something to rebel against in order to propel you forward. They quote the German philosopher Friedrich Nietzsche, the high priest of this school: 'What doesn't kill me makes me stronger.'

But from my experience, even if you did survive being locked in a life-and-death struggle inside your family, you ended up paying a price. It was a hard way to become 'strong', and while it might not kill you outright it often killed something inside you. I blinked away these recollections, the house in Patterson Street, Grandma Lea, my father, the bits of me that had survived, and those that hadn't, for back in Jerusalem, I was almost home.

The reclaimed, re-chained puppy and I climbed the last set of stairs to my apartment and she wound her leash around us one more time. As I inserted my key in the lock, I realised that I was never frightened when Raphael came home. There are many layers behind the choice of who we love.

When we finally made it inside, I collapsed exhausted onto the sofa. Raphael was there, and the puppy ran up to him.

'She's so beautiful she makes me want to cry,' he said, cooing over her as she lay on her back with her paws over her eyes, smiling up at him. I guess they were both in love from the start.

The puppy was very relaxed. She climbed up onto the windowsill and sat there, looking out at the world. When she wanted more human contact she sat at the gate with her head poking out, making friends with passers-by. She never figured out that she could wriggle out through the grille and run away. It was the most obvious escape route, but it was the only one that small Houdini dog didn't nail.

After a few days, when we still hadn't been able to trace her owners, I began to admit to myself that this puppy we'd picked up so casually might be here to stay.

Raphael was thrilled. 'Great, she's ours!'

My reaction was slightly different. 'Oh no, she's ours!'

That was when he confessed that he'd actually wanted to steal the puppy the first moment he saw her. 'She's special. I've never wanted to steal a dog before.'

My cautious approach never stood a chance.

If she was going to be ours we had to name her. We tried out different names but couldn't agree on any. Honey suited her colouring but felt too sweet in English, and the words in Hebrew and Arabic weren't pretty or easy to say. I thought Foxy suited her personality better but Raphael didn't like it. We decided to take another day to consider. She was still at my apartment and I found myself calling her Foxy more than anything else.

When I was on the phone to Raphael that evening, I spotted the puppy chewing my sandals and said sternly, 'Foxy, no!'

Raphael interrupted me, 'Don't call her Foxy!'

He came over later that night and said decisively, 'Let's call her Mia.'

'*Mia?* Why Mia?'

The female lead in Raphael's favourite film, *Pulp Fiction*, was called Mia, but I wasn't convinced.

'Why don't we just call her Uma Thurman and be done with it?'

I thought food names worked better for dogs than human ones. I knew a very cute cream-coloured Labrador called Amaretto and another one called Halva, after the local sesame sweet. Later I learned that place names were also good, when I met a Ridgeback called Memphis and a Red Setter called Boston. But finders have naming rights, so Raphael's choice of Mia stuck.

She soon thought her name was '*MiaNo!*' or when Raphael said it in Hebrew, '*MiaLo!*' She turned out to be so energetic and badly behaved that she couldn't be left alone for more than five minutes. She ate radio cables, underwear and my favourite new sandals, the pink Arche ones from New York, which I'd only worn twice.

'You have the same taste in shoes – so what?' Orla asked kindly.

Once I'd locked up my shoes, the puppy turned to the curtains. They came with the flat and were floor-length, made from Indian sari material, light, gauzy and lovely, another example of my landlord's exquisite taste. Mia apparently thought so too, for when I went out to work and left her alone at home, she methodically attacked each curtain in turn, finishing one before she started on another. I tied the tattered material in elegant knots, above her head, and began working on a story to explain it to my landlord.

Then Mia changed tack and set to work on the sofas, scratching the corners with her claws, and biting at the material she pulled off so that it hung in strips. She also dug beneath the sofa cushions, making large airy holes from two angles, top and bottom. Unfortunately, the sofas also belonged to my landlord. They would cost more to replace than the curtains, but I found that I couldn't dream up a second story that would convince anyone.

'Maybe it would just be easier to tell him the truth?' Orla suggested.

Next Mia ate through the internet cable. My patience was starting to wear thin. I couldn't work without the internet, not to mention that it was starting to become expensive to fix all the things she was destroying. Luckily, the internet service provider sent out an emergency repairman the next day. He was a stocky, smiley middle-aged man, wearing a *kippah*, a Jewish head covering, who turned out to be a dog lover. He played happily with Mia before settling down to fix the cable and explained that his father, who had migrated to Israel from Yemen, had been a dog trainer. Mia watched intently as he worked, so after he'd finished, he put up an extra barrier around the area where she chewed through the cable.

Then he filled out the docket, writing 'ordinary wear and tear' as the reason for the call-out. Before leaving he bent down to pat her one more time. His last words were 'Dogs were my father's life.'

It was a long time since I'd had a puppy, years actually, and perhaps I'd simply forgotten how naughty they could be. Maybe it was a trick of memory, like old folk telling you that summers were hotter when they were young. *Dogs were more obedient when I was a girl …*

We always had dogs when I was growing up. When I was too young too look after them, any trouble was my mother's. The first dog that was really mine was Alfie, our Old English sheepdog. I was in high school and I chose the breed, and then had to pester my parents for months until they agreed, since those long-haired dogs weren't really built for an Australian summer.

My mother made it clear that if I wanted that dog, I would have to look after him. It would be my job to toilet train, and to feed, walk and brush him. I did all that uncomplainingly because I loved Alfie from the moment we first met him sitting among his brothers and sisters at the breeder's, more like a pack of fluffy black-and-white wind-up toys than real animals. Their tails were docked, giving them the look of tiny bears as they tumbled over each other. Alfie had a black patch over his left eye and ear, and conquered all our hearts from the start, not just mine, when he became our own personal family panda.

As English Sheepdogs age, their dramatic colouring fades. Their coats grow longer and shaggier, and the black spots turn grey. Their fur grows down over their eyes, increasing their resemblance to bears, though no longer to pandas. I didn't always brush Alfie enough, and sometimes we'd have to take him to the dog groomer to cut out the knots so we could start again, but I uncomplainingly did most of the jobs my mother insisted on, since I loved Alfie. No, I *loved* Alfie. I *adored* Alfie.

My father was becoming increasingly erratic. He longed for a son, like the Tudor King Henry VIII, and started calling us by male names and referring to us as 'he'. A father to three girls, the best thing he could think to say about women was that you could tell a clever one because she came in under cover when it rained. And clever wasn't much good anyway. Why weren't we beautiful? Why weren't we *thin*?

He could no longer hide how much he felt we tied him down, his albatross of a family. We saw less and less of him as he worked late or stayed away from home, for reasons that were never explained. That should have made things easier, but it had the opposite effect, for when he did come home, he was angrier and more unpredictable. My sisters and I tiptoed around the house. Going out proved to be no protection either. He was prepared to hit us no matter where he was or who was around. He had no boundaries and so neither did we.

During the winter when I was fourteen we went to the school fete. My father arrived separately, there was no need for us to know why or where he'd been, but he thought I wasn't happy enough to see him. I'd presented him with 'a sour face', he said, so he gave me a hard slap, backhanded, across that same sour face.

'Don't you dare look at me like that,' he shouted, in front of everybody – strangers, classmates, friends, enemies. I tried surreptitiously to rub my swollen red cheek, though I pretended it didn't hurt. It felt as if the whole world was watching but I don't remember who was actually nearby. My mother? My teachers? No one said anything. I made an effort not to cry until I reached the school bathroom, where I sobbed. I leaned against the pink, purple and grey tiles in squares on the wall and cooled my hot cheek against the mirror, which had brown splodges at its edges. I splashed water on my face and saw myself reflected back, ugly and swollen, between the rust stains. I felt humiliated and utterly alone.

Despite all this, we believed it was our fault when my father finally left later that year. I was fourteen, my sisters eleven and five, and each of us was certain that it was something she had done that had finally driven him away. In fact, my parents separated when my father's latest mistress became pregnant, but that wasn't so clearly explained at the time. We were left to blame ourselves. Or maybe it was explained, and we just blamed ourselves anyhow.

It is possible that the events at the school fete happened after my parents separated. This is where memory is at its most slippery, and I'm not really sure, like Dylan Thomas, whether it snowed for six days when I was twelve, or twelve days when I was six. One thing is undeniable. My father was finally to have the son he had so longed for, but he would go on to mistreat him too.

I was the first child in my class whose parents divorced, but I didn't talk to my friends about it. I poured all my sadness into my Sheepdog's uncomplaining ears instead. He became my anchor. There was nothing as comforting as burying my face in Alfie's coat, along the line where it changed from white to grey, while I held onto his sturdy supportive body. With his unswerving loyalty, he smoothed over all manner of teenage hurts, my one true friend as I walked with him every afternoon after school and tried to make sense of life. The patch over his left eye was grey now, but whichever way I looked at him, left or right, grey or white, the world looked like a better place because he was in it.

All an adolescent girl's love for an animal was invested in that wonderful consoling pet, from age thirteen till two years later when a florist's van smashed into Alfie on a pedestrian crossing. It ran over my pet in front of me and then kept driving. I was left to drag the poor injured dog off the road, and in an age before mobile phones, to find a way to watch over him and to contact my mother so we could get him to a vet for treatment. For many years, that was the most traumatic experience of my life. Even now I can't stop the tears welling up as I remember that sickening thud and Alfie in so much pain that he bit me for the first time when I tried to touch his mangled leg. We got him to the vet but he didn't survive the operation.

Maybe that ordeal erased all earlier memories, for I certainly don't remember Alfie, the best dog in Australia, the World, the Universe, as we used to write in our First Grade exercise books, being a difficult puppy. I know you shouldn't compare your dogs, your children or your lovers, so here in Jerusalem, I reminded myself that naughty Mia had one huge, positive attribute. She was friendly, clever and cute as a button, but most importantly she had basically toilet trained herself. You can forgive a dog a lot for that.

She woke us when she wanted to go out in the morning, leaping onto the bed to lick our faces. This was truly commendable, since it meant that she wouldn't pee inside, but it was barely 6.00am, forgodsake. Raphael rarely went to bed before 3.00am – I was starting to suspect that he was one of those fashionable vampires – and he turned over and ignored her. Mia focused her attention back on me, licking my face and ears. I hid under my pillow to avoid her raspy little tongue and kicked Raphael feebly. It was his turn.

But I'd struck the conundrum at the core of the male soul. Raphael loved her more than I did, but he didn't love her enough to get up and walk her in the morning. He took refuge under his pillow and didn't come out. Inevitably it was me that ended up leaving our warm bed. Raphael lay blissfully with the doona pulled up tight around him, and I took Mia out no matter how little sleep I'd had. As I often stayed up late with Raphael, I soon became very tired. And very, very grumpy.

Childcare is an issue in lots of relationships. It had just become one in ours and we didn't even have a child.

9

One of the factors I didn't consider when I made my list of why I couldn't have a puppy – no garden, no balcony, no time – was perhaps the most significant. I worked from home to tight deadlines.

A deadline is a state of being, like suspended animation or entering a tunnel, where you need total focus if you are to reach the other end alive. Nothing else matters or exists but the bulletin ahead of you. A childhood friend you haven't seen for twenty-five years can turn up and you tell them to go away. Your ninety-year-old grandmother can call from the hospital on her birthday and you hang up. If you really love her you will find time to say, 'I'll call you after the top of the hour, Grandma.'

The work must be finished, the piece written, recorded, edited and fed by the top of the next hour and nothing can interrupt that. Certainly not looking for a disappearing dog.

'We have to get her a name tag,' Raphael said, after Mia went missing for six hours, stretching my nerves and his. We did and she lost the first tag on the day we bought it, and the replacement a week later, forcing us to get serious. We upgraded to a steel tag, bone-shaped because functional didn't mean it couldn't be cute, and engraved her name on it. That turned out to be a good investment. When I let her run off-leash in the park and she ran away, about an hour later on a good day, and a bit longer on a bad day, the call would come.

'Hello, I'm ringing from the French embassy, I've found a small blond dog and tied her up to a railing here.'

'Hello, I'm ringing from the Greek monastery ...'

'Hello, I'm walking in the Old City near the Jaffa Gate and I've found a very friendly dog wandering on its own ...'

But one day Mia disappeared into thin air right in front of me. I was instantly nervous, because it occurred during the time of the Great Dognapping scam, the latest blight facing pet owners in the Holy City. A gang was stealing dogs and demanding large ransoms for their return. They were highly organised criminals, who usually ran drugs and guns, and who had just figured out they could make large sums for little effort by lifting dogs as well.

Any dog was fair game. Big. Small. Old. Young. Purebreds. Mutts. The previous week, one of my favourite dogs from the park was nabbed, despite the fact that he weighed more than forty kilos. Pasha the Bernese mountain dog was so heavy partly because of his breed and partly because he was owned by the Sausage King and spent his days eating leftovers in Jerusalem's finest sausage restaurant. Pasha wasn't an easy heist, but he was such a beautiful specimen that the gang didn't ring to demand a ransom. They wanted to keep him. The Sausage King was beside himself. Then a week after Pasha disappeared, fate intervened. One of the restaurant workers spotted him on his way home, in an alley in the Old City. The loyal employee called the dog over, freed him and brought him home safely. He was treated as a hero. Everyone in the dog park celebrated Pasha's return but it didn't help us to relax. We met, chirruping with fear as we exchanged stories about wretched dogs and sky-high ransoms.

These events made me even more jumpy. Mia had the luck of the Irish, but when she vanished in front of me that day I had a bad feeling I couldn't shake. I took a shortcut through the brush where she liked to run, the lavender and thyme scratching at my calves, and tried to talk myself round. *What dognapping gang would operate in a park in broad daylight?* The heady scent of fresh herbs followed me as I rounded the corner underneath a beautifully restored historic building. It had

101

been occupied since the year 453, when the Roman Empress Eudokia built a monastery there.

Eudokia began life as a pagan, converted to Christianity, came to Jerusalem and got the syndrome. She separated from the emperor and stayed, ruling Jerusalem as the representative of Rome, writing poems, building churches and monasteries, and being kind to minorities, which at that time included Jews.

Over the centuries, the monastery she built underwent a number of incarnations. For many years, it was a guesthouse for Greek Orthodox pilgrims, run by an Arab Muslim family. Today it had evolved into a centre for the Zionist workers' movement. It had an auditorium and a vegan restaurant. They held world music concerts and an annual festival devoted to the oud, the pear-shaped Middle Eastern string instrument. I had a feeling Empress Eudokia would have approved.

The poster for last month's Oud Festival was still on the wall, as I turned a second corner. There, against the backdrop of the creamy Old City walls, three people were sitting on a bench. There were two men and one woman, with dirty clothes and blurry eyes, who looked like they were living rough. I couldn't tell how old they were. Nearby, tied to a railing, was Mia. I felt relieved, perhaps stupidly, because they looked like drug addicts rather than professional criminals. I decided to ignore them and focus on the dog.

'What are you doing here, you naughty girl?' I said, walking towards her.

Mia wagged her tail perfunctorily and looked away. So far she didn't seem to mind her new owners. They all started to speak at once, and I could hear from their accents that it was a mixed group of Arabs and Jews. Here at last was the unity so hard to find in this conflict. When they cut to the chase, they wanted 200 shekels for my dog.

Nice work if you can get it.

'We didn't take her!' The ringleader oozed fake friendliness. 'Someone came and sold her to us for 100 shekels. So now it's just that we have to make our money back. We're out of pocket but we were only thinking of you, the poor owner,' he wheedled.

He was mesmerising, like the character in the old joke who is in court for murdering his parents and begs for mercy because he is an orphan. But the gall of it was too much for me.

'And since you spent 100 shekels, you need to make an instant 100 per cent profit for what reason?' I snapped.

I was so angry that they'd taken Mia and were now trying to shake me down that I didn't stop to think through whether this tough talk was safe or not. Instead I told them that I had no money and showed them all I did have, my keys in one hand and my phone in the other. I said that I didn't intend to pay to get my own dog back after she'd been missing for less than five minutes. We sized each other up. I looked at them, then leaned down and began to untie the small blond hostage.

Once they realised they weren't going to win, what I have come to recognise as a typically local reversal took place. On the principle that attack is the best defence, they started telling me off. All three of them.

'Really, she's a beautiful dog, you should take better care of her!' the ringleader scolded me.

'What were you thinking? There are thieves *everywhere*,' the girl said meaningfully, as if she were talking about someone else, while the other two nodded.

'Don't be so careless in the future,' the ringleader added.

I stalked off, Mia held tightly by my side. She was not even a bit repentant. I saw them around the park for months afterwards and they always came to say hello and ask after Mia.

'I hope you're looking after her better!'

They infuriated me at the time but they were partly right. They say a dog's bad habits begin with its owner, and in my case I can see that was probably true. Part of the reason that I walked Mia without a leash inside the suburb of Yemin Moshe was that I was just so tired.

There were no cars there, so she wasn't in immediate danger, and after only a few hours' sleep I simply couldn't keep up with her.

I began every morning trailing behind her like a zombie, while she ran ahead sniffing happily. I woke up slowly. The only consolation at that hour was the chance to explore the area where I lived. One of the gardeners suggested that you only really knew a place when you saw it on foot, in all weathers and seasons. I suspected he was right, though 6.15am was a little early for philosophy. Naturally, I'd only met him since we'd found the puppy.

Mia's favourite route was down the main sandstone stairs of Yemin Moshe, across a small dead-end road, and on to the Sultan's Pool, an open-air amphitheatre built by Herod, the 'King of the Jews', appointed by Rome at the time of Jesus. Here Mia ran at great speed, raising clouds of dust, as if she wanted to avoid being thrown to the lions. The ruins were still in use, though taste in entertainment had changed. Bob Dylan had played there and so had The Black Eyed Peas. It was a magical venue, especially at night when the moon was full, the air warm and the Old City walls, lit up against the night sky, glowed above the audience.

Sometimes we encountered hedgehogs there and Mia was thrilled. The first time we saw a hedgehog was at night. I thought she was barking hysterically at a rock. It was only when I bent down that I noticed that the small brown rock had bristles. The hedgehog had curled itself up into a ball the size of a man's fist, and was quivering slightly. I'd be quivering too if Mia was barking non-stop an inch from my head.

I was scared she would give the hedgehog a heart attack – do they have hearts? – or that it would hurt her with one of its spines. (Spikes? Quills? There was a lot I didn't know about hedgehogs.) I tried to catch Mia, but she ran around it in circles, barking frenziedly. I raced behind her, with each of us then changing direction, and I don't know how I did catch her in the end, actually, but by then we were both dizzy and panting. I tugged her away from the hedgehog, and over my shoulder I saw it scuttling away across the sand, a small rock on the move in the moonlight.

From the Sultan's Pool we continued through a dank, dark tunnel under the road. We didn't do this at night, it was too dangerous, and even during the day it was a relief when we emerged back into the sunshine, in the Valley of Gei-Hinnom. Like most of the area, this site was known from the Old Testament. Today it was a green belt, an empty ravine which marked the divide between the Jewish and Arab sections of Jerusalem. In biblical times fires had burned constantly, while pagan rituals were carried out. The Canaanites worshipped a god called Moloch, who demanded child sacrifices. His priests banged on drums so that fathers wouldn't hear their children's screams as they were carried off to be killed. You can't help but wonder what deranged person would invent such a form of worship, what human need it satisfied. The cacophony of cries and drumbeats, smoke and sacrifice, was so dreadful that the name of this place became synonymous with hell for three religions. Gehenna for Christians; Gei-Hinnom for Jews; Gehannam for Muslims.

So much history, so much evil in one spot, I reflected as I watched Mia scampering down the ravine, still shaded in the early-morning light. On one of these walks we met a local Greek Orthodox nun, Sister Serafima. She was actually from Melbourne, but she'd lived here so long she qualified as a local. Her convent sat at the bottom of the Gei-Hinnom Valley, overlooking another area of empty parkland, which was known as the Field of Blood, the Akeldama. It was where Judas Iscariot hanged himself after betraying Jesus in return for thirty pieces of silver. Sister Serafima explained that Jesus knew His fate.

'One of you will betray me,' He told His twelve disciples at the Passover meal they held in Jerusalem, which would become known as the Last Supper. The apostles all denied the accusation, until unsettled by His certainty, each asked fearfully, 'Is it I, Lord?'

Jesus said the traitor would suffer and wish he had never been born, but that didn't deter Judas. He betrayed Jesus to the High Priest from the Temple, identifying Him with a kiss. Within days of their Passover meal, Jesus was crucified.

Afterwards, overcome with guilt, Judas returned the 'blood money' to the Temple and committed suicide here in this field. There is more than one account of his death in the New Testament, and they contradict each other. In the most poetic version, he hanged himself from a tree, known to this day as a Judas tree. It produces flowers of a brilliant deep pink in the spring, around Easter time, flowers that are said to have 'blushed with shame' after Judas's death.

Could all that really have happened here? It didn't seem possible, especially on sunny mornings, when the wild irises and lilies gleamed in the long grass, and small cotton-wool clouds puffed across a bright sky. There was a steep rock face on one side, where novice Jerusalem abseilers perched, tied to ropes, as they learned how to throw themselves backwards off a cliff. But on cloudy days the mood was bleaker. The olive trees looked menacing, and the ravine felt desolate, perhaps because of all these dark deeds.

Packs of wild dogs lived between the ravine and the nearby Palestinian villages. They ran down the hill barking loudly, five or six tall, thin, ragged dogs, with long foxy faces and curly tails like Mia's. She sat very still, looking and listening intently. I wondered what they were saying. Was it news of other dogs from the villages beyond, or were they trying to persuade her to join their pack? 'Don't bow your head to man! Leave that human! Come and join us and you will be a proud beast and will never have to wear a collar again.'

Mia looked a bit uncertain, actually, and I clipped the leash to her collar just in case. After listening for a while, Mia shook her head, as if she had made a decision, and started walking back with me, sticking uncharacteristically close. Once we'd left the ravine, she ran with her lopsided gait through a bed of lavender, tearing first one way and then another, and came home smelling delicious, like a dog of Provence.

The following week Mia ramped up the pressure. She abandoned shoes and sofas, and gnawed on an electricity cable. I don't know how she didn't electrocute herself. She just left the chewed cable cunningly positioned for us to electrocute ourselves instead.

Mia's unsuspecting victim was Esther, the Ethiopian woman who helped me clean the house. Esther was a sunny-natured immigrant in her twenties, whose main language was Amharic. We communicated in pidgin English, and I wasn't sure we understood each other, but the one person Esther always understood was Raphael.

She'd developed a crush on him which brought with it a form of telepathy. When he came out of the bedroom and said, 'Have you seen my ...' Esther would finish his sentence – 'Socks?' – and show him where they were. She knew when he wanted his cigarettes, his lighter, his coffee, and repeated any words he said in Hebrew as if she were in an intensive language class.

'*Eyfo ha tik sheli?*' said Raphael to himself.

'*Tik sheli*,' Esther repeated the last words after him, looking worried.

Raphael flashed her his heart-melting smile.

'*Tik sheli* means "my bag", Esther. I was saying: "Where is my bag?"' Raphael intoned, suddenly sounding like a Hebrew instruction recording. Esther brightened and immediately located it for him.

That afternoon, when it was just the two of us, Esther was telling me about the fiancé she'd left behind in Ethiopia.

'Promise, promise!' she repeated, turning the ring on her finger and looking at me meaningfully.

I asked how long it had been since she'd seen him, and how much longer they would have to wait, but without Raphael there, Esther's intuition dimmed. She shook her head uncomprehendingly. I tried to ask another way, but Esther just frowned at me and then repeated, 'Promise!' which I guess meant they could wait forever. I looked at my watch and realised that I was the one who was running out of time. The new US Secretary of State, Condoleezza Rice, was in town and I had to file a story on her visit.

Rice, or Condi as everyone called her, had been appointed at the start of 2005. One of her first official visits as Secretary of State had been to Jerusalem, and now only weeks later she was back again. She was here to show Washington's support for Israel's plan to withdraw 8,000 Jewish settlers from the Gaza Strip. As Condi flew in, angry opponents of the withdrawal held protests across Israel.

For the Palestinians, the planned withdrawal was welcome, indeed overdue. But in Israel it was tearing society apart. On a rough division, you could say that most secular Israelis supported it and most religious Israelis did not. They feared that next to go would be the settlements in the West Bank, where some 250,000 Israelis – mostly religious Jews – were then living.

Still, most galling for Gaza's Jewish settlers was that the man behind the plan was one of their own: Prime Minister Ariel Sharon. He was a big man in every sense. A former general who led Israel's main right-wing party, he had been one of the founders of the Jewish settlement movement. Now he simply said that times had changed, and that since becoming Prime Minister he viewed Israel's strategic needs differently. He quoted the words of an Israeli pop song to explain this change of heart, 'Things you see from here, you don't see from there.' Perhaps it sounded better in the original, for it became the most repeated phrase of the year.

None of that helped placate the settlers. They declared war on the government they had helped to elect. It was a long, hot summer of protest. Thousands attended demonstrations in the south, near the Gaza border. At the protest I had been to that morning, there were settlers and also right-wing members of parliament, some from Ariel

Sharon's own party. Twenty thousand police surrounded them. It had the feeling of imminent civil war.

On the way back I attended Condi's Jerusalem press conference. She generally appeared slightly troubled when answering questions, as if it really mattered to her to get the answer right. She re-affirmed that Israel's withdrawal from Gaza was vital for Washington. She appeared as neat, and her sentences as convoluted, as ever.

With all this material to edit together, I turned regretfully from Esther's love life back to my computer. At that moment, Esther turned the power on at the wall so that she could use the vacuum cleaner. But Mia had chewed the cable to the multi-plug adapter, and it sparked up in Esther's hands. She hopped back in fear. The entire house short-circuited and my computer shut down with a sudden final PHUT. Esther said that she was fine, so I ran to the fuse box and fiddled with all the levers. There was a hum and everything slowly jerked back to life, except the electrical appliances centred around one plug – where my desktop was, of course.

The deadline was now looming but I couldn't work without the computer. It was how I edited and sent my stories overseas. I took a deep breath and told myself it was important not to panic. Squatting under my desk I tried each plug in turn. Nothing happened. I sat back on my heels, sighing.

I am not that technical and couldn't tell whether it was the computer which had been damaged by the power outage, or simply one of the plugs attached to the power point. It looked like I would need some time to figure it out and might not get the report done before the top of the next hour when it had to be on a news bulletin in Canada. An hour later a second version had to be on a news bulletin in Germany.

Mia was sleeping soundly on the couch, for which she didn't need any electricity, as I rang the CBC news desk in Toronto. It's not a good look to miss a bulletin, especially with this flimsy 'The dog ate my homework' kind of excuse. But not for nothing do Canadians have the reputation of being the nicest people in the world. The standard response, in news-desk speak, would be, 'I don't give a fuck about you and your fucking dog, just get me the story for the top of the clock!' But instead of giving me a bollocking, the Toronto chief of staff said, 'Please be careful! Don't electrocute yourself.'

Esther went home. I missed both deadlines sorting out the power problems. By the time I was finally back in business, electricity on, computer rebooting, ready to file, Mia woke up, refreshed. She climbed down from the couch, stretched, shook herself out, and went to sit by the door. She started whining.

I looked at her with narrowed eyes. Although I felt I could kill her, I judged that it would be quicker to give in. Experience had taught me that when she knew I had to record a voice track, which needed complete silence, she would sit at the door crying, producing an urgent low sound like a cello. If I ignored that she moved into a higher register, like a violin, before beginning to yelp. When I was desperate − and so was she − I had to edit out barking from a sign-off that went 'Irris Makler, woof, CBC News, WOOOF WOOF WOOOF WOOF, Jerusalem.'

'Okay, five minutes is all you have, Mia. This isn't a walk, it's a pit stop.'

Mia jumped up and ran in happy circles around me. She was thrilled, as ever, to leave the house. She barrelled out of the gate like a cannonball and ran down the stairs, bleached white in the midday sun. It was hot and Yemin Moshe felt sleepy. Not to Mia, of course. She was attached to a leash so that I could catch her when I needed to, but running free so that she could pee quickly, which she always preferred to do by herself under difficult-to-reach bushes. That was another lesson I had learned. But today, experience didn't help. The gremlins had taken over the machine.

Mia ran off and wriggled under a bush, completely disappearing. I was antsy as I watched her vanish where I couldn't follow. *Come on,*

Mia, we haven't got time for this, I muttered, looking at my watch. When she finally crawled back out she had slipped out of both her leash and her collar. I couldn't believe my eyes. How was I going to get her home? She was not a dog you could rely on to come when she was called. In fact, if she sensed that you really wanted her to come she ran in the other direction.

I started searching in the bushes, grumbling to myself as I crawled under the branches to look for her leash. *I have to be at my desk, I can't be any later on this story because of this dog today, Condoleezza Rice will be back in Washington before I file at this rate …*

On my hands and knees, twigs scratching my face, I didn't find anything except some old dog droppings. I was tempted to ask the question you should never ask when things are spiralling out of control – *What else could go wrong?* – and concluded that there was nothing for it but to pick Mia up and carry her home. She wasn't particularly heavy, but she didn't like being carried and we had to climb more than sixty steps from the park to reach the house. I started casting about wildly for someone except myself to blame as I cornered her.

Raphael! Aaagh! I can't believe that these crises always happen when he's not here.

I picked up my resisting hot furry bundle. She wriggled and squirmed, I sweated and groaned. She suddenly felt much heavier than her fifteen kilos, and the stairs seemed to have multiplied. Halfway up, they swam before my eyes and I almost toppled over. I regained my balance and kept going. When we neared the top, Mia made one final effort to break free, wriggling and biting my hands. It was all I could do not to bite her back.

We made it inside, sweaty – speaking for myself – and frazzled. I deposited Mia on the floor, sat down at the computer and tried to remember who Condoleezza Rice was.

I just made my deadline. In an exhausted stupor, I watched the little green bar on the computer screen that let me know how quickly the item was speeding its way towards Toronto. That was generally a soothing experience. But today was different. I looked back, horrified, at what had just taken place.

I had missed three deadlines, two for the first broadcaster and one for the second. It was as bad as I had feared at the beginning: the dog was with me here in Jerusalem more than she was with Raphael in Tel Aviv, and she was killing my work. If you said I hadn't done everything right, I couldn't argue with that. But I also couldn't afford to be missing stories because my dog had eaten the internet cable or an electricity plug or simply slipped her leash and wouldn't come when she was called. The freelance world is tough and competitive. If you can't file on time, the broadcasters will get someone else who will. As the dark Australian saying has it, 'It's a dog-eat-dog world out there, and there's not enough dog to go round.'

Once we were back inside, Mia had turned into an angelic pet, wagging her tail happily and curling up again in a ball, but could I have a puppy this naughty in my office, which unfortunately was also my home? I looked down at her, sleeping contentedly at my feet, and wondered how long it could also continue to be her home, even part-time.

10

Raphael tried to talk me round. He was up north, performing at another biblical location, the Sea of Galilee. When he called, I bombarded him with complaints about the dog, and he diagnosed a bad mood because we hadn't seen each other for two weeks.

'Yes, you're right – that's part of it. It feels like ages …' I said. Hearing his voice made me happy. It was an instant infusion of tranquillity. He always made me see the funny side of things, and I knew that I might not take the puppy's naughtiness so hard if he were here right now, but I had to talk this through with him. 'Mia has been a very naughty dog. We have to figure out a better way to share her.'

'Who looked after her for four days when you were in Gaza?'

'You did. But …'

He cut me off. 'And I couldn't take her this past week because I've been travelling and performing.'

'Two weeks, it's been two weeks,' I reminded him. 'And I've been busy too and there was no power and Esther was nearly electrocuted. I don't know if I can look after her even when it's my turn. Maybe we're just both too busy to have a dog.'

'Wow! You really have got it bad, haven't you? Don't worry. I'll be back in Tel Aviv in three days. Can you hang on till then? Are you sure all this isn't because you miss me?'

I said I didn't think so.

'What? Don't you miss me?'

I said that I did. We talked some more, teasing each other about who missed the other more and how many more sleeps till we would see each other again. It was a sweet exchange, filled with laughter and longing. Mia's naughtiness was forgotten for a moment.

Since Mia had arrived, my apartment felt smaller and messier. I threw myself into projects around the house, hanging paintings and tidying shelves, but it didn't make much difference. I was still climbing over piles of papers and disks and recording equipment and could never seem to find anything. *Storage* was obviously what I needed. It was time to tackle a long-overdue job and to build some furniture.

I trooped down to IKEA and chose bookshelves and a chest of drawers. According to the pictures, they would help me achieve a gleaming, orderly Swedish life. Next, I was dragging the flat packs down the long path to my house, stopping along the way when they got too heavy. Surely this wasn't how they did it in Stockholm? Mia watched, fascinated, as I unwrapped the packages and sat on the floor with the components around me: pieces of wood, sheets of cardboard, sliding steel connectors to make the drawers roll, and the exact number of screws, little wooden plugs and rubber rings, as well as the vital part that held everything together, the Allen key.

I enjoy building furniture the Swedish way – it's a bit like Lego – though I have learned that you need to concentrate to avoid irreversible mistakes. I studied the pictured instructions as if I were an Arctic explorer clutching her only map. It turned out Mia liked making furniture too. She decided to try her hand at carpentry, inserting her paw above the nail just as I was about to bring down the hammer. Next she tried to master the mysteries of the Allen key, and then she snatched one of the wooden pegs that held the shelves together and made off with it in her mouth. I ran after her, wrestled it from her, and wondered if the wet, slightly chewed peg in my hand would fit into its hole in this condition, or if the shelf was ruined. There's no margin for error, since IKEA rations them out, giving you only the precise number you need, even though they are basically one step above toothpicks.

Before I could check, Mia was already back at the pile, grabbing another peg and running off proudly. This time, instead of chasing her again, I scooped up all the pegs and put them out of her reach to prevent this turning into an episode of *Keystone Kops*. By the time I removed the second peg from her mouth, it was even wetter and more chewed than the first one. After that, I grabbed her leash and tied her to the kitchen table to free me up to finish the job.

Raphael phoned at that moment, and when I told him what Mia had been up to, he said that he thought she would look good advertising Swedish furniture and maybe we should try to get her a gig as the IKEA dog. I told him that right then, I'd happily give her to IKEA for good. He apologised for not helping me. He was still away and he wasn't much good at building things anyway. I accepted that, because I think you have to play to your strengths and help where you can, and not get angry when the other person can't do everything. If they can help, great, and if they can't, that's fine too. I guess that having been independent for so long also meant I was just used to getting on and doing things by myself. I was not as demanding as a woman his age might be … and maybe that suited Raphael too.

With Mia out of the way, I completed the frame and the drawers and only had to do the last crucial section and join them so that the drawers rolled smoothly. That, of course, could take hours. Mia was lying near the table, nose between her paws snoozing, when I heard a rattle at the gate. As usual on a warm evening, the front door was open, the gate in front of it locked. I looked up to see a tiny white Labrador puppy tumble in. He fell on his stomach, got up and ran over, throwing himself into my lap. Standing outside the gate was his owner, a neighbour I hadn't met before. Through the bars, Itzik apologised for the intrusion, and introduced himself and his new puppy, Mondo.

'Mondo has just arrived from the Guide Dog Association. They have this project where the puppies are raised in a family home for a year before they go on to become working dogs,' he said. 'So I am Mondo's new family.'

'What – and then you give him back when he's twelve months old?' I asked, cradling wriggly Mondo, who felt like he had too much skin for his body. 'How will you be able to bear that?'

The Guide Dog Association had strict rules. You weren't allowed to pick the puppies up or to carry them, they were never to sit on furniture or to sleep on a bed. I felt even sorrier for poor wriggly Mondo and hugged him close. Mia was not impressed. She wasn't keen on unvetted canine visitors, especially when she was tied up and they were running free inside her house, indeed in my lap. If she could, she would have called the Guide Dog Association to report the infringement herself.

I wouldn't ordinarily invite a stranger into my house, but Itzik was part of the brotherhood of dog owners, which changed everything. As I unlocked the gate, I could see Itzik glancing across at Mia, tied to the table. It didn't look too good, so I hastily assured him that I'd only tied her up for ten minutes to allow me to finish building a piece of furniture. As a show of good faith I untied Mia. She went straight for the puppy's throat. After we'd separated the dogs, Itzik demonstrated he had no hard feelings by asking, 'How are you going with those drawers?'

I sensed that this was not a casual inquiry and that Itzik might be a man who was interested in building. I launched into a detailed description of my problems attaching the drawers to the rollers. He didn't fail me.

'I'm an engineer! Maybe I can help?'

I tied Mia back to the table again, to keep her away from Mondo and to let Itzik work in peace. Guess I am a wicked dog owner after all … In no time Itzik had done that last fiddly step that would have taken me an hour. When the drawers were properly in place, I untied

116

Miss IKEA so that we could join Itzik and Mondo as they completed their walk.

'Look, Mia, a new friend,' I said brightly as she growled menacingly at Mondo.

We walked along, both dogs happily off-leash. The puppy jumped on Mia, while she swatted him away, or, fed up, zoomed in circles around and around him, till he sat down, dazed.

Once she'd put Mondo in his place, Mia trotted dismissively ahead. When we reached the park a minute after her, she was rolling on the ground. With Mia there was no such thing as an innocent roll, in the hay or even the dirt. Some dogs roll to scratch their spines or just for the fun of it, for the delicious feel of the grass on their backs and the knowledge that they are living life to the full. Mia only bothered if there was a dead animal, or some other putrid, rotting, stinking mass to enjoy.

I had become familiar with the final resting place of every ex-Yemin Moshe cat, bat, rat, mouse, jackal and fox. I was hopeful that this wouldn't be too bad because it wasn't any of them. I shouted my trusty 'MIANO!!!' but it was too late. When she stood up, there was something thick and gooey smeared all over her fur, and we could smell it at a distance. Itzik broke the Guide Dog rules and rushed to scoop Mondo up and carry him off home. He disappeared before I had time to thank him for his help.

I caught Mia and we went home too. She was looking proud of herself, so I told her sternly that at this rate we wouldn't have any friends in the 'hood. I wasn't really worried, though, dogs always find each other again. I don't know what it was that she rolled in, but it was a smell you couldn't ignore, even out of doors. Once we were inside it became overpowering, and actually made me dizzy.

'God, Mia!!!' I groaned, holding her leash tight so that she didn't smear it on any furniture before we reached the bathroom. 'What is this – mustard gas?'

Mia didn't like being washed, and up till now it had always been a two-person job. Raphael and I both got in the bath with her, one holding her and the other wielding the handheld shower and applying the shampoo. Inevitably we all ended up equally drenched. Now I badly needed him here to help, but there was no choice. I'd have to do it by myself. I stripped down to my underwear. Mia was shaking with terror as I lifted her in, and stood there shuddering in huge, involuntary spasms of fear. My heart went out to her, she looked so miserable, but there was nothing I could do; I wasn't the one who rolled in something noxious when I was lucky enough to get an extra walk.

When all the sticky, stinking stuff finally appeared to be gone, I let go of the leash and Mia jumped out of the bath. She shook herself off, spraying every surface in the bathroom with water, as well as me, of course, and when I let her out of there, she ran around the house like a small tornado, wiping herself on each piece of furniture in turn. I followed in disbelief, watching her overturn carpets and bite pillows before jumping onto my bed and rolling on the fresh sheets like a creature possessed. She came to rest upside down, on her back, her fur in spiky wet tufts, sighing and looking up at me happily, as if the djinn had finally left her. I didn't have the energy to change the sheets. When I went to bed, they were damp and smelt of wet dog, a dispiriting odour, more old socks and mould than live animal.

I woke in the morning to see Mia looking oddly guilty. She didn't hop up onto the bed and lick my face like she usually did. Instead, she was sitting on the floor, staring at me intently, as if willing me to wake up. *That's funny,* I thought, but it was only when I walked out into the living room that I understood why. She'd been sick all over my favourite rug. My landlord's rug, naturally.

I looked at the three large piles of dog vomit drying on the beautiful Moroccan kilim and looked back at Mia. Before I could say anything, she lowered her ears, and opened her eyes wide. She seemed to shrink into herself, transforming into a pale, sad shivery creature in front of my eyes. I swear she was only half her previous size, while her eyes had become huge, taking up most of her face. It was impossible for any animal to be sadder or sorrier.

Who teaches them to do that?

'You look just like the Spanish cat in *Shrek*!' I said severely. 'And I don't believe you any more than him.'

She held on to the sad, small persona for a little while longer, until she was certain that she wouldn't be punished, then scampered around me as I filled a bucket with warm water so that I could clean her vomit off the rug. Some things are too disgusting to describe, so I will spare you.

I wanted to share this predicament with someone, and Raphael was closest to hand. Metaphorically that is. Physically – where *was* he?

Raphael had never had a dog as a child. Sometimes when he hugged Mia, he held her close just like a nine-year-old would, awkwardly, his hands high under her front paws, and his expressions were the same as those on the face of a child holding his first pet. Maybe it's true that for everything there is a season and you have to do certain things at certain times or you spend the rest of your life longing for them. Perhaps we all need rock-star boyfriends when we're young. Then we wouldn't be disappointed when they weren't there to clean up dog vomit, because we wouldn't have these ridiculous expectations. We'd know that no rock star cleans up vomit, not even his own.

Some of it was ordinary puppy naughtiness. But some of it was something else, a nonchalant wildness that was beyond my capacity to deal with.

'Don't worry, it won't last,' Orla advised airily. 'She's just discovering her inner fox!'

Orla could always make me laugh. And she'd hit the nail on the head. I did feel as if I were living with a fox rather than a dog. But should you have a fox in your bedroom?

That night when I got into bed, I jack-knifed up because something sharp was digging into the small of my back. I pulled out a dried half-chewed bone with spiky edges. It was like a weapon used by Neanderthal man, with a bit of dog saliva thrown in. I tossed it on the floor in disgust. What had happened to my nice clean bed, my nice clean life? Orla said this *was* love but I wasn't so sure.

It was another week before Raphael and I finally got to see each other. As soon as he'd finished his gigs up north he was offered some acting work in Tel Aviv.

'It's a TV ad for the lottery and I've got a proper role,' he called to tell me gleefully, counting the cash and spending it even before he'd been paid. He wasn't one of those fussy actors who were disappointed if they weren't doing art films. Music was his first love and his real calling.

'You can act in a student film for a week and barely get paid. Here they pay you and they feed you. Well, I guess it is for the lottery after all ...'

I couldn't keep talking. My Palestinian translator, Nuha Musleh, was on the other line. There were riots in the Old City of Jerusalem. Israeli police on horseback were clashing with young Palestinians who were throwing stones, and we had to race down there. The numbers of police had been bolstered following rumours that right-wing Jewish activists were planning to march on the Al-Aqsa Mosque as a protest against the planned withdrawal from Gaza. Over the week, hundreds of young Muslims had gathered inside the mosque to wait for them. In order to prevent the two groups meeting, police had refused permission for the Jewish activists' march and limited the access of any more Muslim worshippers. Following this announcement, the young men inside the Al-Aqsa Mosque began to riot. I said goodbye to Raphael and planned where I would meet Nuha. I grabbed my equipment and ran down to the Old City.

Nuha was a Palestinian woman of fifty, with short red-brown hair and a beak-like nose set in a wide face. She appeared gruff until she laughed, which was often. She was born in Silwan, a Palestinian village just outside the Old City walls, about two kilometres from my flat, when the area was ruled by Jordan. She was twelve years old in 1967 when Israel conquered East Jerusalem and reunited the city into an uneasy whole, turning her into a resident of the Jewish state. Nuha was unequivocal. This was occupation and it had to be brought to an end.

Nuha was wealthy and had two young children, and she could have been one of the ladies who lunch in Ramallah. But, fizzing with energy, she was prepared to spend her days on the front line instead. Her English was excellent; in fact she was one of the best translators I have ever worked with. She had the deep voice and impassioned delivery of an actress, so I was able to use her translations directly in my stories, without revoicing them, which I have never been able to do with anyone else. She was a small woman, but had such a huge presence that she often seemed overpowering. A Palestinian man watching her work with me in the markets in the West Bank town of Jenin came up to confide, 'Your translator, she is a dynamo.'

Nuha was also a business dynamo. She and her husband were collectors of antiques and artwork. They bought and sold jewellery, carpets, saddle bags and beautiful pieces of enamel-inlaid furniture. Central Asian wall hangings were their specialty. At first these treasures were spilling out of two rooms in their home, until they gathered them into a gallery shop, the most beautiful in Ramallah. Nuha was always looking to snap up bargains when we were out working, no matter how dangerous the story or how tight my deadline.

'Sweetie, wait just one more minute, we can't leave yet! These Bedouins are bringing some of their carpets and they promised me they are old ones!'

She was clever and also fearless, striding ahead in her designer shoes, unconstrained by dirt or danger. Her resonant voice often drowned out the sound of stones, stun grenades and even gunfire on my recordings. I knew from experience that she would find it hard to stay quiet for long, and I would often move closer to the line of fire just to get away from her.

It was Nuha who would be with me four years later when I was injured, during riots in the same part of the Old City where we were headed now. This area, known to Jews as the Temple Mount and to Muslims as the Noble Sanctuary, was a flashpoint. It was where the Second Intifada had erupted, and clashes here claimed many lives. When I arrived at the nearby Lions' Gate, I scanned the crowd. Nuha was always easy to spot. Ah, there she was. Who else would be wearing a red suit, black stockings patterned with red roses, and red shoes? She had made her necklace and earrings herself, from large silver coins and stones and ancient beads. Her hat was also red. We kissed each other.

'Do you like the outfit, sweetie? I bought it on sale in Tel Aviv, it was only $500. And since it was seventy per cent off, I bought three!'

Then it was down to business. The Al-Aqsa Mosque compound was shut, and we could hear shouting and stun grenades. We could also see black clouds rising above the walls and feel the tear gas catching at our throats and irritating our eyes.

'Is that live fire? Are the bastards shooting in there?' Nuha turned to me.

We didn't know for sure. Nor did the furious Palestinian men surrounding us. Israeli troops had prevented them from entering Al-Aqsa to pray because they were under fifty years of age. They told us in Arabic that they intended to defend Al-Aqsa with their bodies from any Jewish assailants. They said they suspected the Jews were planning to take over the Mosque area and to divide it in two. 'After that, they will prevent us from entering altogether! So we will fight them.'

When I had gathered sufficient material, I said goodbye to Nuha and went to interview the Israeli police.

The police spokesman said there had been no live fire. As proof, he said there had been injuries during the afternoon's clashes but no deaths. He revealed that for the past six months Israel's security services had gathered intelligence about a planned attack on the Mosque by right-wing Jewish extremists. Their rationale apparently was that an attack there would cause so much trouble that it would stop the Gaza withdrawal in its tracks.

It was hard to absorb. On any ranking, Jerusalem was the main game and Gaza a side issue. Al-Aqsa was the third holiest site in Islam, and Jerusalem was significant to more than one billion Muslims worldwide. One of the Palestinian slogans which had been adopted across the Arab world spoke of a million martyrs marching on Jerusalem to free it with their blood. A million martyrs were not going to march on Gaza. A Jewish attack on the Mosque might stop Israel's withdrawal from Gaza, but it would certainly set the entire Middle East alight, and possibly lead to a war with the Muslim world. It would be a case of a successful operation which killed the patient. As a British colleague said pithily, 'They aren't just extremists; they're brain dead.'

Israeli police were now proposing 'administrative detention' – jail without trial – for those activists. It was a practice regularly used against Palestinians, but rarely against Israelis. The police had arrested their first Jewish suspect, an extremist from the settlement of Yitzhar in the West Bank. If they could persuade the court that he was a security risk, they would be able to hold him for six months, which would put him behind bars when the withdrawal from Gaza took place over the coming summer.

Raphael and I arranged to meet in Jerusalem the next evening. Somehow, without planning to, we had spent three weeks apart. 'At last!' we said to each other longingly. I went down to Gaza and was back in my apartment expecting him when he called with bad news.

He had just been told that he had an audition the next morning in Tel Aviv and he couldn't come up. Couldn't I please come down there now instead, and bring Mia with me?

'I will spoil you,' he lured.

It had been a long, hot day and I had been on the road for most of it. I only agreed to get back into the car again because I missed him. Raphael also persuaded me that Mia would be no trouble and, while I knew that bit wouldn't be entirely true, I didn't expect her to be quite such an edgy passenger. She never really liked the car. Things hadn't much improved since our first day together, when she was in short order sick in the back seat and then climbed into Raphael's lap in the front. A drive always began with her in the back, paws on my shoulders, claws grinding into my neck. On this scorching night, she refused to calm down at all.

I had been in Gaza to do a story about female suicide bombers, which was a sufficiently disturbing subject without the trauma of getting in and out of the Gaza Strip. On the way there I had listened to the BBC World Service. Appropriately enough, it was running a story about stress.

The World Service had been my 'friend', a source of news and interest, over the previous five years, when I'd been living in places without regular English-language broadcasting. In Russia and Afghanistan, it only transmitted on a shortwave frequency for a few hours a day. I knew the times off by heart and had a special radio, which I took with me everywhere, listening to the last second before it would dip into newscasts in other languages, or – my favourite – English lessons for Russians that were so complex no one could hope to learn the language from them. One week they would translate the lyrics of a Beatles song: 'Ob-la-di, Ob-la-da, life goes on, brah … *Ob-la-di, Ob-la-da, Zhizn takaya, brat* …' The next week it would be Edward Lear's nonsense rhymes. It was more like a program to sabotage English learning.

Their story about stress examined how much our internal levels of tension affect external situations. They interviewed a beekeeper who said she never went into the hive if she wasn't feeling tranquil, because if she was even slightly out of sorts, the bees knew instantly and attacked her. I took a deep breath as I anticipated the tension of getting into Gaza.

Israel had built a wall around the Gaza Strip to prevent suicide bombers from leaving, entering mainland Israel and killing Jewish civilians. In the way of walls, it kept everybody else out as well. Israeli troops stationed at the main crossing point, called Erez, monitored who could enter and leave. The wall there was a depressing sight, six metres high, made of concrete, with watchtowers at set distances, like an American prison or a Soviet labour camp. In other areas, it was a barrier made up of wire fencing with posts, sensors and buffer zones. Journalists and diplomats were the only groups with a consistent right of access

So I was fortunate in that sense; I could go in, but the process was inevitably fraught. Journalists had to walk a long way carrying heavy equipment, down a filthy concrete corridor, smelling of urine. The corridor had a metre-high gap along the top, beneath the ceiling, which let in air and light. On the Palestinian side, rolls of barbed wire had been strung along this gap and Palestinians on their way to work in Israel threw their shirts up to wait for their return. They were caught by the barbed wire, and blew in the breeze, the strange, sad form of a man, above the rubbish and rubble on the ground beneath.

Welcome to the Erez crossing point.

When we walked down this corridor from the Palestinian side, on our way back to re-enter Israel, we encountered a closed iron gate. If we tried to push the gate a disembodied voice squawked at us in Hebrew to stop, so someone was watching from a camera somewhere but there was no one to speak to. After a period – it could be an hour or it could be five hours – the gate swung open without warning and we had to scramble through it. There were four narrow lanes, divided by iron railings, resembling nothing more than a sheep pen, and the same disembodied voice instructed us which lane to take. Often when I reached the end the voice squawked again: 'Go back!'

Wrong run, little lamb.

I had to start over, dragging my gear back up the narrow space and going down what I hoped was the right lane this time.

'This one? This one?' I'd shout up at where I thought the camera was, but there was no response. When I reached the metal turnstile this time, there was no more squawking, so I was in the right spot but I couldn't fit through with my gear. Once I'd squashed and pushed and pulled my cases and myself through, praying that I'd done no lasting damage to my equipment, I was at the scanning point.

Scanning required removing the belt from my jeans, leaving all my equipment unguarded, and standing in a machine which I am sure saw right through to my bone marrow. The transparent doors closed and whirled around, leaving me feeling irradiated. That was standard, today there was more.

'We can see something. We have to do it again.'

What did they see?

'Steel. You can't go on.'

'Steel? Where?'

I had an idea what might be causing all the trouble, but could you say, 'Victoria's Secret,' to a disembodied voice that didn't speak English?

After another radioactive whirl, the unseen soldiers conferred some more and released me from the contraption, and the process began over again with my bags. That could take hours too. The record for this belonged to my Danish friend Allan, who'd once taken eleven hours to cross.

Still, no matter how bad it was for us, it was worse for Palestinians. The politicians drove through, but ordinary Palestinians could only pass with a special permit, usually for work or a hospital visit and, like us, they generally did it on foot. Everything took longer and was more problematic. If I managed to get through without removing my bra, a Palestinian woman would not be so lucky.

Today a Palestinian mother was returning from hospital in Israel with her sick daughter. The kindness of the care by Israeli medical staff was offset by the experience of getting the child home. The girl looked about seven years old. She was wearing a pink nylon dress and had a shiny black shoe and white frilly sock on one foot. The other was in plaster. She was attached to a saline drip, which she had been carrying until she grew too weary. Her mother now held it. The mother, in her long black cloak, had to carry the girl down the sheep run, put her down and return for her bags, put them down and then lift the girl and push her through the steel turnstile. Both were crying from effort and pain, and no Israeli soldier opened the side gate for them, which would have avoided this pushing and pulling and was presumably what that gate was for. Nor did they allow any of the Palestinian men behind her to help the mother in this hazardous, humiliating process. I will never forget the look on that child's face.

Everyone had their own way of dealing with these experiences. Orla shouted at the soldiers. It took her longer and made her – and them – angrier, but maintaining the rage was what got her through. I did it differently. I tried to make it as smooth and quick and pleasant as possible. I put myself in a good mood. It had to be genuine or, like with the bees and their out-of-sorts keeper, it didn't work. And generally, I sailed through. But afterwards, back in Jerusalem, I found myself having bitter fights in shopping queues or while I was driving. It took me some time to realise that this road rage or fury about who was next at the cheese counter was actually displaced stress.

On this occasion, I emerged from Erez unsettled as always, though the bra issue had only delayed me by half an hour. Now at night, I was heading back down the same highway from Jerusalem, where you had to concentrate on driving, because the road was winding and steep and full of speeding cars. But I was distracted, thinking about my day in Gaza and what makes a suicide bomber.

My mind kept going back to the Al Bass family, whom I had interviewed. Their eldest daughter, Wafa, had been caught at Erez ten days before, trying to cross while wearing an explosive belt, the standard equipment of the suicide bomber. She had hidden it under the long dark coat-dress she was wearing, but the Israeli soldiers, suspicious, had asked her to open her coat. At that point, realising that she wasn't going to get any further, she had tried to blow herself up. The explosives had failed to detonate. All this had been filmed by the Erez security camera. There was no sound but the footage was devastating. It showed a short, wiry young woman crying and running her hands up and down her body in a frenzy of agitation and fury, exhibiting the extreme reaction of someone who believed she was about to die. It is not a moment we see in the ordinary course of our lives. After witnessing the contorted expressions on her face, I believe it's not a moment that we should see.

Wafa was barely twenty-one years old with a pretty dark-skinned face and burns covering her entire body. Her health problems were critical to this story. Six months earlier, she had been in the kitchen of the white breeze-block house in the north of Gaza where she lived with her parents and six brothers and sisters. A gas cylinder near the stove had blown up while she was cooking. Wafa was engulfed in flames and received burns to ninety per cent of her body. At first it appeared she would not survive. The hospitals in Gaza couldn't treat her. Wafa was transferred to a hospital in Israel, where doctors performed a series of operations, including skin grafts. They saved her life. She wrote them letters of gratitude. When she required further operations, these were also carried out in Israel, and she was returning for yet another one when she was caught at the checkpoint with the bomb.

By surviving, Wafa had turned into a propaganda prize. Israeli police paraded her for the media, permitting her to give a number of interviews. I gathered up all the interviews from that day, and it was telling to observe how she changed. First, she said that she'd planned to detonate her bomb at the hospital, and spoke in slogans about a Palestinian victory. As time went on and the interviewers succeeded one another, there were fewer slogans and she began to cry. By the end, she retracted her confession. Her family didn't believe she could do such a thing and I didn't know what to believe.

'I looked after and fed her like a bird,' her mother said to me, distraught. 'She was in so much pain, her body and her hands were all burnt, I had to do everything for her. How could she be involved with a bomb?'

The idea that you would go back to kill the people who saved your life was incomprehensible, although the reality was that Wafa Al Bass would never have made it out of Erez with a bomb. As indeed she hadn't. Since 1996, every suicide bomber who had tried had ended up detonating their explosives at the crossing. It still wasn't clear to me how much Wafa knew, or what she intended, but the militants who sent her knew her 'best' chance was an explosion at Erez, killing some Israeli soldiers, or possibly only herself, but making a statement on their behalf.

Wafa's parents criticised the militants for preying on a sick girl, an unusual step in the Palestinian territories, where armed gangs exact swift revenge against citizens who speak out against them. Wafa said that the militants had approached her and told her that no one would marry her now that she was injured, so she might as well die for the cause. She had enough savvy to ask them why *they* weren't going to blow themselves up. They told her that they had children and reminded her that she, however, would never have children now, so she was better placed to make the sacrifice.

In her final interview, Wafa brushed away tears, holding her manacled hands up to her face and revealing badly scarred wrists.

The reality of her bleak future in an Israeli prison, always in pain, seemed to be sinking in. She apologised to her mother and referred to herself as a bird, echoing her mother's words to me.

'I am sorry, Mother,' she said. 'I was once free and now I am a chained bird.'

I was jolted out of this disturbing reverie, because Mia was pawing at my neck and my mobile phone was ringing. We were almost halfway to Tel Aviv and Mia was still standing on her hind legs, whining and scratching at me. As I reached down for the phone it stopped ringing. I dropped it and tried to calm the dog. Then the phone began ringing again and I snapped. I pulled off the highway, onto the hard shoulder, and sat with my head in my hands, crying, my silly dog finally standing quietly behind me. Cars flashed by, their red tail lights disappearing into the hot, dark night. My tears made them look blurry. At that moment, Raphael rang for the third time, to check where we were. Boy was he sorry.

'This is the worst drive I've ever done, the dog is driving me crazy, I can't believe I agreed to go from Gaza to Jerusalem and then drive back down this road again to bring her to you, and I don't think I can keep going,' I sobbed into the phone.

I rubbed at the claw marks Mia had left on my neck as Raphael persuaded me not to turn around and go back to Jerusalem.

'I wouldn't do this for anyone else.'

Mia, unaware of any mood but her own, continued to be difficult all the way to Tel Aviv. Or perhaps – to be charitable – like the bees, she sensed my mood and that was what prompted her behaviour. Either way, by the time we reached Raphael's, I handed her over to him and never wanted to see her again.

11

It doesn't work like that, of course. Dogs, like babies, are always there, needing to be walked and fed, no matter how naughty they've been the night before. Raphael energetically took on the role of the peacemaker, calming Mia down and cheering me up. He was singing in the morning, another reason it was lovely to be around him when he woke up. By the time we walked around the corner for breakfast, a truce had been declared.

Raphael and I were holding hands. He was holding Mia's leash. The air was humid and our clothes were sticking to us. Tel Aviv in summer is a three-shirt-a-day town. I don't know how Raphael coped in jeans. My way of fighting the heat was long, loose sleeveless cotton dresses. I was wearing my favourite one, in turquoise, a colour that made me feel calm and strong. Raphael's shiny black hair was back in a ponytail, mine was clipped up. The only one who couldn't remove her coat seemed unaffected by the heat. Mia was filled with excitement at an excursion with the two of us, and ran around us and between our legs, making everyone who passed us on the pavement smile.

We reached the restaurant and chose an outside table under a magnolia tree. Raphael smoked as we ordered, Mia at our feet. A sumptuous Israeli breakfast made its way to our table – large wooden platters piled high with omelettes, cheeses, salads, olives, tuna, salmon, various breads, fruit, Granola, yoghurt and jam. Cups of excellent coffee followed. Mia dug herself a hole in the gravel, creating a cool spot where she could fall asleep.

After this repast, I exhaled. My Gaza story wasn't due for two days, so we had a whole twenty-four hours free together. It was simple to be with Raphael, in the best sense of the word. He soothed me. Problems that had seemed overwhelming now appeared insignificant in his company. But we had to discuss how we could better handle this small naughty dog that seemed to be upending our lives. Well, my life. I could see that it wasn't Mia's fault that I'd had a hard day in Gaza, or that she didn't like long drives. But I told Raphael it did make me doubt if I was ready for a dog, especially such a spirited one.

Raphael smoked and listened. I looked down at Mia, stretched out with her pretty foxy face between her paws and felt something tighten in my chest. It was one thing to think these things, another to say them out loud. I was smitten with this small wild creature, who made strangers smile. But was love enough? I looked back at Raphael.

'Sometimes you need more than love,' I started and then stopped, not sure why I was pushing this conversation in a direction I didn't want it to go.

Raphael looked at me for a moment before replying.

'Yes, you do need more than love,' he said brightly. 'You need training! The answer isn't to give her away, it's to improve ourselves.'

Of course, *training*! Raphael's optimism was one of his most appealing characteristics. I felt relief coursing through me. I wanted a reprieve and he was giving me one.

'Does that mean you'll help a bit more, and walk her more often?'

Raphael said he would, though I wasn't sure I believed him. I gave him a quizzical look. We never used to have conversations like this. I was beginning to suspect we'd found this dog too early in our relationship. The 'baby' had come too soon.

Mia woke and shook herself out. She stretched, first backwards and then forwards, a quick canine Salute to the Sun, and sat back on her haunches, looking up at us expectantly. 'Do you think you'll be able to step up to the plate and improve a bit too?' I asked affectionately as I reached down to scratch behind her ears. 'You dog with nine lives …'

Mia gave me an inscrutable look, not unlike Raphael's, and turned her head away. It looked like I'd be stepping up to that plate by myself. But that was alright too. Raphael was giving me permission to do what I wanted to, which was to keep her, rather than what was sensible, which was to give her over to him or to someone else.

A tall, stooped man walked past us on the way to his table on the other side of the magnolia tree. He was thin and grey-haired, and seemed sunk in on himself until Mia ran up to greet him. We started to pull her back but he didn't seem to mind.

He stopped and said, 'What a beautiful dog!'

She stood with her paws on his thighs, eyes up, ears back, a seductress intent on conquest. He let go of whatever gloomy thoughts were consuming him and gave her a smile, the genuine one that only a dog or a small child elicits, as he stroked her head.

'And she's so friendly! Is she your dog?'

I looked at her and at Raphael.

'Of course!' he replied confidently.

'Yes, yes, she is,' I said more slowly.

That was the moment that I made my real commitment to her. I understood that it didn't matter who had originally saved her or how naughty she was, or would be again, she wasn't going anywhere. We could encourage Cesar Millan to come and do a show in Jerusalem, or we could find a local Cesar, but she was here to stay. Mia was ours, but also mine, for better or for worse, to have and to hold, leash or no leash. We loved her too much to give her away.

One friend who was one hundred per cent behind the decision to keep Mia was the American journalist Meg Coker. She was part of my 'Russian Mafia', the journalists who had come to Jerusalem from Moscow, where we had first met.

Meg was in her early thirties, clever, funny and a devoted dog owner, as well as a great friend. She had soft brown hair, which she wore bobbed, and the alluring traces of a southern accent that became more pronounced after a few drinks, or if she met anyone from Texas or Atlanta. She had striking light blue-green eyes, cat's eyes, and was always poised, no matter what sandy pit we were stuck in doing interviews. Flea pit. Mosh pit. Bear pit. Wherever we went, whatever the story, Meg always maintained that glossy American cover-girl look.

Despite being as wholesome as apple pie, Meg was an 'old Russia hand', having worked in Moscow on and off for ten years following the collapse of the Soviet Union. When I arrived as a newbie in the year 2000, overawed by the vast, impenetrable Russian capital, perhaps the quintessential insider's city, Meg showed me the ropes. As much sister as friend, she was decent, sceptical, hard-working and also practical. The first three are standard issue for journalists – well, maybe not so many are decent, now I come to think of it, but far fewer are practical. Journalists will turn up on stories without pen or paper, or the name of the person they are there to interview; they will arrive at the airport heading for a war zone without their passports, and they are always losing things – addresses, money, equipment, keys, tickets, receipts. Almost alone among us, Meg was organised.

There was one way in which she was a typical journalist, though. She was involved in a long-distance relationship. Meg was in Moscow and her boyfriend was in Nairobi. Craig Nelson was also a journalist whom I first met when he came to Moscow to visit Meg, and liked immediately. A kind, handsome man with a strong jaw and a boxer's body, he was a reporter of the old school – *Just the facts, Ma'am* – uncompromising about the search for information, never satisfied with opinion, or 'What the journalist was feeling', instead of the story. He also passed that most important girlfriend's test – he appeared to genuinely love Meg, and she was light and happy in his company. It was difficult to maintain a relationship over such vast distances, but they made the effort, flying across continents for months, until Craig gave up his job in Africa and relocated to Moscow. Two years later, they moved together to Jerusalem.

Meg and I often went out on stories and were good on the road together. We watched each other's backs, and were lucky, an unquantifiable but important factor on difficult stories. We also had fun. We ate lentil soup in restaurants and hotels across the Middle East, and if I ventured into a hotel lobby without her, assorted managers would run up in concern, saying, 'Hello, Miss Irris, but where is Miss Margaret?' We went to Baghdad together after Saddam Hussein was captured in December 2003 and visited the statue of my literary heroine, Scheherazade. As far as I am concerned the brave and brilliant storyteller of the *Thousand and One Nights* is the patron saint of female journalists. It was lovely to see her recognised with her own statue in a park on the banks of the Euphrates River.

Scheherazade stood in bronze, with her arms apart, her hair in a wave down her back, a half smile on her lips, spinning another tale for her survival. The king sat opposite, listening. Meg and I gazed up at her, on a cold winter's day, the river sparkling in the sun. We weren't the only visitors. One of the men sitting nearby said he came to see her whenever he felt down. There was something about the statue of this woman who lived on her wits, like everyone in Baghdad now had to, which helped his ill-feelings disappear.

Scheherazade's story is very satisfying. It starts with a king whose heart has been broken when his queen betrays him. He decides upon a murderous revenge. He marries a virgin, sleeps with her for one night and then has her killed, so she will not have the chance to betray him too. He does this night after night, striking terror into the hearts of the young women in his kingdom. All except one. Against her family's wishes, Scheherazade volunteers to marry the king and proceeds to talk her way out of trouble. She tells him fascinating tales, stopping at the most suspenseful spot, so that night after night he spares her life. Naturally, he falls in love with her, and like in all good fairytales, they live happily ever after, though I never got the feeling that she loved him back. She was smarter than that …

The sculptor of the Baghdad statue said his Scheherazade was a strong figure, standing while the king was reclining, but I thought he had given her something of the look of a mermaid. She was certainly a secular, unashamedly female figure, unveiled and self-assured. That at least was something. There wasn't that much happily-ever-after in present-day Iraq, although that was the period before the descent into civil war, when you could still move about and do investigative stories.

Meg and I travelled to the town of Al-Hilla, the site of ancient Babylon. It is one of the oldest centres of civilisation in the world, where right then another layer of history was being excavated. Six months earlier, Iraqis had discovered two mass graves, and I had been there when they had begun digging up some three thousand bodies. These were Shia men killed by Saddam Hussein for taking part in the rebellion against him, following the first Gulf War. They had been shot in the space of one month between March and April 1991.

It was one of the most terrible sights I've seen in my career as a journalist. Bulldozers worked around the clock to dig up the skeletons, which were packed tightly together. Volunteers gathered the remains in plastic bags and put any identifying clothes or dog tags nearby. These were laid out in rows in the dirt as far as the eye could see. The sweet, sickly smell of death hung in the air, intensified by the heat, and people from all over Iraq poured in, stepping over the skeletons in the search for missing loved ones. Black-clad Shia women marched among the bags of bones, looking, from a distance, like scavenging birds. They were carrying photos and ID numbers of the long-lost sons and brothers they hoped to find, and sobbed and ululated when they made a match, the other women simultaneously jealous and relieved that they had not yet received a confirmation of death.

Locals in Al-Hilla had known where to dig and they knew who was responsible. They accused the owner of the field where the mass graves were found, Sheikh Mohammed Al-Neifus. Some of them had actually watched him carry out the massacres. US forces took Al-Neifus into custody but four weeks later they released him, apparently in error. They issued a reward for his return, but it was too late, he had melted from view. Meg and I went to the Al-Neifus clan home and pieced together the family connections. With the new material we uncovered we had a strong story. It was fascinating but also dangerous, and Meg was so relieved when we were safely in the car on our way back to Baghdad that she initiated a round of carol singing.

'It's so close to Christmas we have to sing,' she said.

She taught our Iraqi driver and our translator the words to 'Jingle Bells', so they could join in. It was a very funny process and the two men laughed constantly. They were letting their guard down for the first time after years of living under a dictatorship, and it felt as if mirth – or pent-up relief – was exploding out of them. During Saddam's time, they'd suspected their neighbours and nearest family members of spying on them, and had censored even their own thoughts. As we sang, the driver, Samer, became interested in the Christmas story, quizzing us closely on theological points. Meg was the daughter of a Catholic deacon, and though her faith had now lapsed, she made a valiant effort to explain the concept of the Holy Trinity. She didn't have much success. The Virgin Birth was beyond them.

'But Mary was not a virgin, was she? It could not be!' Samer exclaimed, astonished. 'You do not believe this, do you, Meg?'

It seemed easier to go back to another rousing chorus of 'Jingle Bells'. I recorded us singing and sent the Baghdad Christmas carol to Craig in Jerusalem.

Craig had reported from Rwanda during the genocide in 1994, Afghanistan during the 2001 war, and Baghdad during the US invasion. He was brave, resourceful and persistent, qualities which were about to be tested in Jerusalem.

On a warm autumn evening in 2003, Craig was driving back to Jerusalem from Tel Aviv. He had been there reporting on a suicide bombing at a bus stop used by Israeli soldiers. He called Meg to see what they should do about dinner. They were foodies and great cooks, and even a casual meal at their place was always worth staying for. But they were both writing that night and neither had time to prepare a meal, so Craig offered to pick up some pizza on his way home. He stopped in at their local favourite, the Pizza Meter.

While he was waiting to collect the take-away, Craig noticed a young Palestinian man wearing a backpack standing outside and focused on him for a moment, before turning back to the pizza oven. Craig didn't see him scuffling with the Israeli guard, who prevented him from entering the pizzeria. He didn't see the young Palestinian then run on to the busy cafe next door.

Cafe Hillel was brand spanking new. It had floor-to-ceiling glass walls, and from the street you could see the new wooden floors and furniture, and the spectacular quiches, tarts, chocolate cakes and cheesecakes covered in berries invitingly displayed at the front counter. Ramez Abu Salim, from a village near Ramallah, stopped at the entrance to the shiny room, its floor not yet scuffed, its tables not yet scratched, looked at the customers and detonated his bomb.

The sound and the force of the explosion almost knocked Craig over next door. Sometimes the noise alone is enough to incapacitate people, paralysing them or sending them into shock, but Craig kept his cool. There was a moment's silence, as if the air had been sucked out of both restaurants, and then pandemonium, as the blast set off all the car alarms in the area and people began screaming. Clambering over the wreckage, Craig was there before the rescue services.

The cafe was black with smoke. Bleeding victims were stumbling out. The badly injured lay unable to move. Seven people were dead and more than fifty wounded. The bomber's head had become separated from his body and rolled into the middle of the road, where it sat upright. Craig looked away from that grisly sight and focused instead on the survivors. He saw a young Israeli woman thrown on her side nearby, bleeding profusely from her neck. He went over to help.

Her name was Nava Applebaum, and it was the day before her wedding. She had been in the cafe having a final 'date' with her dad. They were ordering take-away to bring back to the rest of the family, who were working at home on wedding decorations when the explosion took place.

Her father, Dr David Applebaum, ran the Emergency department at one of Jerusalem's main hospitals, Shaare Zedek, where they treated Palestinian patients, as well as the victims of Jerusalem's many suicide bombings. An American immigrant, Dr Applebaum had revolutionised the practice of emergency medicine in Israel. He was just back from New York, where he'd been lecturing at a 9/11 commemorative conference on how hospitals should deal with mass casualties. He was always the first on the scene at Jerusalem bombings – no other doctor could beat him there – and it was true on this night too. But Dr Applebaum wouldn't be treating any more victims, he had just become one himself. He died instantly. Craig struggled to save Nava, holding her wound to staunch the blood, gratefully giving way to the paramedics when they arrived. But they weren't able to help her either. Soon after arriving at hospital, Nava died, the bomb's eighth victim.

Friends and relatives who had come from all over the world to celebrate her wedding attended a double funeral in its place. Nava's husband-to-be led hundreds of mourners, dressed in their bridal finery, an indescribably sad sight. Before Nava's coffin was lowered into the ground, her lover threw in a final gift: her wedding ring.

It reminded me of the funeral of Ophelia from Shakespeare's *Hamlet*, where Hamlet's mother places flowers on Ophelia's grave and says:

I thought thy bride-bed to have deck'd, sweet maid,
And not have strew'd thy grave.

They buried Nava next to her father, and when the first clods of earth were thrown in over the coffins, the hundreds of mourners seemed to sob in unison, a collective intake of breath, followed by a long, low desperate wail.

Like many of the people we interview, Craig brooded on his lucky escape. Sitting over a cup of coffee in his sunny kitchen the next day he said, 'I was about to go into that cafe, but then I remembered that Meg is always nagging me about not drinking coffee late at night …' Craig smiled at Meg and leaned over to kiss her cheek. 'So I didn't.'

That suicide bombing took place on Craig's birthday. He seemed taken aback when I told him that this year his present was survival.

Journalists don't always cope with the terrible things they see. For weeks after the bombing, Craig battled feelings of guilt about failing to save the doctor's daughter. Seeing how troubled he was, Meg persuaded him to go up to the hospital and talk to the staff there. They took Craig seriously and spent time explaining the nature of Nava's injuries and reassuring him that he had done all he could. They said they couldn't have saved her either, even if the attack had happened at the hospital itself. Her injuries were so critical she could not have lived. In this context, that terrible truth was consoling. Craig got back in the saddle.

There are large tragedies, when you are part of a national event that is bigger than you, and smaller, more personal losses, and each affects you in its own way. Sometimes a small loss can take a great toll. At the end of the year, just after we came back from Baghdad, Meg's beloved old dog, Fred, died. She'd had him for more than ten years, and he had travelled with her to all her postings, from the US to Russia and then here. Meg was devastated. She was so knowledgeable about dogs that people sought her advice. I nicknamed her Dr Dog, and Orla and I considered having cards printed for her setting out her two specialties, *War Reporting and Pet Care*. After teary discussions, Meg and I agreed that having a pet was part of her life. Dr Dog needed to own a dog again. So did Craig, who loved animals, and had been devoted to Fred. When they said they would go to the Jerusalem dog pound to choose a new pet, I offered to come.

I arrived at their place the next morning to see that Meg had spent the morning crying. She didn't want a new dog at all, she wanted her old dog back. By the time we got into the car she promised she was over that. She still seemed sad to me but she was being positive, and had her sunglasses firmly on her nose, so the new dog wouldn't see her red-rimmed eyes.

We drove towards Atarot. Jerusalem's main dog pound is actually closer to the Palestinian town of Ramallah. It sits just off Road 443, the road that separates the West Bank from Israel, with Israeli towns on one side and Palestinian ones on the other. The road itself is built on Palestinian land, which Israeli authorities had requisitioned, overcoming Palestinian protests by arguing that the road would be of benefit to them too. However, after a series of shootings targeting Israeli cars, no Palestinian vehicles were permitted to drive on it. I felt uneasy taking a road prohibited to an entire group on the basis of their nationality. It was part of the compromise that this strange, divided society forced on you.

We reached the dog pound and parked outside. The air was filled with howls, the bereft, miserable, aching cries of homeless animals. It was a daunting welcome. We steadied ourselves and went in through a rusty gate set between two high walls. The early morning sun lit up a series of large concrete pens separated by wire fences, with small paths in between. They were filled to bursting with dogs. One plus was that they didn't kill them. But the pound was so overcrowded that many mornings the workers would find two or three animals dead, victims of health problems or struggles over food or simply their position in the pack. There were literally hundreds of dogs. They were

141

of all shapes, sizes and colours, in various states of health and fitness, but they shared one common characteristic: they were desperate. They jumped up as high as they could, or hurled themselves at the wire fence, barking wildly.

Pick me, pick me!

The sound was bloodcurdling. Some dogs threw themselves so hard I began to fear the fence would give way. No dog was still. Even the weaker ones, who couldn't reach the fence, were running backwards and forwards behind the rest of the deafening pack, though they weren't jumping up or daring to catch our eyes.

There's no point, you won't pick me.

I couldn't tell which was worse.

Dogs can convey many messages when they bark – menace, triumph, friendly inquiry, fear, even boredom. These dogs just sounded wretched. They had room to run around and there were buckets of water and food in each pen. It wasn't the worst pound in the world, by any means, but even here the conflict intruded. Few people came any more and the problem, once again, was the location. Israeli authorities had established the pound here, in the West Bank, in the 1990s. Once the Second Intifada began in the year 2000, Israelis stopped coming out. They became too scared. The pound was much closer to Palestinians but it was on the Israeli side of the line, and by mid 2004 when we came to choose a pet for Meg and Craig, it was also on the Israeli side of the wall which Israeli authorities were building around Ramallah to separate the Palestinian territories from Israel.

Palestinians now needed special entry and exit permits to go to the dog pound legally. Few were so attached to rescue dogs that they would go through all the hassle and humiliation of arranging a permit – or having it refused by Israeli military authorities – just in order to go to the pound. They saved that for when they needed to go to the hospital.

All in all, not many people came to Atarot to collect pets any more, and my head was spinning and my heart breaking from the sheer number of dogs around us. Soft-hearted Craig wanted every abandoned animal, including a tiny puppy with distemper and laboured breathing, and a dog so old and sick she wouldn't have lasted the month. I knew I could never choose just one out of all these, so I took refuge in a pen where there were puppies playing. I sat under a tree while a tiny warm puppy clambered in and out of my lap. He was white with fawn spots, and gave me sideways looks from slightly oddly angled eyes. I played him with him and ached for his future. While I escaped from my responsibilities, practical Meg narrowed it down to a shortlist of four possible pets. When they couldn't choose between two finalists, a handsome mutt and a stylish brown pointer, Meg proved why she was Dr Dog.

'Which one would you rather have on the bed with us?' she asked her boyfriend.

It was the killer question. Craig pointed to the mutt, a large dog with Alsatian colouring and a Rottweiler's build. So we took him and left the pointer behind, standing and watching us sadly from behind a wire gate before going back to his old life as one of hundreds in a pen. The mutt came with us, out past the wall, to his bright new future and a spot on the bed.

They named him Chucho. He sat nervously in one spot, trembling, for a week and never lay down, not even to sleep. Meg placed pieces of chicken on the steps leading up to her bedroom to lure him to climb them, but it took days before he dared to follow her up. The sight of a steel leash, which had belonged to Meg's old dog, caused him to shake like a leaf. Meg put it away, tears in her eyes at the thought of how cruel someone must have been to this poor animal.

The one piece of luck in his miserable life was that it was Meg and Craig who found him. He responded to their kindness by latching onto them like a duckling. He was soon following Meg from room to room, including waiting for her outside the bathroom, but he didn't let anyone else near him.

He barked wildly at every person who approached, and even a few who were simply walking quietly, minding their own business, on the other side of the street. He sounded like he wanted to kill them. And he was big and strong enough to convince them that he could. Chucho was terrified and terrifying, resembling one of those angry people who lashes out but is actually frightened underneath.

'You're a lion!' Raphael would say to him, urging him to be brave, but like the damaged lion in the *Wizard of Oz*, Chucho had no idea how fearsome he actually was.

One plus, he was a dog's dog, as happy and friendly with his own kind as he was terrified of people. Once we introduced him to Mia they became instant friends. She, of course, was a Dog of the Universe, and loved just about everyone, canine and human, that crossed her path, but there was no doubt that she loved Chucho most of all.

Meg and Craig's apartment was a ten-minute walk away from my place. Mia and I would head up the hill and as soon as we turned into their street she started wagging her tail excitedly. The process of getting from the front door of their building to Chucho's apartment on the top floor involved so much pent-up emotion I felt I had stepped into a nineteenth-century Victorian romance.

Mia could hardly bear the ten seconds involved in buzzing upstairs to be allowed into the building. As soon as the door opened, she strained against the leash until we reached the lift, where she also added whining to her repertoire if the doors didn't open immediately. Once inside the lift, she positioned herself, nose tight in against the door, front legs down, back legs up, because that was the point closest to Chucho. When the doors opened, she hurtled out and adopted the same position at Meg and Craig's front door, her entire being suffused with longing. When that door finally opened and she could see Chucho, she ran in between the feet of whatever human was in her way and flung herself on him.

Mia had the energy but Chucho had the skill. While she jumped on him, attacking him from all sides, it seemed, he stood still, disposing of her with one perfectly timed shoulder roll. He never used his full strength, judging exactly what the boisterous puppy could take. She was not so considerate, clamping herself onto his cheek with her needle sharp teeth. He tried to wriggle away but she wouldn't let go, and he would end up standing on top of her, so that they looked like a double-decker dog. Still she didn't budge, hanging underneath him determinedly. Meg and I agreed that she gave new meaning to the word 'dogged'.

When Chucho had finally had enough, an eruption of jumping, rolling, biting and chasing followed. They skidded on Meg's beautiful Afghan rugs, then ran in the opposite direction, skidding again. Meg automatically straightened the rugs behind them when they whizzed by.

'Maybe we should have called her Dervish?'

The dogs played games they devised, with complex rules, attacking each other on Chucho's dog bed and then howling and squealing indignantly when either landed on the floor in contravention of their strict rules.

We sat on Meg's balcony, where she'd planted citrus trees in clay pots. She tended the limes and cumquats as we drank coffee and the dogs skidded around us. From her balcony you could see the Jerusalem section of the wall Israel was building in the West Bank, an ugly grey gash on the stony landscape, cementing the separation between peoples here. Still, if you didn't look out but only down at the dogs it was possible to be distracted from all those restrictions and sorrows. We spent many easy afternoons like that, coming back from difficult reporting assignments, taking an hour before we started writing to enjoy the comic relief the dogs provided.

Standing on Meg's lovely balcony, I savoured a spectrum of feelings. Sometimes owning a dog was very tense, but at other times it was wonderfully light. Love can illuminate your life whenever and wherever you are lucky enough to find it. Even the love of a dog who seems to be part fox, or the love of a man who is so unlike you that all the matchmakers and computer dating agencies would rule him out immediately.

The film *Shakespeare in Love* always seems to me to give the best and most detailed explanation of how love works: 'No one knows. It's a mystery.'

Raphael had big news. He had just landed a role in an upcoming Israeli film. It was a dramatisation of the novel *Someone to Run With*, by one of Israel's best known authors, David Grossman.

The novel was a coming-of-age love story set in Jerusalem. It was about a group of street children who were dependent on drugs, and lived under the care of an underworld figure. He sheltered and also exploited them and the story turned on how they tried to escape. Raphael was to play one of the bad guys. I was fascinated to see what he would do with the role, since it seemed to me against his natural type. I was also very happy for him. You're always struggling in creative professions, like music and acting – or, for that matter, journalism – so it's wonderful when a solid block of work comes along. It's even better when it's a project that you can be proud of. It was a step up from doing commercials, and if the film was a success, it could be a big career boost. The producers also knew that Raphael was a musician who wrote his own material, and they commissioned some music for the film. He was thrilled.

The hero of the story, with the biggest part, was a dog. In the book the dog was a Golden Retriever. In the film, it was played by two Retrievers, Casey and Naana. Raphael said I should bring Mia to visit when they were filming in town, near the Jerusalem farmers' market, an area I knew well, as I'd become a regular ever since Raphael led me there.

The location was a steakhouse called Sima, a Jerusalem landmark. Cars, props, lights, cameras and boom mikes filled the busy, narrow street. A large truck was parked on the pavement, blocking the way of pedestrians. Cables were taped on the ground, and heavily made-up actors and, in this case, dogs as well were mingling with the shoppers.

The two Retrievers were waiting to go 'on' and Mia went over to pay her respects and drink some of their water. When the three caramel-coloured dogs sat facing the steakhouse, Mia looked just like a small 'Mini-Me' Retriever. The adult dogs put their feet into the water bowl when they'd finished drinking, as if they wanted to swim, a habit she had too.

'Oh, I was hoping she'd grow out of that …' I said to the dog handler. He was a fat, confident man in his fifties, with yellowing teeth and short grey hair. When we met that morning, he was content to drink coffee and to tell dog stories. He didn't have to do much more because his animals were so well trained. He seemed relaxed, but after the filming was over, he had a nervous breakdown, a reminder that you can never tell what is really going on in people's hearts.

'Quiet on set!'

It was time to work. The trainer watched while his 2IC took charge.

'Action!'

Golden-haired, calm-eyed, reliable Naana – which means 'Mint' in Arabic and Hebrew – listened for his orders.

'Naana, break through the door!' and Naana did, three times, for three different camera angles.

'Naana, speak!' Naana barked.

'Naana, run!' Naana ran.

'Naana, look at the camera!'

'Naana, look away from the camera!'

Then they held up a sign saying 'bark' and Naana barked. Raphael and I looked at each other in disbelief. The dog could *read*.

After that, to give Naana a rest, Casey went into action. She also did what she was told, repeating each action over and over again until the director had everything he needed. I watched in awe. They made fewer mistakes than the human actors. I saw a large neon sign in the sky pointing down at these remarkable animals and pulsing on and off as it changed colour. It said, 'Training for Mia'. Raphael said to go for it, so trailing our naughty dog, held on a tight leash, I asked the dog handler if he could recommend anyone.

'The only condition is that I don't want to use violence but I can see that I do need help with discipline.'

He was happy to recommend a woman he'd worked with. Two days later Einav Carmel arrived on a motorbike. She put her helmet under one arm as she extended the other in a strong handshake. She was of medium build with a wide face and a sleek head, almost bald, like a young Sinead O'Connor. She seemed tough, and she was firm with dogs but never mean. She had a deep love of animals and a belief that you could get the best out of them by reward rather than punishment.

'There is no need to hit a dog if you can get him to obey by other means instead. You will see how much we can teach a dog to do for a small piece of sausage.'

In this land of hard-hitting military solutions, Einav believed in the soft option. I liked her from the first moment.

She suggested that we start out to the park so she could see how Mia and I interacted together there. I kept Mia on the leash, since I didn't want to waste Einav's hour running after her.

After watching us, Einav said, 'Do you see that she has never made eye contact with you once? It's as if she is not going for a walk with you. She is going out on her own and you happen to be coming with her. We'll have to work on that.'

Then Einav watched Mia ignore me back in the apartment as well, and laid it on the line. Our work would be cut out for us, because Mia might be part Golden Retriever, but she was also part local Bedouin desert dog.

'The Bedouin desert dogs are among the most recently domesticated dogs in the world. Essentially they are wild dogs who've just come in near the campfire, like the Australian dingo or the American coyote.'

'*Ohmigod!* I've got a half dingo in the house. No wonder she's like this,' I muttered to myself.

'And although Mia has the appearance of the domesticated dog, in her nature she is more truly like the wild one,' Einav continued.

As I listened, I felt relief wash over me. So this wasn't all my fault. I told Einav that I'd always felt I was living with a fox, rather than a dog, and confessed that at times it made me so desperate that I worried about whether we could keep her. Einav replied reassuringly that she often heard that from people who owned these desert dogs, and that some of them really couldn't be kept as pets because they would never adjust to domestic life. But she didn't think Mia was like that.

Oh yeah, you just wait ... I had to stop myself from saying it out loud, and wondered if I was starting to channel my dog.

Einav said the dogs were smart, and often cunning as well, but despite this they proved difficult to train. They learned every order quickly but they ended up obeying only if they wanted to, which wasn't actually the point of training a dog. Or being a dog. She said we were lucky that Mia was a mix of two breeds, and that her wild heart was tempered by the good nature of a domesticated Retriever.

'Mia is as clever as Naana, the Retriever in the film, I could see that immediately – you could teach her to do anything. But,' Einav looked at me sternly, 'she is a dog without boundaries.'

As if to underscore this point, Mia hopped up onto the couch, turned in a circle three times, yawned and closed her eyes.

'We have to set some boundaries and sooner rather than later. We will embark on a serious training course. We won't hit her, but we will control her every moment. In the end, you will take charge.'

It sounded scary but I told Einav I was ready. I'd finally realised that with these dogs, like with the locals, you had to go all the way. It was war. Either Mia won or we did.

Once you knew, everything seemed different. I started noticing the Bedouin dog features – long sharp faces, curly tails, lean, rangy bodies with something of the look of a fox – in many dogs being walked on the street. Some were thinner, like the wind-swift Salukis; others were stockier, like the Canaanite dogs. All had a similar look of alert self-possession.

They were territorial and frequently aggressive, and carried some of that in their bearing. For a tough dog, they were also surprisingly pretty, their foxy faces dominated by dark-rimmed eyes, as if they were wearing eyeliner. 'M'kahhal – born wearing kohl,' they say in Arabic about people with this naturally occurring marking. On a blonde like Mia it was especially fetching.

These kohl-lined eyes, curly tails and white socks were so common, it was as if there should have been a designated breed: the Jerusalem Street Dog. Mia was one of the prototypes. When a dog called Toffee went missing, her owners put up pictures and signs everywhere. It was sad for me, since Toffee was so similar to Mia. More than once when I entered a park, a stranger rushed up to me and said excitedly, 'You've found Toffee!'

When I replied that this dog wasn't Toffee, their eyes narrowed and they looked at me suspiciously, as if they'd found the dognapper instead. I could see them thinking, *You've stolen Toffee!*

I don't know if Toffee ever came home.

One afternoon, when Meg and I were walking our dogs, a Bassett Hound was running through the park. We agreed that we'd never seen a low-slung Hush Puppy dog move so nimbly or quickly. It was really covering some turf. But when we looked more closely we saw that, despite its size and colouring, which were all Bassett, the face was just a bit too narrow and long, and the tail was just a bit too curly … a Bedouin wild dog had crept in there, too, to give this dog more oomph.

'Animals here are more bestial,' Meg said, in her best Dr Dog voice, as we watched our dogs jumping on one another, teeth bared. They were noisy, their expressions aggressive. If you didn't know better you'd say they were fighting.

'They're territorial, they fight,' Meg continued, looking around at the motley crew in the park. 'Most dogs in my home town aren't like this.'

Nor in mine. They'd be muzzled and leashed and probably on Prozac if they behaved like this in Sydney. I couldn't imagine Paris Hilton's rat-sized micro-dog attacking the one in her friend's handbag the way these dogs went at each other.

They were strong dogs who aroused strong feelings. Later that week, when I was walking Mia in town, a plump middle-aged man came up to ask if he could pat her. He had an open, kindly face with trusting eyes behind thick glasses, and Mia decided that he was a good person because she sat and looked up at him obligingly, which she won't do for everyone when we're so close to the park.

He told me that his name was Abdullah. As he stroked Mia he explained sadly that two weeks earlier he had been visiting relatives in Bethlehem with his wife, children and their beloved family dog Foosky, when Foosky had been run over. Foosky was identical to Mia, *identical*, he repeated, looking down at her in astonishment.

'I just want to pat Foosky again,' he said, reaching down to scratch behind Mia's ears, adding, 'I can't believe it, I can't believe how similar they are …' And then he stopped because tears were welling up in his eyes and rolling down his cheeks.

All the ordinary noise and bustle of the street – people walking past, cars honking, cranes and excavators working at a nearby building site, the pneumatic squeal of brakes as large trucks drove by – faded into the background. The man wasn't ashamed of his distress and didn't try to hide his tears or to wipe them away. He just kept patting Mia, and as she leaned into him I found that I couldn't stop the tears gathering in my own eyes. I was caught up in this man's grief for his departed pet, an animal I'd never seen, but which was so like my own dog that I understood his feelings of loss and sadness intimately.

Mia was introducing me to the city of Jerusalem in a new way. I was meeting my neighbours and making friends in the same streets I'd been walking for the previous two years without speaking to anyone. I was getting to know the city's alleys and its stories and its people. And they knew my dog.

'She's become your guardian angel,' Meg said approvingly.

12

In the mornings inside our garden suburb, my guardian angel befriended the early-bird walkers and exercisers. Funny to think I was now one of them. On a green hill across from the walls of the Old City, we often met Sarah the English doctor. She was visible from a distance, wearing a scraggy T-shirt and sweatpants, and making slow, controlled balletic movements. She did tai-chi in front of that rolled-gold million-dollar view until Mia interrupted her, running up, tail wagging, ears down, to say hello.

Sarah was perhaps my most eccentric and fascinating neighbour. A thin woman whose dark hair was flecked with grey, she was that unlikely combination, a traditional Jewish Buddhist. She kept a kosher home and observed the Sabbath, as well as meditating and travelling to Buddhist retreats around the world. A paediatrician, she no longer treated patients, instead running a centre studying Tibetan medicinal plants at Jerusalem's famous Hadassah hospital.

She was clever, principled, kind and selfish all at once, with an impish laugh and infectious enthusiasm for every project she undertook. Her latest idea was to study all the medicinal plants mentioned in the Bible and to scientifically evaluate their healing properties. She said she was convinced there was a Jewish book of healing, which God had removed from man in biblical times. Like a medical Indiana Jones, she was on its trail.

'I want to unlock its secrets!' Sarah announced grandly.

You always need a vision to inspire you on the long march through research. In addition to the plants mentioned in the Bible, she was studying local traditional medicines and the treatises of brilliant physicians from earlier times, like the medieval Jewish doctor Maimonides and the great tenth-century Muslim doctor Avicenna. Once she found that they all used a certain herb to treat an illness – say, diabetes – then she would test that herb in the lab to see if it did have any effect on diabetes.

'I want to find a way to treat diseases that are plagues of modern medicine,' she explained.

Sarah had a nine-year-old son called Uri and three other loves: classical music, the Dalai Lama and Mia. Sarah's affections were cemented one evening when she wasn't feeling well. She rang to say feebly that she was too ill to cook and to ask me to bring over some food. Forget herbal remedies; Sarah had something else in mind.

'Bring chicken soup! I'm *so* sick!'

I ran down to the markets, cooked up some soup and took it over, pot in one hand, Mia on her leash in the other. Sarah's son, Uri, let us in because Sarah was too weak to come to the door. She lay on the sofa in her welcoming messy lounge room, where shelves of books lined the walls.

In between were framed sketches drawn by Sarah's father, Ralph Sallon, who was a famous British cartoonist. His pictures of Einstein, Churchill and members of the Sallon family stared down at you companionably when you sank into Sarah's couch. Sarah sat up only to eat some soup, and Mia spent the whole evening lying in the crook behind Sarah's legs, a warm, living bandage.

'I love this dog.' Sarah gazed at Mia and Mia gazed back, in that unfathomable, reassuring way dogs have. 'She is a most unusual animal – look at those eyes, she is actually thinking, you know. I have the strongest feeling that she was a person in a previous life. Were you a person, Mia? Who were you?' Sarah cooed at Mia.

Living opposite the Old City of Jerusalem, I spent hours in its streets. Here at the beating heart of the Middle East conflict, Jews believe the Jewish Temple once stood, Christians believe Jesus was crucified, and Muslims believe that Mohammed ascended to heaven on a winged horse. The ancient walled town is tiny, only one mile square, no wonder they end up fighting!

The ornate sign to my street, in Hebrew, Arabic and English. *Hatiqwa* means 'hope' in Hebrew. When I moved in during the Palestinian uprising, the Second Intifada, hope seemed in short supply. Thousands were dying in Palestinian suicide bombings in Israeli cities, and Israeli military incursions in the West Bank.

I took this photo after Israeli troops withdrew from Bethlehem in May 2002. They imposed lengthy curfews on Palestinian residents, and surrounded the Church of the Nativity, where Palestinian militants had taken refuge. The church is built on the spot where Christians believe Jesus was born. After the militants were released and the curfew was lifted, this Palestinian boy climbed into a car destroyed during the fighting.

The dove of peace, wearing a flak jacket, in someone's gunsights. Always in someone's gunsights. British graffiti artist Banksy painted this on a wall in Bethlehem for a Christmas exhibition in 2007.

Another Banksy mural on the Separation Wall, Bethlehem, shows a Palestinian girl patting down an Israeli soldier.

A Palestinian refugee on Nakba Day in Ramallah. Israelis celebrate the creation of their state as Independence Day, the Palestinians mourn it as Catastrophe Day. The names say it all. The woman is holding the key to her family home inside Israel. She has never been there, since her parents fled in 1948, before she was born.

The view from my house in Hope Street, Jerusalem. This is a Benedictine abbey, the Hagia Maria Sion, on the slopes of Mount Zion, just outside the walls of the Old City.

I am broadcasting for an international TV news channel from Jerusalem, with the symbol of the city, the Dome of the Rock Mosque, on the skyline behind me. They just open the window on this rolled-gold million-dollar view from their front room in a house turned into a TV studio in East Jerusalem, the Palestinian side of the city.

Easter in the Old City of Jerusalem. Greek Orthodox nuns walk the Fourteen Stations of the Cross, from the Lions' Gate to the Church of the Holy Sepulchre, built on the site where it's believed Jesus was crucified. The church is shared by six Christian denominations.

The Israeli farmers' market, Mahane Yehuda, Jerusalem. The *challah*, or Sabbath bread, is going fast. I enjoy shopping here because the produce and the stall holders are both great value.

My friend the American journalist Meg Coker. We worked together on stories across Russia, Central Asia and the Middle East, and were often the only women in all-male crowds. Here she is in a cafe in Amman in 2003, on our way to Iraq after Saddam Hussein was captured.

The compound of Palestinian leader Yasser Arafat in Ramallah, on the day Israeli troops withdrew in May 2002. They had re-occupied it during Operation Defensive Shield, Israel's largest military operation in the West Bank since the 1967 war. I returned in November 2004, squashed in the huge crowds that turned out for Arafat's funeral.

Children on their way to a rally in Gaza, 2005. Gaza is an Islamist stronghold, where many forms of entertainment such as movie theatres have been banned. Restaurants serving alcohol have been burned to the ground. Funerals and political rallies are some of the only public gatherings left, and the children are as involved as the adults.

Al-Araqib, a Bedouin village in Israel's south. Israeli authorities destroyed this village four times in July 2010, arguing that it was built on land that did not belong to the Bedouins, but to the state. The Bedouins of course dispute this, which is why they rebuild.

Photos of rabbis watching over a drinks stall in the Mahane Yehuda farmers' market. The stall holder reveals a lot about himself – including what community he's from and how religious he is – by the photos of the rabbis he reveres.

Palestinians stand next to a wall with graffiti painted by Banksy. Ironically, the owner of the wall later painted over this, unaware of its value.

Children in Gaza, 2005, holding political flags, on their way to a rally.
They are photographed so often that they are very relaxed around cameras.

Raphael, my Israeli musician boyfriend. We met by chance in the same cafe – twice. Can you meet someone by accident twice? Here, in the superstitious Middle East, they tell me that's not chance, it's fate.

Mia, the dog who changed my life. It was unplanned of course. Raphael saved her as a tiny puppy from under the wheels of an oncoming car. More chance, or fate. Here she sits in the window after a visit to the vet.

Raphael performing with his band in Tel Aviv. He is also an actor and a writer.

We are a family now, though at first it did seem as if 'the baby' had come too soon. Suddenly we were fighting about looking after Mia, and especially who would get up for the 6am walk.

Mia comes with me to visit Nabil the Palestinian money changer in East Jerusalem. He says Mia is his favourite customer.

I lived in this beautiful sandstone suburb, Yemin Moshe, built on a hill opposite the Old City of Jerusalem. Its streets were closed to traffic, which is a plus for owning a dog. But there were also lots of stairs to run up and down in pursuit of a runaway like Mia.

Mia at the front gate to my Jerusalem apartment. She spent a lot of time here looking out and supervising the street.

Mia loves children, but in the area where we live she encounters many religious Jewish and Muslim children who are terrified of dogs. She has taken it as her mission to convince all children, no matter how frightened, to love her back.

Yemin Moshe, with its cobbled lanes and sandstone houses, is like a village in the centre of town. It was the first Jewish area built outside the Old City, but initially the frightened occupants only stayed here by day, returning to the safety of the walled city at night. Between 1948 and 1967, when Jerusalem was divided between Israel and Jordan, this area sat just above No Man's Land and was often dangerous.

My street in a Jerusalem winter. Snow falls on palm fronds and bougainvillea, which always appear indignant in their white coats.

Baghdad 2003. I am standing in front of a defaced mural of Saddam Hussein in Abu Ghraib prison. Then the cells had been emptied and the feeling was somewhat optimistic. However, the American military soon reinstated it as a prison, and also a torture centre. The shocking evidence was revealed in photos taken by the US soldiers themselves.

At the ransacked Ministry of Culture office in Baghdad, 2003. I smuggled a poster of Saddam out of Baghdad after removing it from a wall in one of these offices. It was my only piece of war loot. Raphael was horrified when he saw it on my Jerusalem apartment wall. So Saddam had to be put away.

A Palestinian protester in the alley near the Lions' Gate on the day I was injured. I was hit in the face by a rock thrown down into the alley by masked Palestinians running along the flat rooftops above. They were protesting the Israeli decision to limit the number of Muslim worshippers at the Al-Aqsa Mosque. My jaw was broken in three places. Given the size of those rocks, I'm lucky my injury wasn't more serious.

Later that same day, waiting in a Jerusalem hospital to have my jaw wired shut. I couldn't talk or eat for six weeks. As well as breaking my jaw, the rock had damaged some of my facial nerves. My smile was crooked and the left side of my face was frozen. The doctors said it might stay frozen for the rest of my life.

With Mia on the first anniversary of the day my jaw was broken in the Old City. Luckily, some of my facial nerves recovered and I no longer had a crooked smile. Whenever I'm in a bad mood, I tell myself to keep smiling, because I'm lucky to be able to.

Mingling her core beliefs, Sarah pronounced that in an earlier incarnation Mia had probably been a rabbi.

'Yes, a rabbi! She is always running into the synagogue when you walk by,' she pronounced.

It didn't seem likely to me, but I was happy to see that Mia and the chicken soup had done their work and that Sarah was looking perkier.

'What terrible thing did you do to be demoted to a dog, hmm?' I asked Mia fondly, still in her little lair, wedged behind Sarah's knees.

Sarah was not alone in believing that dogs were part of a reincarnation cycle. Many ultra-Orthodox Jews believe that after a person dies, the soul can have difficulty in going to heaven due to unresolved issues with people left behind on earth. In these cases, the lost soul takes possession of the body of an animal, usually a dog, as a place to 'hover' until it sorts out its problems and can finally leave this world. Rabbi Yitzhak Basri, a scholar of the Jewish book of mysticism, the Kabbalah, takes it one step further.

'Sometimes the souls of sinners, such as adulterers or people who slept with non-Jews, enter the body of a dog. It is known that when a righteous man dies, the souls of people in need of redemption come to him so they can be healed as a result of his death.'

If a dog suddenly appears at a synagogue or the home of a religious person after they die, and refuses to leave of its own accord, the ultra-Orthodox sometimes perform an exorcism to free the soul of the person trapped inside. One such exorcism was filmed by an enterprising documentary maker and shown on Israeli TV. Sitting on my sofa, with Mia curled up beside me, I watched ultra-Orthodox Jews from the Jerusalem suburb of Mea Shearim describe how shortly after their rabbi's death, a thin disturbed dog arrived at the late rabbi's apartment.

Mourners were crammed into the rooms, all wearing their traditional black clothes. They were segregated, men in one room, women in another, as required by their beliefs. No one had ever seen the dog before, but it refused to leave the house. They considered all animals to be unclean, and were afraid to touch any dog, even an ordinary non-possessed one, and they called in someone from outside the community to remove the intruder. To no avail. The dog wouldn't go.

The community buried its leader and then gathered in his house for the traditional week-long Jewish mourning services. The dog stayed for the lot. It sat with its head down, appearing to follow the prayers. The congregation agreed that the dog seemed moved when they sang the 'Kaddish', the Jewish mourner's prayer. They held an exorcism ceremony, which as far as I could see involved more prayers, this time directed at the dog, until it finally departed.

I watched the film amazed, first by the content and second by how much that dog resembled Mia. Tan, lean, sharp-faced, curly-tailed, the main difference was sleeker fur and a far more troubled expression than you would ever see in the eyes of my protected pet. The outstanding feature of the film was how solemn everyone was. There wasn't a twinkle in the eye of anyone being interviewed. Possessed pooches were serious business here.

But to each his own. One afternoon when Mia chased a cat up a tree, and was at its base, barking bossily at the terrified but victorious creature above her, a woman came up to me and said confidingly, 'That dog is barking the words of Jesus.'

Dogs are a screen onto which we project our own beliefs.

The other people out at all times and in all weathers were the gardeners. They befriended me and had lately taken to providing me with a much needed boost – a cup of coffee in the morning. There's nothing that can equal being given something *just* when you need it.

The Palestinian national poet Mahmoud Darwish describes coffee as a journey, begun thousands of years ago, which still goes on. 'Coffee is a place. Coffee is pores that let the inside seep through to the outside. Coffee is geography.'

The gardeners were up before dawn, and by the time Mia dragged me out of bed, two hours later, they were ready for breakfast. They gathered in the small park nearest my house, beneath a large, ancient olive tree. It was a popular spot. Children climbed on the tree's gnarled branches during the day while lovers sat entwined beneath it at night.

Tsadok, the head gardener, was a tall, fair-haired Israeli who came prepared. He brought a suitcase, with a camp stove folded neatly inside, as well as coffee, sugar and glass cups. He unpacked with a flourish, sat in the shade and proceeded to brew a perfect cup of coffee, the way the locals liked it – black, strong, sweet and electrified by cardamon. Sometimes Jamil, his Palestinian 2IC, was allowed to step in, but when he did, they inevitably ended up squabbling.

'I make better coffee than you,' Jamil announced, stirring in sugar by the spoonful.

'No, you don't because you always make it too sweet,' Tsadok replied, watching him closely. 'Not so much! *Ach*, you always do that!'

Darwish said no coffee was like another because no soul was like another. That was certainly true here.

Tsadok made a dismissive downward action, waving the air with an open hand, the local sign for a waste of time and effort. They were like an old married couple, one of those rare Arab-Israeli ones. Mia ran up to defuse the tension.

'Mia!' they stopped bickering to greet her.

When the coffee was ready they poured it, steaming, into small coloured glasses. They handed me the dark-blue glass with light blue curls picked out in enamel along the rim. It was the only one that wasn't chipped and I appreciated the honour.

'Better than a restaurant,' Tsadok boasted and he was right.

But inevitably by that time, Mia was on her way to the next park and I had to drain the cup quickly, till only sweet muddy grounds were left, rinse it with the garden hose, and run off after her, waving to them.

Often when she ran away or became separated from her leash or collar, it was the gardeners who helped me find her, running up to my house when they'd see her on her own in one of the parks, or knocking at the door with a big smile, holding up my missing leash, sometimes with dog attached, sometimes without. I thanked them, amazed that Mia had found herself such a wide circle of helpers. Hillary Clinton was right: it takes a village to raise a dog.

With three days to go before Mia's training program began, I went down to Gaza. It was the last working day at the Jewish settlement of Ganei Tal, a small collection of red-roofed homes in the south of the Strip.

Ganei Tal – Hebrew for Gardens of Dew – was home to about one hundred families, some five hundred people. It looked like an ordinary well-off Israeli suburb, except that it was surrounded by a barbed-wire fence and backed on to the large town of Khan Yunis, where some 200,000 Palestinians lived. This tiny number of Israelis could not have survived here without a massive military presence guarding them day and night. The settlers were mostly farmers. Their hothouses were filled with plastic-covered rows of geraniums, peppers and cherry tomatoes, grown for export to Europe. There was lush vegetation inside the Ganei Tal fence; sand outside it.

The Israeli government had sent Jewish volunteers to settle Gaza from 1967 onwards, spending huge amounts building their homes, subsidising their businesses and connecting them to electricity and sewerage. The roads and other infrastructure built for the settlers were much better than those of the surrounding Palestinian population. Over time, the settlers ended up consuming around forty per cent of the land. The amount of water directed to the Jewish settlers and away from the Palestinian population was another source of conflict created by the Israeli presence in Gaza.

While most of the families in Ganei Tal opposed the edict to pack up and leave, they were reluctantly obeying. I was there with Aaron Schachter, a funny, easy-going American radio journalist. We often went out on stories together, since we both worked with the eccentric, brilliant – and brilliantly clothed – Nuha as our translator and could share costs and transport. After the settlers paid their Palestinian workers for the last time, Aaron and I recorded the workers trooping out of the back of the settlement, across a sandy stretch of ground to their village on the outskirts of Khan Yunis. Standing in the late-afternoon sunshine, gauging the distance at no more than a couple of hundred metres, it struck me how closely some Jews and Arabs lived.

A single cart and donkey stood waiting. The Palestinians were leaving Ganei Tal carrying the possessions the departing Jewish settlers had left behind. The settlers would trade up when they began their new lives back inside Israel, but that was almost impossible to do in Gaza, where the import and export of goods was tightly controlled by the Israeli military. Gazans evaded this economic blockade by smuggling goods in from Egypt, via tunnels dug deep under the ground. The smuggled goods were inevitably more expensive – and often of lower quality, since large items such as cars had to be sawed into bits so they could be squeezed through the tunnels and then welded back together once they reached Gaza.

Second-hand goods that Jewish settlers were prepared to discard had a different value here. At the back of Ganei Tal, Palestinians loaded up the wooden cart with fridges, stoves, microwaves, computers, cupboards, tables and chairs, shelves, coils of aluminium, plastic sheeting and gardening pots. Children's shoes were tied on top. Women sat in the sand minding their piles of possessions until the donkey returned for the next load.

The cart's first stop was in the closest Palestinian village, where someone had brought out a set of large old-fashioned butcher's scales to weigh the piles of aluminium. These had been frames in Israeli greenhouses until yesterday. The Palestinian men weighed and measured them, crouched on the sandy ground, shaded by green flowering shrubs in the village square, while a crowd watched to make sure there was no cheating.

This transfer of property symbolised what would happen next – the return of the land to Palestinian control. We went to see Osama al Farra, Palestinian Governor of Khan Yunis. He said his town would increase in size by one-third after the Israelis pulled out.

'I think our people are counting the days and the hours and the seconds. It is our dream for a long period.'

He explained that the Palestinian Authority had multi-million-dollar plans for the land, which also included the largest Israeli settlement in Gaza – actually a town – called Neve Dekalim.

All they were waiting for was Israel's final withdrawal.

When I returned from Gaza, it was time to begin Mia's new training program. She must have sniffed the end of freedom on the wind, for she ran away again, only this time she did it in spectacular style. We were out in the park, and yes, she was without a leash again. I was instantly anxious, and there was no one to blame but myself. I let her run free partly because I couldn't get this romantic image of the ideal dog out of my head. It was not a dog I had ever owned, rather a prototype for what all dogs should be: an Australian working dog, perhaps a Kelpie or a Blue Heeler. The breed wasn't crucial, it was the attitude. My ideal dog was hard-working and obedient, out on a farm, rounding up sheep and cattle in the furthest dry, red paddock till it heard my whistle. Then it loyally returned and hopped up onto the back of my ute, where it stood steadily while we drove home. The sun set, the vehicle threw up clouds of red dust, and no matter how bumpy the road, the dog stayed aboard, silhouetted against the vast skyline. There was no leash in sight, just wordless communication between dog and owner. I had this image firmly fixed in my mind, even though I was strictly a big city girl and had never lived in the Australian bush, and definitely hadn't rounded up sheep or cattle.

All that romantic guff was out the window now. It was late on Sunday, and instead of enjoying a hot, lazy afternoon, I was once again trudging anxiously through the local parks. Mia's name tag had fallen off, and buying a new one was on my To Do list for the next morning. Knowing that no one could call me if they found her made me more desperate. The shadows lengthened on the bleached grass. My breathing became shallow and I had a sick feeling in the pit of my stomach. It was a beautiful evening, the cicadas chirruping, the warm air scented with pine needles and herbs. But I was oblivious, calling Mia's name over and over, until my voice grew hoarse. I phoned Raphael and he steadied me, but the fear wouldn't go away.

I climbed the stairs back to the top park and met one of my neighbours. Damira was an émigré from St Petersburg who had lived in Israel for more than fifteen years. A slender woman in her fifties, she had greying hair which she swept back from a face at once both plain and pretty. She often looked ineffably sad, until she smiled, at which point you momentarily saw what she would have looked like as a girl. Damira was a Christian woman who had come to Israel in 1990 with her Jewish husband, part of the wave of Russian Jews who left the Soviet Union after the Communist system collapsed. These migrants now make up almost twenty per cent of Israel's population.

Being part of this large group had not been easy. The state of Israel plonked Damira and her husband and hundreds of others in caravans in a partially built 'absorption centre' on the outskirts of Jerusalem. The pre-fab dwellings were boiling in summer, muddy in winter, and far from public transport and other services. Damira described this pioneering start as a shock after St Petersburg, the most sophisticated, romantic city in Russia. She and her husband soldiered on, learning Hebrew and trying to find jobs. In Russia her husband had worked in the aerospace industry, in charge of producing the space suits worn by cosmonauts. There was no equivalent in Israel, and he needed to find a new field of endeavour. But he didn't manage to.

'He was too old for that,' Damira explained sadly.

She sometimes felt that her only connection to this new homeland came from an abandoned puppy that she was feeding. She named him Chips. When Chips was still small, her husband began feeling unwell. They found a Russian-speaking doctor who diagnosed cancer. Damira nursed her husband devotedly until his death six months later. By the time I met her, she was completely alone, for Chips had died too. She'd ended up here, with no roots, no contacts and now little money.

'*Sudba* – Fate,' she said with a Russian shrug. You couldn't explain or understand it.

I had only learned Damira's life story after Mia had introduced us. Now I explained urgently that Mia was lost, and Damira said she would help me to look. I could do a sweep of the parks again, and she would do the streets around my house. It was comforting not to be searching alone.

I tramped back through the top park, calling Mia's name and recalling Damira's last visit to my house. She had come leading a stray with attractive dark markings, a lovely 'Jerusalem street dog' face and a shy expression. But something was wrong. The dog's tail was barely attached to its body. Someone had tried to hack it off with a knife. The cruelty had made my eyes water. The assailants hadn't succeeded in doing the job properly, either because they got bored or because, maddened by pain, the animal had escaped. Its tail was starting to rot and Damira had come to see if I would drive them to a vet.

The dog went with us happily enough and at the clinic the staff said they would have to dock its tail. The vet was a striking young Israeli woman with delicate features and creamy skin. She looked like she had stepped out of the Bible, perhaps an ancient Hebrew judge, as she pushed her dark curls back from her face and said sadly that this kind of 'surgery' without anaesthetic on the tails and ears of dogs happened all too regularly. She also told us that she became a vet because she loved dogs and cats, all animals really, and she chose to work at this charity clinic in order to help them, but instead each day she witnessed the terrible suffering humans inflicted on animals.

This memory was making me so frightened I couldn't think straight. As I scanned the horizon, terrified that some nameless cruel boy had taken Mia into the Old City, and was hacking at her tail with a knife, I decided to confront my fears and report my lost dog to the Old City police. I called Raphael again. He said that was a good idea, though Mia would most likely be waiting for me at home when I got back.

'Call and let me know what happens.'

I left Yemin Moshe and climbed up the hill to the Old City. The light was soft, before the quick fade to dusk, and the air was cooling slowly. Despite centuries of bloodshed, Jerusalem always looked so serene. The lights were switched on and the Old City walls glowed orange. People all over the world directed their prayers here, but the mystical walls remained inscrutable tonight, offering me no help. I walked in through the Jaffa Gate, an entrance arched over a roadway near the city's Armenian Quarter. There was one last wheelbarrow selling bread, and one last tout who offered me a tour of the Old City.

'Maybe another time,' I said.

'Perhaps you are looking for a rich husband?' he asked, lifting my mood for a moment – no, not a husband today, not even a poor one, just a dog. I rounded the corner and headed towards the police station. Israeli soldiers were posted there to check my bags, but I didn't have any, only keys, a mobile phone and a worried look.

When I told them I'd lost my dog, they asked in disbelief, 'Is that really what you're here for?'

They were used to more serious cases. This had been a police station during Jordanian, British and before that Ottoman times.

Once inside, it could have been a cop shop anywhere in the world. Dark, dank, even in summer, with faded posters urging women to report domestic violence tacked onto the thick stone walls. A sergeant, one of the many Arabs in the Israeli police force, was sitting behind a desk. He had red hair, blue eyes and pale skin. He was Circassian, like Jordan's King Abdullah. His ancestors had come here from the Russian Caucasus one hundred and fifty years ago, to guard the Ottoman kings. Wearing his blue Israeli uniform, his name in Hebrew on his badge, the fair-skinned Arab officer was part of the incomprehensible mix of races and religions that makes up Jerusalem.

He said no one had seen a dog like mine nor heard about one being taken. I asked him to keep an eye out and said I would come back with a picture if the dog hadn't come home by tomorrow. He was bemused, but said politely that that would be a good idea, and then looked down at his desk, making it clear he wanted to return to some real policing.

After more than two hours of fruitless searching I returned home, uncertain if the excursion to the Old City had helped me in any way. I unlocked the door and couldn't stop myself expecting to see Mia, doing the funny jump that she did when I'd been away a long time, rising up on her hind legs and shimmying sideways in the air, like an Indian dancer auditioning for a Bollywood movie.

She wasn't there, of course, and the room looked dark and empty. I threw myself down on the couch, deflated. When I reached across to turn on the nearest light, the bulb died with a small 'bink'. It was hard not to see it as an omen. The bells from the Old City churches began pealing, reminding me that it was Sunday evening. Sitting in the dark listening to that rich, sweet sound, I tried not to give in to a pervasive ill-feeling, part PMT, part fear, that this time Mia had used up the last of her nine lives and I wouldn't see her again. Damira came by to say she'd had no luck, and Meg called and offered to come over but I preferred to be on my own. I kept the front door open as I prepared dinner, returning to stand at the gate and check the street every ten minutes or so, looking out like Mia did when she was here. Nothing. Raphael called for an update.

'Has she come back yet?' he inquired optimistically.

'No! And I just hope the person who's found her isn't being cruel to her,' I wailed. I didn't want to voice the fear that some evil person was hacking away at her ears or tail – her beautiful tail! – but Raphael sensed that I was really scared.

'Don't worry. You know how lucky she is. Some good person has found her and is being kind to her and it will be alright.'

His next suggestion threw me. He said gently that now was the time for me to learn to pray. This re-opened an old argument between us, for I didn't believe in an interventionist God who had time to help individuals with lost dogs and new jobs.

'There are more than six billion people on the planet – how can He have time? And if He does, why are most people's lives so bad?'

Raphael just repeated patiently that the time had come for me to pray.

'She'll come back, you'll see!' he said with certainty.

Perhaps it was easier to be optimistic in Tel Aviv.

'And when she does, another thing I've learned is that after your prayers are answered, it's important to say thank you.'

I was so desperate that I did try to pray but I felt foolish and soon gave up. I was convinced that it only worked if you did it mindfully, and I couldn't see how the half-hearted, self-doubting prayers of a non-believer who'd lost her dog could be high on God's list of priorities for Jerusalem tonight.

In the morning the house felt very quiet. No small butterscotch-coloured dog hopped up onto the bed to lick my face. I opened the door and looked outside, but of course she was not there either. To push away the fear that I might not see her again, I decided to keep busy and sat down at the computer to create some posters.

The process of typing 'Mia has gone missing in Yemin Moshe' had me in tears, but I concentrated on choosing the best photos and printed off ten copies. Outside my empty apartment it was a perfect Monday morning, the air dry, the sky cloudless and a deep comforting blue, the sun already warm on my skin. Shame it was a war zone, people would kill for this climate.

At the park I put up my posters on trees and benches, and spoke to a number of people, including the gardeners, but no one had seen Mia. One woman suggested that I call the Jerusalem SPCA, which had a lost dog hotline. *Why didn't I think of that?* I ran back home and rang.

My voice was wobbly. 'My dog has run away and ...'

'And her name is Mia?' the hotline worker asked.

Like a small child I said, 'Yes, how did you know?'

It seemed like a miracle and I felt tears in my eyes again, tears of relief this time. I couldn't stop myself from asking, 'Do you – do you have her?'

The woman replied sympathetically that someone had found Mia almost as soon as she ran away and had brought her in. My details were on Mia's identifying microchip, but their computer was down and they could find basics like an address but no phone number. The woman who'd picked Mia up drove her back here to try to find my house, but she'd got lost in the maze of streets without names in Yemin Moshe. So much kindness while I was suffering so much anguish.

I jumped in my car and called Raphael in Tel Aviv to tell him the good news. He was on his way back to Jerusalem, so we would all be re-united. He agreed that Mia's rescue was like a miracle and sounded smug when he asked if I finally believed in the power of prayer. I decided to leave that thorny issue to one side and to put my faith in training. I did say thank you to a Higher Power, though, just in case ... and also made a donation to the SPCA. You have to cover all bases.

Raphael was coming to Jerusalem for a week of work on his film. They had an early start and the entire crew had been booked into a hotel so that they could wake them at 5.00 and start filming promptly at 6.00am.

'We're like prisoners; you'll have to come over here. And bring Mia! I have to see her, to make sure she really has come back.'

The hotel was one of three tall buildings near the entrance to the city, across from the main bus station. They stood out clearly, but were surrounded by a spaghetti of roads and flyovers. Each time I approached, I found myself directed into a new one-way system, away from where I wanted to go, and ended up driving around in wider and wider circles. On my third try, I spotted a small sign saying 'Hotels' and followed that gratefully. I finally arrived at the entrance to Raphael's hotel to find a huge ultra-Orthodox wedding taking place.

A klezmer band was pumping out the sound of eastern Europe. Clarinet, violin and accordion worked together energetically to produce harmonies that made you want to dance or to break some plates. Peeking in from the path, I saw hundreds of men in black dancing together, and knew that the women would be in another garden dancing with each other there. I didn't think either group would be happy to see a dog, so I called Raphael to check how we were going to smuggle Mia past the wedding. He came outside, hugged me close and then crouched down and hugged Mia too.

'I'm so happy to see you, you funny little dog. Why do you run away from us? We're you're family and we love you!'

She smiled up at Raphael winningly. A plump black-suited man wandered around the corner, wiping sweat from his face, and almost jumped out of his skin at the sight of her. I held her close, in case he began thinking of performing an exorcism. I was ready to admit defeat but Raphael still seemed to think we could spirit Mia up to his room.

'There's no one at reception, but it wouldn't matter anyhow, since there are stairs you can't see from the front desk.'

I crept up the stairs behind him, astounded at his chutzpah. But it turned out I was the only one creeping. Raphael and Mia were quite brazen. When we reached his room, Raphael moved his bag from a chair for me. Before I could sit down, Mia hopped up and curled into a small ball there, ready to the stay the night. We laughed and settled on the bed. When I decided not to stay for the 5.00am start, Raphael led us back downstairs, past reception and the unruly wedding, still going strong, and Mia and I headed home for our big day with the trainer.

Einav came over the next afternoon and, as the sun streamed into the living room, she explained the new rules aimed at reclaiming my house and my life and making *me* Top Dog. Mia would learn that there was a pack – Raphael, me, and whoever else we allowed in – but that she was not the one who led it. She was a lower grade member who took orders, just as she would in the wild. However strong-willed and dominating Mia might be, she was not an alpha dog, Einav said sternly. She had only ever seen one true alpha dog and it had been an amazing creature.

'Most of them end up being killed because they are deemed to be difficult dogs. They simply will not take orders,' she said.

Einav could see I was losing myself in the romance of the alpha dog with the unbreakable spirit, and called me back to reality.

'Now, to work. We have to pick a spot that Mia likes and tie her up there.'

I felt uncertain, but Einav assured me it would soon become Mia's favourite place, where she would feel safe and to which she would go when I told her to, and when she wanted time out for herself.

I nodded uncertainly and wrote 'Hook for wall' in my notebook.

Whenever I fed Mia, I was to take her food bowl away after ten minutes. Food came when I said so, it wasn't there for her to have whenever she wanted. We would teach her tricks – starting simply with the instructions to sit and to stay – so that she would learn to obey me. When she was not at her place at the wall, Mia would be tied to the chair where I was working. This was tough love.

'Now, you'll see, she will do everything for a small piece of sausage,' Einav exclaimed gleefully, supervising as I cut some up.

'That's too big!' she said, stopping me and cutting a tiny sliver instead. '*That's* the size. This is a reward, it's not to take the place of her meal, so keep the pieces small and repeat these exercises every morning.'

I wrote 'Sausage' in my notebook.

We started, and during that first class Mia mastered sit, down and stay. I was amazed.

'I saw straight away that she was as clever as those movie dogs,' Einav said, smiling.

I was proud of Mia and I could see that she was proud of herself, and that she had enjoyed the process – the learning, the praise and, yes, the sausage. Einav looked at us, both preening, and said, 'The word for dog in Hebrew is *kelev*. Do you know where it comes from?'

I shook my head.

'*Kelev* means "like the heart", because a dog is like the heart of man.'

She smiled at me. 'That's a strong connection. It will be alright, you won't have to give her away.'

13

I decided to take Mia to the Mahane Yehuda markets. I plucked up the courage after seeing a man shopping there with his dog, which had been very well behaved. I wasn't sure which way Mia would jump but Meg said to give it a try, since she knew I liked a multi-function outing, on which I could walk the dog and do chores.

It took us about half an hour to reach the markets and, once we entered, I held Mia's leash tight. The crowds and particularly the smells were so overwhelming that they dazed her into obedience. I did my shopping, Mia behaved impeccably, and on the way home I called Meg to report an unmitigated triumph. From then on Mia became a market regular too. With her talent for making useful friends, she quickly won the heart of a butcher across from Haim the fish man.

Ahmad the butcher was a character. Thin and small, with curly hair and a weedy voice, he reminded me of an Arab Popeye. He worked with two religious Jewish butchers, and gave me discounts on bags of bones. Although young, he seemed old, perhaps because of his exaggerated, almost cartoonish, features. As Mia sat gazing up at him winningly, he told me that he loved dogs.

'I have twenty-five dogs. And it all started with one female!' he said, holding his hands up in amazement like a small child. 'You don't want a puppy, do you?'

I shook my head. One was enough.

'I used to drive a truck all over Israel and the West Bank, but that's very tiring work. And dangerous. It's much better here,' he said as he handed over the latest collection of bones, which I whisked past Mia's nose and stuffed into my trolley.

Yes, I am about to confess to a style crime. I own a trolley. One of those ugly and irredeemably uncool dark-plaid one-hundred-per-cent plastic ones. They are very practical and allow you to fit in an enormous amount, far more than you could ever carry, but simply standing near one instantly turns you into a Russian grandmother, so I resisted for as long as I could – until one day my arms felt as if they were breaking under the weight of the bags full of bones, fish and fruit I was carrying, as well as the need to keep Mia in line. A trolley was hanging from the ceiling, dangling enticingly about level with my nose, right where I'd stopped. I deposited all my bags on the floor, made them take it down and bought that very one. Salvation! Who'd have thought surrender could be so pleasurable?

As I walked home that first day, I learned that it takes a degree of skill to manoeuvre a heavy trolley and a dog who likes to career off in every direction. Mia could only promise good behaviour inside the market itself; once we left all bets were off. The sun was pounding and I could feel the sweat gathering on my neck as I tried to pull her back when she ran in front of me. Her leash was cutting into my forearm – 'MiaNo!' – but I couldn't stop her as she yanked me behind her into a store. Not just any store, an air-conditioned store. In fact a cafe. When she and I and the trolley came to a halt, she threw herself down on the ground, back legs splayed out behind her, and looked up at me, panting. She wasn't moving.

From behind the counter, a tall guy with dreadlocks, wearing a faded Guns N' Roses T-shirt, watched our dramatic entry and said, 'I suppose you'll be needing a coffee?'

I looked helplessly at Mia before I understood it was exactly what I needed.

'And some water for the dog?' he offered.

171

'Yes, some water for this clever, thirsty dog,' I said, patting her as I pushed the trolley in behind the nearest table. *Like the heart of man*, and she knows what I want before I do.

At other times, I shopped on the Palestinian side in East Jerusalem. Raphael, who had blithely led me to the Mahane Yehuda markets, the scene of so many suicide bombings, didn't dare to come here. Like many Israelis he didn't feel safe on the east side, in the midst of an Arab majority. On those excursions, I went by myself, or with Orla or Meg.

I shopped at a small fruit and vegetable shop called the Garden of Eden, where all the produce was laid out in rows, like a painting; nearby a chocolate shop sold sweets and nuts, spicy roasted almonds and rich caramelised pecans. Further up was the best fish shop in East Jerusalem, where you could buy fresh prawns and they would even peel them for you and give you the shells to take home separately so you could make stock. All these shops were further out than Mahane Yehuda, and I needed to drive to reach them. My favourite greengrocer within walking distance of my home was on East Jerusalem's main shopping drag, Salah-a-Din Street. It was a curving avenue of low stone buildings, a distinctly Arab street, filled with hotels, shops, cafes and money changers. Salahaddin, who had liberated Jerusalem from the Crusaders, was the hero on this side of town. Maimonides, the hero in West Jerusalem, had been his doctor.

The greengrocer sat at the centre of a very handy little shopping hub. Across the street was Nabil, the money changer of choice for most journalists, and the best hummus in Jerusalem was around the corner. That's a hotly contested title, and not everyone would let me get away with that one. Hummus is rated here the way foodies in France grade wine or cheese.

The hummus at Abu Ali's was rich and sweet, not too tangy, not too much tahini. It's a breakfast dish, so he made one batch fresh each morning, and served it until it was finished. Then he shut up shop and didn't return till the following day, when he prepared another perfect batch.

On special occasions Nabil ordered in Abu Ali's hummus, with pickled cucumbers and chillies, and large falafels, which had onions fried in sumac in the centre, a repast fit for a queen. Nabil was a dog lover and always encouraged me to bring Mia.

'It's good exercise for you to walk here – and I love that dog.'

He happily minded her while I scooted across the road to buy vegetables. The greengrocer was an older man who wore a white cap indicating that he had made the hajj to Mecca. His sons and brothers helped out. It was not as neat as the Garden of Eden, but they had wonderful produce, including many items which were *baladi*, 'home-grown in the village', in this case their village near Hebron in the West Bank.

The grapes and plums they grew were never as large or as perfect as the ones grown for the supermarket chains, but they were infinitely more flavoursome and sweet. The apricots – the real apricots that only appear for two weeks a year – were small, pale and unprepossessing, but so delicious that Meg and I would fall on them the instant we saw them, calling each other to drop everything and come immediately. We bought up all we could and ate them, juice running down our chins, marvelling that the taste could be so different to what was available anywhere else.

The hajji also sold peppery olive oil, pressed in his village. At the front of his shop there were herbs and greens, parsley, coriander, shallots and vine leaves. Large carrots and zucchinis were in bags nearby, hollowed out to make it easier for busy Palestinian housewives to fill them with meat or rice, for the traditional dish called *mahshi*. Above the greens, there was a TV. It was usually tuned to an Arab satellite news channel, which meant that I didn't have to miss out on any news while I was shopping.

Sometimes the TV was tuned to Al-Manar, the official channel of the Islamist Hezbollah party in Lebanon. It's a propaganda channel, specialising in endless speeches by Hezbollah leader Sheikh Hassan Nasrallah, hate-filled rants spiced up with stirring music and military scenes. Soldiers ran by, drums went boom boom, a male chorus sang 'Allahu Akbar' and then boom boom, a tank went up in flames, 'Allahu Akbar', another tank exploded … and so it went, on and on, a bizarre rousing accompaniment to buying your tomatoes.

I chose my vegetables, watching the world according to Nasrallah, Israel's number-one enemy in the Middle East. It was part of the strange pluralism of united but essentially divided Jerusalem. And as I carried home the sweetest apricots from the east side, and the creamiest goat's cheese from the west side, I appreciated that I had what the locals longed for, though it eluded them: the best of both worlds.

A newly built suburb was emerging on the rim of the valley along from Yemin Moshe. Named David's City, it was a gated community, where sandstone houses towered over forbidding avenues, with none of the charm of the higgledy-piggledy streets where we lived. Still, the Jerusalem municipality's latest contribution to housing for the very rich was closed to traffic and almost entirely empty, appealing qualities for anyone walking a dog.

Early on a warm summer's morning, Mia and I climbed around the back of the new suburb, along a rough path that had not yet been landscaped. The gravel was hot and the sandstone white, almost blinding. Through the glare, I saw that up ahead a small dog was walking towards us. Prancing might be a better word. As it got closer I saw that it was a pug with cream fur and a dark face. The first thing I noticed was how slim and shapely it was. For a moment I didn't think it *was* a pug. Most of the ones I'd encountered up till then were overweight and somehow comical, with slightly bug eyes and laboured breathing, like small overworked machines. This pug, on the other hand, was slender and dainty and somehow elegant.

Mia and the pug greeted one another, tails wagging, hesitantly at first and then more confidently, windscreen wipers on high speed. They began running, first in one direction then the other, a sign they liked each other. On a scorching day, with the heat reflected back off the stones and gravel, the pug kept up with Mia and wasn't out of breath. That was one fit pug.

When they slowed down slightly, I noticed that the pug was wearing a very glam collar. It was both garish and tasteful at the same time, the kind of mixture of tartans, cowboy motifs and gold that you can only get away with if it's very expensive. It was a designer collar. The pug wore Versace.

The last thing I noticed was what I should have noticed first. It – she! – had red toenails. Each nail was scarlet, shiny and perfectly painted. Her pedicure put mine to shame. I instinctively curled my own toes under as I stood staring, transfixed, at this vision. Versace and nail polish weren't common on dogs here. In fact, I'd never seen anything like her before.

Her owner came panting up the hill behind her. He was a balding energetic New Yorker in his sixties, and I had to ask him about the nail polish. Owning a dog is a licence to question a stranger on almost any issue. The man said his wife did the dog's nails, or the hairdresser would, if they were taking the dog there anyway for a shampoo and set. Then he launched into his dog's life story.

'Her name is Fancy,' he began.

Of course, I found myself thinking, what else could it be?

He told me proudly that her remarkable figure was the result of a vigorously policed diet, comprised mostly of tinned vegetables.

'It's hard work to keep her so thin; nobody's ever seen a pug who looks like her. Each time we take her to a new vet, they go wild.'

Fancy's owners divided their time between New York and Jerusalem, and planned all their travel around her. They monitored her diet so that she'd stay under nine kilos and could travel with them

175

in the cabin when they flew. Anything over nine kilos and she was luggage. Fancy's owners flew only to dog-friendly cities – 'We'll never stop over in London, the rules are too complex!' – and used only dog-friendly airlines. German carrier Lufthansa was best, he explained, because they sometimes let Fancy travel in the cabin even when she weighed ten kilos. And once she was there the kind staff sometimes let her out of her crate. Needless to say, Fancy, like her owners, flew only first class. At that point, the energetic smiling man turned serious.

'You won't believe this but Fancy was a rescue dog,' he said, looking down at his svelte pet. 'She'd been a breeding dog, which means she had a litter every eight months for six years. And then, when she couldn't have any more puppies, they just threw her out onto the street.' He was squinting in the bright light but his eyes were noticeably shiny for a moment when he described the dog's traumatic past. The outrage hadn't left him.

'Can you believe that people could be so cruel?'

Fancy looked up at this point. She knew her own rags-to-riches story, of course, and how fortunate she was to have been taken in by this kind, wealthy family. Her tale could have ended very differently. She could have spent the rest of her days in a dog pound like Atarot, or even worse, a pound like those in the US and Australia, where, after a certain period, unwanted dogs are put down. Fancy leaned against her owner's legs, an almost feline action, before sitting back on her shapely haunches.

He was right, it was an amazing story. I decided that after what she'd been through, Fancy deserved her red toenails and first-class flights. I am attracted to people, stray dogs and even houses which come with a good story. We said goodbye and I watched her mincing off into the distance, living proof that your luck can turn and that sometimes the cards will fall in your favour. It was hard to stay optimistic when reporting on this conflict. I took my inspiration where I could find it, and let a chance encounter with a dog light up my day.

The stately King David Hotel was a West Jerusalem landmark. It sat on the opposite side of the city from the Mount of Olives, looking out over my neighbourhood. In the 1930s, during the time of the British Mandate, it was used as a headquarters for British troops. In 1946, right-wing Jewish militants placed a bomb there and killed dozens of people. In the 1950s, the hotel was rebuilt, and over the decades the rich and famous returned to stay. They included world leaders such as US President Bill Clinton, and before him Egyptian President Anwar Sadat. Sadat's visit led to the peace treaty between Israel and Egypt, and to his assassination two years after that.

There was a grove of fir trees behind the hotel, a lovely place to sit on a hot afternoon, and it was there that I first met Mustafa the Palestinian carpenter. He was sitting on a shady patch of grass and pine needles with his dog, a remarkably unattractive creature, like a stubby Alsatian chopped off at the knees. We only spoke because of the dogs. He introduced himself and said his dog's name was Steve.

I was initially distracted by that – 'Steve? Your name is Mustafa and you've called your dog *Steve?*' – so it took me more than a moment to appreciate that this squat-ugly mutt was possibly the best trained animal I'd ever seen.

Steve was sitting neat and alert, near his owner, when Mia ran up and jumped on him. He ignored her. His first allegiance was to Mustafa. She tried his other side. He ignored that too. He ran to play with her only after Mustafa gave him a nod. I watched, impressed. When the dogs returned, Mia to sniff just out of my reach, Steve to sit by his owner again, I tried to pat this obedient creature, but Steve was not very interested in me.

'*Quuelha kiifhaalek.* Say "How are you?" to her,' Mustafa instructed his dog softly in Arabic. He gave all his orders softly.

When he heard this order, Steve trooped up to Mustafa and put his head in his owner's lap instead of mine. Mustafa laughed. The only time Steve disobeyed was when he misunderstood.

'*Mish ili, ilha!* Not to *me*, to *her!*' he said, and Steve, keen to make up for his error, came over to me and put his head in my lap this time, gazing up at me obediently.

I gazed back into his sweet ugly face, even more impressed. He was not on a lead, Mustafa didn't raise his voice, and Steve did what he was told. Even when he failed to follow orders, he was actually trying to be obedient.

I looked at Mustafa with respect. He had a serious square face and short cropped hair, and every dog in the park responded to his mixture of serenity and authority. Amongst the Palestinians I'd met, fear, or cruelty, appeared to be the two most common responses to dogs. There were exceptions, of course, but it was not generally a dog-friendly culture. When Mustafa told me that he lived in the Muslim Quarter of the Old City, without Steve disturbing any of his neighbours, I realised that we'd stumbled upon a dog whisperer. A *Palestinian* dog whisperer!

In the way that you do when you meet an expert, 'Oh, you're an orthopaedic surgeon? I've got this problem with my knee …', 'A Buddhist monk? Now about these meditation techniques …', I was soon asking Mustafa for advice about my wayward dog. I was sure that if he had her for a week, she would stop running away.

'You have to give her some freedom,' he said thoughtfully, like the Oracle of Delphi, or a New Age sage. 'Let her go out of your sight, she will come back.'

I told him that I did that and that she inevitably took the first opportunity to scarper.

'No, no, if you wait, she will return,' he advised with tranquil certainty.

After that encounter I resolved to become a better and more disciplined dog owner, relaxed and wise, like Mustafa. But I sensed it would be a long-term project, perhaps even a lifetime's work, and I had urgent business in the United States. My friends Meg and Craig were getting married.

A poem brimming with the ache and wonder of love by the charismatic, persecuted Russian genius Boris Pasternak graced their wedding invitation, just right for two people who first lived together in Moscow. The wedding was to take place in Santa Fe in New Mexico, and the invitation promised 'dinner and dancing under the full moon'.

I was very excited until Raphael checked the date and said he couldn't make it. He had to sit music exams. We talked it through, slightly spiky with each other, since I couldn't help feeling that he could come if he *really* wanted to and he thought I was being unreasonable.

'I can't come. You know that. I don't have the money, but more than that, I don't have the time. Even if I scraped the money together I couldn't come. I haven't been studying properly because of the filming.'

He looked at me but I didn't say anything.

'And the film's not done yet. The main filming's over, but there are still a few scenes left to do, and I don't know when they will be – only that it's in the next month. I can't just up and leave now. What happens if they call me when we're in the US? I can barely juggle my work and my exams as it is.'

Raphael said that he would look after Mia while I was away. Sometimes when we were both busy, we had sent Mia to a kennel, which I guiltily thought of as a dog prison, even though I knew it was a good place because Meg had found it and a difficult dog like Chucho was happy there.

'I'll make time for her, and you won't have to put her in one of those dog prisons. You won't have to worry about her and you can enjoy the wedding,' he said eagerly.

Of course, I would rather Mia was with Raphael than in a dog prison. But I'd rather Raphael would come with me to Santa Fe, even if Mia had to go to the dog prison. Still, I could see that that wasn't going to happen. Raphael said he would most likely be in Jerusalem while I was away, as his classes were finished now, and any extra filming would be up here, so we agreed that he would stay with Mia in my apartment. Right. Sorted. But when I told him that there was a support network of friends and neighbours who would be able to help him out he was offended.

Now it was Raphael's turn to be grumpy and we had one of those silly fights that you sometimes have when one of you is going away.

'I can't do it on my own. Why should you? The neighbours all help me, why shouldn't they help you?' I asked, reasonably, I thought.

'She's *my* dog, and *I'll* look after her!' Raphael replied crossly.

'I'm sorry I tried to make things easier for you.'

We were both in a huff now. Separation anxiety, I told myself, and once we got over it, I grew excited about the wedding. Foreign correspondents would be flying in from all over the world. People who connected, scattered and reconnected, often in war zones, were finally meeting for a celebration. For us, the film would be *Forty Funerals and a Wedding*, and it was lovely to be the lucky ones attending the wedding.

Before I was due to leave, Raphael invited me to join him on a family walk in the hills behind Haifa in the north of Israel. He had a large, warm, sprawling family. Raphael's parents gathered children and grandchildren happily around them like a duvet, and they simply invited me to clamber in too. They held noisy family get-togethers, where the house gleamed and his mother Hannah's face shone with joy, real clan gatherings, everyone talking and laughing loudly as they ate the wondrous meals she prepared.

They married young – tall, thin uncles and short plump aunties, who still seemed to like each other decades later, laughing when they heard each other's stories, with as much pleasure as if they were hearing them for the first time. Raphael's dad glowed as he took pictures of every child and grandchild. That family was everyone's anchor.

One element that tied them together was Raphael's mother's sublime cooking. Here, food really was love. One of Hannah's great dishes was a soup with meat dumplings, a staple of cooking in Central Asia, where Raphael's father's family was from. Since Hannah's family was from Iraq, after she married, her mother-in-law had taught her to prepare all these Central Asian and Russian Jewish dishes. Raphael's dad was so lucky. He had simply moved from one home where the meals were superb to another, eating food of this quality all his life. No wonder he was so easy-going.

'My mother-in-law was a great cook, a truly great cook,' Raphael's mother said the first time I complimented her on the soup. 'I try to emulate her but I don't always succeed.'

I was revelling in the dumplings swimming in a clear broth, which was fragrant with fresh herbs, but I knew there was no point protesting. I frequently heard this homage to their female ancestors from women here.

'My grandmother prepared this pastry much better than I do ...'

'My aunt's cooking was extraordinary – you've never tasted anything like it. When she made these meatballs ...'

It was a lovely feature of life in both Israel and the Palestinian territories, so many women preserving their mothers' and grandmothers' dishes, and with it their love, certain that no matter how delectable, today's versions didn't quite measure up to the great dishes of the past.

Raphael and I drove up the coast road to Haifa, the sea on one side, farms and villages on the other. When we veered inland, the hills were carpeted with bluebells. At the nature spot, Raphael's parents were bursting with pride at having all of their children and grandchildren together. I recognised that look; it was the same one on my mother's face on the increasingly rare occasions when her three daughters were all together in Sydney for a short time.

The children ran, their long dark hair flying out behind them, laughing and shouting in Hebrew. Then they turned, running the

181

other away, unaffected by the heat. Raphael's nieces came up to me, a posse of beautiful giggling girls, to ask what job I did and how old I was. Oh no, how old was I? Was that a trick question? I struggled to remember what I'd told Raphael so I could tell them the same thing. *God, how do spies do it* ... Interview over, the girls ran off, whispering to each other, before trotting up to Raphael to announce they had an important secret to tell him.

'They say we should get married,' Raphael said, once the giggling strike force departed. We both smiled. The oldest girl was just eight. The matchmaking instinct starts early here.

He paused and added reflectively, 'They've never told me that about anyone before.'

Later, as we were driving back to Jerusalem, Raphael looked out the window and said in a sad voice, apropos of nothing, 'But you know I can't marry you. I've understood that now.'

He was right, and I'd known it from the start. He would have to leave me and find a girl his own age, someone who wasn't passing through, so that he could start a family. I could already imagine them, more beautiful dark-haired children who would run with their cousins through the bluebells. But the fact that he'd said it suddenly like that smarted, more than I would have believed it could, as did the mixture of hurt and world-weariness in his voice.

'Still, I'll be waiting for you here, while you're in America,' he said, smiling again.

I tried to smile back at him but I'm not sure I succeeded.

The next night, the taxi was due at 3.00am. Mia had watched me pack and now she ran to the door, understanding something was happening though she was not sure what.

'Look after Raphael,' I said as I patted her and closed the door. I watched her confused face through the glass squares for a moment with a lump in my throat, before dragging my bag down sixty stairs to the waiting taxi.

14

Before we met, Meg and I had each believed that we were the only women in the world who hadn't dreamed of being a bride or never imagined walking down the aisle in a white dress, queen for a day.

'What – really? Me neither!' we'd exclaimed with delight, happy to have our worldwide minority of one expanded to a group of two.

But never say never, for here we were in Santa Fe, with Meg's white dress hanging splendidly in its own cupboard. She may not have dreamed of this as a girl, but I could see that she had met the right person to share her adventurous, high-octane life. Craig had waited till he was in his forties to propose for the first time. They had found each other, and knowing and loving them both I was happy for them. As for me, it wasn't hard to go back to being a subset of one. I've come to accept that the only constant is change.

Friends and relatives began flying in from all over the world. None of the guests lived in New Mexico, including the Americans, which gave the event an extra festive quality. It was a wedding but it was also a holiday. I joined up with various groups of Meg and Craig's friends, getting to know them as we went exploring Santa Fe, an old Spanish frontier town nestled in the foothills of the Rocky Mountains. Low-rise pink adobe buildings, many now converted into fashionable art galleries and boutiques, sat on a grid of wide streets. Beyond were mountains and desert. The sky seemed vast. I felt like I was in a cowboy film.

On the day before the ceremony, Meg carted all the girls off into the mountains. She had found a Japanese spa with outdoor hot tubs and saunas, and we immersed ourselves in the bubbling water, looking up at pine trees and the big sky. For someone who spent so much of her time in grungy places, Meg sure knew how to organise treats.

After the spa, I could no longer put off my last outstanding job. I had been asked to do a reading at the wedding, but still hadn't settled on one. Now I came across a poem by the American poet Walt Whitman which seemed right. 'Song of the Open Road' was romantic and optimistic, about lovers and the lure of adventure, as if he'd written it with Craig and Meg in mind. The poem described the joy and lightness of being able to follow a path, wherever it led.

Henceforth I ask not good-fortune, I myself am good-fortune,
Henceforth I whimper no more, postpone no more, need nothing.

But in the end the traveller found he did need something – a companion to walk with him along the path. When he found her, he extended his hand and asked if she would share his adventures. Beautiful and apt. The only drawback was that I couldn't read it aloud without crying. Two of Meg's American girlfriends said that they weren't as soft as me, and offered to come and help.

'You can read it to us! Over and over, till you stop crying,' they said.

We had moved to the pink-walled hacienda in the hills where the wedding was to take place. They trooped up to my bedroom. It was beautifully fitted out in dusky pink and dark blue, with elegant earth-coloured fixtures and paintings, but suddenly it felt like we were at boarding school, chapter ten of *What Meg Did Next*. The tough girls sat giggling on my bed, and I pulled out my poem, gazed out at the mountains visible through the window and began reading. When I looked up they were both crying.

'Oh no!' I wailed. 'I haven't even reached the sad bit yet!'

By the morning of the wedding I'd memorised the poem, though I hadn't succeeded in reciting it once all the way through without my voice breaking. I called Raphael because he always steadied me. It was lovely to hear his voice, and at the end of our conversation he suggested that maybe some exercise would help calm my wedding nerves. 'You know how you like that ...'

One of my best friends from Sydney was a photographer called Davo, who'd flown in to shoot the wedding. Davo agreed with Raphael that a walk would do me good and said he'd come along.

'It will help me get over my jet lag.'

Tall, funny and almost lethally charming, Davo was a compelling talker, with a penchant for giving advice. What gave him an extra edge was that he was also a great listener. People were drawn to tell him their darkest secrets, often within minutes of meeting him. He would have made a good journalist, or a good priest. Davo was delighted to be in Santa Fe, meeting my friends from Jerusalem and Moscow. I also enjoyed the two halves of my life connecting.

As we were leaving on our walk, one of the American wedding guests came over and said she'd driven down here with her young dog which needed some exercise. His name was Paco, he was very good-natured, would we mind taking him along? We said we'd love to. At the last minute a local dog from the hacienda ran up too. So we set out, two dogs and two people, for a brisk morning constitutional. We didn't even take a phone. We were on holiday. What could happen?

'We'll be back in about half an hour, forty minutes tops.'

We waved to Meg and walked along a path through brush land, talking and laughing. It turned into more of a catch-up than serious exercise. After about fifteen minutes, the local dog peeled off, but by the time we'd clocked that he was gone, it was too late, the woodland had suddenly grown over the path and we were deep inside it.

'Which is the way back?' we asked each other.

I must have looked panicked because Davo said reassuringly, 'Don't worry. Wedding photographers are renowned for their sense of direction.'

'That's what I was afraid of.'

We agreed on one route but only found ourselves fighting our way deeper into the bush. We tried the opposite direction. Same thing. The path appeared to have been swallowed up completely. We had one overheating dog, one bottle of water and no phone. And I had the wedding photographer!

'Why didn't we follow that wily local dog?' Davo and I asked each other as we started to climb upwards so we could gain some height and look for a landmark.

Thirty minutes later we had to admit it. We were utterly *Picnic at Hanging Rock* lost. We fed docile, tired Paco gulps of water from our cupped hands. He was a large dog, but he was only eight months old and this was probably the longest walk he'd ever done in his young life.

I didn't discuss with Davo what would happen if we didn't find our way out in time for the ceremony that he had flown all the way from Australia to shoot. Once those negative ideas worm their way in they can take over. Instead, I just focused on getting out. We climbed for another hour through dense unyielding brush, which scratched our hands and legs. I was starting to get really worried, unable to stop those unthinkable *Could we possibly miss the wedding?* thoughts, when we reached a wire fence. It was quite high, but through it we could see a paved footpath and some houses. Paco wriggled under and we heaved ourselves over. We still couldn't see our hacienda, but we walked with renewed energy. Paco came to a halt in the shade of the first parked car he saw, and lay down, panting.

I looked at my watch. So far, it had taken us a bit over two hours, and the wedding was due to start in ninety minutes. We gave Paco the last of the water, then coaxed him up and walked another half a kilometre, to a fork in the road. Nothing looked familiar. We were in what appeared to be a new suburb, still under construction. We walked up to the nearest house. There were no curtains in the windows and no flowers in the garden. We knocked and then pushed at the door. It was open. The room inside was empty, but there was a ladder, tins of paint and some tools, and we could hear the sound of men talking in the next room. Davo and I looked at each other, weak with relief.

Two workmen in spattered overalls came through the doorway. It turned out that they spoke only Spanish, as you'd expect in New Mexico. I was trying to convert the little bit of Italian I knew into a useful sentence, and to remember the name of our hotel, but I could only come up with 'Hacienda'. It turned out that was enough. One of the guys had worked there and had the number in his mobile phone. We called and they said they'd send a car. I tried to explain to the bemused workman that he was our saviour, and we sat down to wait.

I kept looking at my watch.

'We've got an hour left till the wedding starts. So depending how long it takes them to get here, we might be okay or we might still be in trouble,' I said to Davo, trying to keep the tone light and conversational, as if it were no big deal.

'You mean it ain't over till the fat photographer sings?' Davo asked.

I laughed. 'Let's hope it won't *start* till the fat photographer sings!'

Davo is very even-tempered, but after ten minutes waiting and trying to make pidgin conversation with the workmen – *You are from Australia!?! Do you have kangaroos in your house? You are here for wedding? Wedding is good!* – I could see that he was becoming anxious too. We both jumped up as if we'd been shot when a car pulled into the driveway. Thankfully, it was our rescue vehicle and we scrambled in. Poor tired Paco curled up on the back seat and was asleep before the car turned out of the street. We arrived a little more than thirty minutes before the wedding was due to begin and found Meg seated before a mirror in one of the bedrooms. She was wearing an apron over a pale shift and a makeup artist was applying powder to her face with a brush. She stood up, looking tense.

'Everyone else has already had their hair and makeup done,' she said. 'What happened?' Her tone conveyed both concern and 'I don't need this extra stress on my wedding day', which was justified.

While I launched into the story of our saga and lucky return, Davo picked up his camera, as if this were the moment he was meant to start work all along, and began taking photos of the bride being made up. We were hot, sweaty and dusty, but Davo barely stopped to wipe his face. He began cracking jokes, confiding to Meg how a nice little death march just put him in the mood. She was soon giggling, and before I knew it she was absolving him of responsibility. Did he know that, after years in Jerusalem, Orla and I had not been able to find the Mount of Olives, ten minutes from my front door? A sense of humour like his is a blessing.

'That was a close call!' we agreed as Meg rustled off to get dressed, her good mood restored.

'Was there ever a moment when you didn't think we'd make it?' I asked.

'Sure! I actually can't believe we *did* make it,' Davo replied as we ran off to clean up.

The wedding took place on an outdoor terrace. Davo was already there, taking photos of the guests, when I reached my seat. The desert stretched out before us, the mountains of New Mexico rolling away into the distance, like an open-air church. The sun shone down from a wide, approving sky onto the heads of all the guests. Meg was ravishing, face matt, eyes smoky, and hair swept up in a glamorous 1940s coil, her cream silk dress shimmering as she strode down the aisle. Craig was handsome on her arm, the wedding speech he'd finished as the music began folded in his pocket. Craig was one of those journalists who always file right on deadline. Nothing wrong with that; I'm one myself.

The service was beautiful. Everyone was overflowing with happiness and goodwill. Even the pastor had tears in his eyes. I cried during all the speeches, including the one I gave, which is bad form, but it was the same section that got me every time.

Camerado, I give you my hand!
I give you my love more precious than money,
I give you myself before preaching or law;
Will you give me yourself? Will you come travel with me?
Shall we stick by each other as long as we live?

I looked up to see Meg and Craig both in tears too. Still, Meg's brother-in-law won the cry-o-meter reciting a love poem he'd written himself. To lighten the mood, I read a rhyme by Ogden Nash, whose relationship counselling was brief and to the point: Say sorry when you're wrong, say nothing when you're right. It's good advice. I laughed through my tears, and so did everyone else.

Weddings make you think about your own relationship – you can't help it. This lovely ceremony confronted me with the fact that I was involved with someone I would never marry. I'd known that going in and he felt the same way. It began nine months ago – *nine months!* – as an adventure in the moment, so that I would know the feeling of a wild ride with the warm wind in my hair and have no regrets.

But now, under the influence of all the emotions being churned up here, I wondered why I was pursuing something that wouldn't last. What if Woody Allen was right and a relationship was like a shark and needed to keep moving forward or it would die. Were Raphael and I paddling in circles in the shallows, waiting until our relationship expired? Were we passing time, wasting time? Or was every moment precious, the paddling in the shallows – in the lovely cool, clear water there – the whole point? And what was I doing listening to Woody Allen anyway? What if nothing would ever be this good again? I

189

couldn't answer those questions, so I decided to rejoice for Meg and Craig and to dance under the full moon.

When I returned to Israel after the wedding, the lead items on the news were about sex, not politics. In the Israeli way, the news hit you immediately, from the radio blaring at the airport taxi stand. There was no mention of Israeli Prime Minister Ariel Sharon, nor of Palestinian President Mahmoud Abbas. Instead there were allegations of rape against a rabbi in the West Bank, allegations of child abuse involving neighbouring families on the coast, and an investigation into fraudulent advertising by a Jewish dating agency. It seemed that in their ubiquitous ads – *Meet Jewish singles near you!* – the happy sexy blondes 'looking for love' were first of all not Jewish and second of all not available … it turned out they were Polish porn stars. The police were now investigating.

Still, that bad news for internet daters was great for me, because all those items were what they call 'inside baseball' in the newsroom – stories that were interesting but not big enough to report for overseas, because everyone has their own home-grown sex scandals. It meant I wouldn't have to work the second I walked through my front door.

We had to wait for the taxi to fill up. It was a cheapie, which drove ten people to Jerusalem for $10 each, dropping each person at their door. I'd grabbed the best seat – a place for one at the front. It was very early in the morning, but it was already hot; that moist heat that wraps itself around you and seems to weigh on your skin like a blanket. Most of the passengers so far were ultra-Orthodox Jews, men in black sweat-stained suits with black hats and mounds of luggage. They literally recoiled when they saw me. There were two other women waiting in the taxi, but they were wearing long dark skirts, long-sleeved shirts and ill-fitting wigs. I was the only problematic one who was dressed for the summer in leggings and a tank top.

I put my hair up in a clip, to keep it off my neck, happy that I had a seat on my own. After the dry New Mexico desert, the humidity was overwhelming; it was like swimming through the air. We were waiting for one more passenger to make up our quorum of ten when another ultra-Orthodox man walked up. He was young and plump, with pale skin and fair hair, wearing the uniform of black suit, white shirt and black hat. He spoke almost no English, and though he lived in Israel, no Hebrew either. Still, he was able to make himself understood. He looked at me and, waving his hands back and forth in front of him, shouted two words he had mastered in English, 'No woman! NO WOMAN!'

Then it was relayed to me, like Chinese whispers, as if I hadn't been there watching the whole thing.

'He can't sit near a woman,' the driver said, then asked, 'Will you move?'

'Where?' I asked, looking back down at the full taxi van. The other male passengers were tightly packed into their seats, and the narrow aisle was overflowing with their bags. There was one free seat among the men, but if I moved there it would cause a riot. The driver would lose more customers. I also suspected a 'cunning plan' by the new arrival to snatch the most coveted seat in the taxi from me, so I refused.

'I'm sitting in my own seat here in the front. If he goes down the back, he won't even see me!'

'She's in her own seat, you can sit at the back,' the driver yelled out the window impatiently in English. One of the male passengers in the back translated this into Yiddish, the only language the prospective passenger really understood. He stayed outside the taxi van in an agony of indecision. The others didn't try to influence him, they were from different streams of Orthodoxy, each with its own rules. He had to make his peace with God about this trial in his own way.

The driver tried again, 'Nu, hurry up, make up your mind. You're the last one; if you get in we can get moving.'

191

The ultra-Orthodox man pulled out a mobile phone and made a call. I wondered if he was ringing his rabbi. The driver rolled his eyes. Whoever it was the man spoke to, the effect appeared to be calming. He agreed to travel. He pushed his three suitcases onto the luggage rack behind the seats, now piled up to the ceiling, and leaned against the back door to squeeze it shut. I climbed out so that he would be able to reach the woman-free zone in the back without any disturbance. When I climbed back in, we were finally able to leave.

The driver turned on the AC and said to me confidingly, 'Those religious guys are crazy. Really, they don't know what they're missing.'

I think he meant that by way of apology. I put my head back and closed my eyes. I was definitely not in the US any longer.

As we wound up the hill to Jerusalem the air lost its humidity. It was dry, flint dry, the stones blindingly white in the sun. Spring and autumn were short gentle seasons here, soon gone. Summer was the main game; long, hot and parched. Unlike Australia, there was no rain. I'd always loved Sydney's summer thunderstorms, when plump drops of water fall sizzling onto the hot pavement, lightning illuminates a grey sky, and after the deluge, the air feels clean and smells of wet earth and leaves. Here once summer starts, you just put your head down and endure it, like a camel trudging across the desert. The air becomes so dry it feels as if your hair and skin are cracking. The light is harsh, a knife blade in the eye. If you ask in Arabic, 'Is that clear?' the proper reply is 'Clear as the sun – *Wadha mittel ashshams.*' Nothing is clearer, or more relentless.

When we reached Yemin Moshe, the air smelt of cedars, herbs and dust, the smell of homecoming. I pushed open my front door. The first living creature I laid eyes on was Mia, who was no more than moderately pleased to see me, as if I'd just returned from a ten-minute trip to the corner store. I was very happy to see her though, and hugged her close. I bit her ears, something I couldn't resist in moments of great joy. Raphael had called in New Mexico to say she'd run away again, so now I asked her why she'd done that. In that infuriating way of dogs, she remained silent.

Raphael was happier to see me. All the doubts which had welled up at the wedding receded at the pleasure of seeing him. It was a physical joy. He held me close, and Mia jumped up, suddenly keen to remind us that this was a three-way reunion. I revelled in Raphael's heart-stopping smile, the feel of his skin, his familiar scent. Why would I give this up? Sometimes living in the moment was enough, more than enough, even plenty. Those Buddhists are so wise.

Raphael sat with his arms around me, full of silly, funny stories. He told me that yesterday he'd been catching a bus, that insane behaviour that I could never wrap my mind around, and had got talking to the driver. He'd asked where Raphael's family was from, the standard Israeli question. When Raphael said they were from Iraq, the driver, who was also an Iraqi, was happy.

'And then he said, "Where in Iraq?" And when I told him Mosul he said, "You know the old saying, *Alf wawi afdhal min wahad Moslawi*".' Raphael paused for effect before he translated, 'Be careful. One thousand wolves are better than one guy from Mosul!'

The driver had laughed louder than Raphael, who was still smarting and smiling at once as he recounted the story. He lit a cigarette and I re-arranged our position, moving out of the circle of his arms, sitting with my head on his shoulder, away from the smoke. We sat like that for a long time, checking who had missed the other more. Raphael said he'd taken his dog-minding seriously and that Mia had been good, apart from her major escape, which had been difficult. His life had stopped for forty-eight hours until he and my Spanish neighbour, Josefina, had tracked her down to the dog pound.

'She's turning into a femme fatale,' he said, smiling to distract me from the thought of Mia in the pound, 'though she doesn't know it yet, and still thinks she's a tomboy.'

I soon saw what he meant.

There were yips, yaps and taps at the door, and when I went to see who it was, the guest was on four legs, not two. Dogs now came to visit. They saw her in the park, gave their owners the slip and stayed on her trail till they found our house.

One regular was Miko the Golden Retriever, whose owners I knew, and there was another whom I dubbed the Handsome Husband, because he was large, confident and gorgeous, with a 'love 'em and leave 'em' air. His bark was pretty much 'Hey, babe', and I let him in, since I had a soft spot for playboys – well, canine ones, at least. There were others, a series of huge, gentle males, to whom I hadn't given names, but who all trooped down to pay homage to Mia, the siren of Hope Street. When they appeared at the front door, she took the adulation in her stride, but we all knew – them, her, me – that she had encouraged them.

First, at the park she was excited to see them, sniffing, biting and generally expressing delight. Then she ran in circles around them, faster and faster, wider and wider, kicking up sand and stones and emerging through the dust for her next widening gyre. It was a show-stopping performance designed to induce them to chase her, but at the same time to taunt them and show they couldn't reach her. After a while they gave up and sat stolidly in the middle of her lightning-fast figures of eight, looking dejected. When she felt she had demonstrated her superiority she changed tack. She slowed down and they played again, chasing one another happily. Sometimes she even let them catch her. But as soon as Mia sensed that they were hooked, she turned cool. She stopped playing. She yawned and looked away. Really, they were too dull. Wasn't there another dog, a *wolf*, she could run with instead? She sashayed off, leaving them behind, crushed. Playing hard to get worked in the canine world, just as it did with humans.

Since I was never the most popular girl in the class, it was fascinating to watch Mia in action. It was as if she'd read a 1950s dating manual. Meg thought I was exaggerating until, when she got back from her honeymoon, she came to the park one day and watched all the males queuing up for a moment of Mia's time.

'Okay, okay, you were right,' she said in amazement. 'She could write a dating advice column … or she could have her own website: *Ask a Sex Goddess.com.* You could write it for her. No one needs to know you learned everything you know from a dog.'

Now that the wedding was over it was time to get back into training. Gym for me, and Einav's twelve-step desert dog detox for Mia. The centrepiece of Einav's training program involved attaching your dog to a special extra-long leash. Young dogs learned to open up a three metre gap when they were walking with their owners, Einav explained, because they'd figured out that at that distance you couldn't catch them.

'Aren't they *cunning*?' I asked her in disbelief.

The leash Einav recommended was ten metres in length, to give the dog the feeling of freedom even when it was tied to you. That was the theory. In practice it was more complicated. Mia and I were now bound together by a long dangerous umbilical cord, which soon became wound around benches, statues, trees, barbed wire, and of course us too. She got trapped under bushes and I had to crawl in to untie her, emerging scratched, hot and dirty. Once when I couldn't disentangle her, I had to leave her there, go home, get scissors and come back and cut her out.

The long leash also became a weapon. We created a tripwire for taking out people who were walking along, not paying attention to where they were going, and even those who were paying attention but couldn't jump out of the way fast enough when Mia sped up and raced past them on the right, while I was walking on their left. The cord suddenly went taut, catching them at the ankles, and sending them sprawling.

Einav was very strict about the ten-metre lead. 'Never let it go, NEVER. Now that you two are tied together, Mia is not a solo agent any more.'

But sometimes when I saw that Mia was about to bring down another victim, I simply had to let go. It was generally more dangerous for dogs than people, and most dangerous of all for dogs she liked, because she ran up and wound herself in an excited circle around them. She could bring any dog down within thirty seconds. It would make a SWAT team proud.

Back at home I was trying to fulfil Einav's other requirements. First came setting up the secure spot to tie Mia up. I bought a heavy-duty hook for the wall and called my colleague Aaron Schachter for help. Aaron was another dog-owning journalist. He had known Cesar Millan in the US way back before he became a superstar, when he was just a dog walker with attitude, which gave Aaron street cred on pet-related issues. He was the devoted owner of a brindle Pit Bull rescue dog called Duke, and told me earnestly that Duke had seen him through some hard times. I reminded Aaron that he was happily married, he loved his wife, he loved his job, he loved his dog – what hard times? Aaron said that Duke had been by his side through thick and thin, before he'd met his wife, and I wasn't to say another word. He only looked like a happy guy. Duke knew the truth.

Once Mia arrived, Aaron and I became even better friends. We could branch out from radio gear, one of Aaron's top areas of expertise, to dog gear, which came in a close second. He listened to my hook-in-the-wall problem and said that he'd never heard of anyone tying a dog up like that. Aaron talked tough but in reality he was a softie. Still, he said he had a new electric drill that I was welcome to borrow.

After picking up Aaron's drill, I went home and selected Mia's favourite place, the corner where she loved lying on the cool tiles, and drilled into the wall there. Within seconds there was lots of masonry on the floor and a vast shallow gap, like a moon crater, in the wall, into which no hook would ever fit. You know how it is with drilling. You try to fix a problem and end up making it worse, or maybe I only thought that because I didn't really know anything about drilling. Afraid of bringing down the entire wall, I rang Aaron for advice.

'Look, that drill was a gift. I've never actually used it, I don't know what to do.'

I think the truth was that his heart wasn't in the project. Since home improvement wasn't Raphael's strong point either, I set out to find a guy who owned a drill, but not a dog, to help finish the job. Builders renovating a house on my street agreed to lend me a hand. Now there were no more excuses.

Raphael came from Tel Aviv to help with tying Mia up. I was touched that he was making this effort. We were all stepping up to the plate. Or, in this case, the wall. All that remained was to put down an old rug and some toys and to tie Mia there. At first she was cool, she liked the rug and the corner, so it seemed the only one who was troubled was me, the crying alpha dog.

Raphael smiled and said, 'See, that was easy.'

Then Mia realised that she couldn't leave when she wanted to, or perhaps she got a whiff of my mood, for she started leaping, pulling against the hook like a rodeo pony, crying and then howling. It held fast, but I couldn't bear the sight and even more the sound, and I looked at Raphael in despair.

'This is so cruel ...' I wailed, as Mia jumped and whined. It sounded like the Atarot dog pound in here. To my surprise, Raphael didn't try to untie her or to talk me out of it.

'It can't be helped. Of course it's going to be difficult at the start, but we want her to learn to be obedient, and this is what the trainer says to do.'

I could hardly hear him over the howling, but I could tell he'd drunk the Kool Aid. We sat there for a moment longer, me with my hands over my ears, looking away from Mia. Then Raphael cracked.

'Why don't we ring Einav?'

When we called, the trainer was sympathetic but firm.

'I know it's hard, but if you give in to her now she'll know that this is how she has to behave to be set free. You can only reward good behaviour,' Einav advised. 'So go and pat her and when she calms down you can let her go. You *only* let her go when she is quiet, and then after a while you put her back. I know you don't believe me, but soon she will be going there willingly when you give the order.'

She was right, I didn't believe her. But I did want a more obedient dog, so I gritted my teeth. Raphael and I both patted Mia. We waited till she stopped howling to untie her and then started all over again.

Ever since he tumbled into our front gate, Mondo, the white Labrador puppy from the Blind Society, had become a regular visitor. He was now too big to wriggle his way in, so instead he whimpered with excitement outside, running around and around on the spot. I didn't know if I could tell Mondo apart from any other Labrador – okay, maybe a black one – since I'd never seen him sit still. I couldn't imagine how he would ever make a guide dog.

A little while after Mondo arrived and waited in an impatient frenzy, his owner, Itzik the engineer, would follow, nose in a book. Moscow was the only other place I'd seen people walking in the street reading. One time Itzik was immersed in Solzhenitsyn, the next it was the New Testament. He was a quiet, clever man, who lived alone with Mondo, and we talked about books and dogs on our walks. When Mondo saw Itzik arrive behind him, he increased the speed of his whirring. Mondo was so frenetic and Itzik so relaxed the contrast was comical.

'He just comes straight here,' Itzik offered apologetically, only looking up from page 113 as he reached our door.

While Mondo had loved Mia slavishly from the first moment, in his wriggly, bouncy, dog-in-eternal-motion way, she never forgave him for being free while she'd been tied up and she attacked him each time they met, pinning him to the ground by his neck.

'He's growing, Mia; you won't be able to do this for too much longer,' we warned her, as she growled and Mondo squealed. It was a sign of how laid-back Itzik was that Mia's aggression didn't faze him.

I forced her to release Mondo and then she chased him down the path. Mia was growing too. She had lost her puppy fur. The cute soft down, more like a baby duck than a dog, had been replaced by a proper adult coat. It was also getting darker, changing from straw blond to caramel. Her tail was becoming a plume, honey and white blond mixed together as if she'd been to a hairdresser for expensive highlights. Beneath that Farrah Fawcett tail, a skirt of whitish fur now fell, covering her back legs. The bobbing tail and skirt were very alluring if you walked behind her, which I guess was the purpose of the design. It certainly seemed to work on Mondo, and when he went missing the following weekend, Itzik turned to Mia straight away. He ran up in a panic.

'I don't know where Mondo is. He's just disappeared. Can I borrow Mia while I look? He won't be able to resist coming back if I have her with me.'

Itzik wanted to use her as bait, jail bait in fact. I thought it was a great plan. Never hurts for your dog to redeem herself with the neighbours. Not long after Itzik had taken Mia, the police called from the Old City. They'd found a Blind Society Labrador out with two small boys. Something about the dog's hysterical behaviour had made them suspicious. I smiled to myself. Mondo was *always* like that. The police would have been suspicious if they'd seen him out with Itzik, too.

That's how it was that when Itzik walked into the old sandstone police station near the Jaffa Gate to spring his dog he had my small blond honey trap in tow. Mondo was tied up near the wall. He was reasonably happy to see Itzik, but absolutely thrilled to see Mia. He jumped all over her, licking her ears and pawing at her back. Mia reacted with cool distaste, sitting still and turning her head away.

199

The policewoman who had been looking after Mondo said, 'Look, he's so happy to see her, but she couldn't give a toss.'

At least Mia didn't attack Mondo in front of the cops, pinning him down by his neck till he cried. So much for redeeming herself.

After two months of diligent training and 'controlled barking' I was not certain where it was all going.

Mia ran away less, but that might be because she was off the lead less. She went to 'her place', the corner where I tied her up, as soon as I gave the order. The trainer had been right about that, though Mia didn't go there voluntarily any more. It had become more of a punishment spot. She also did tricks when she thought you had sausage on hand, and sometimes even when you didn't. But doing tricks is not the same as being obedient, especially for such a clever dog. Had she learned her place in the hierarchy? I wasn't sure.

One day, not long after we'd begun this process, Raphael and I took her for a walk. We stopped at our favourite cafe, the one where we'd met. Raphael suggested we stay instead of taking coffee away to a park where Mia could play. He said that sometimes humans' needs could be taken into account too, and besides, Mia was learning how to be a cafe dog.

We ordered food for us and water for her. After both arrived she decided that she wanted something from my plate, but I was talking to Raphael and didn't notice. Incensed, Mia did all her tricks, one after another. She sat, lay down, sat back up and gave me her paw. She had everyone's attention now. Raphael and I laughed and the guys at the next table clapped. I gave Mia some of my sandwich.

When I stopped laughing and thought about it, though, the aim of teaching Mia these tricks was so that *we* would control *her* … but it seemed she just saw them as a way of manipulating us. I imagined her debriefing with Chucho.

'You know, I had to work really hard to get her to feed me, even though I did all the tricks I've taught her for producing food. I'm a bit worried, her concentration seems to be lapsing ... or is it just that humans never really learn?'

Perhaps Top Dog was in the eye of the beholder.

Love comes in many forms. There's the uncomplicated devotion we feel for animals and the far more complex emotions that humans elicit, especially the deep and yet paradoxically fragile bond we have with lovers.

Raphael's love was a wonderful source of light in my life. He was constant and accepting, which still seemed incredible to me, since I was so self-critical. When I said – as I did regularly – that I was going on a diet, Raphael replied that I didn't have to; he didn't like it when I got too thin. I shook my head in disbelief, the words as incomprehensible as if he'd spoken Chinese, since a majority of women at any given time are on diets, binging, purging, starving, weighing, measuring, calculating – glycaemic index, carbs, or just plain old-fashioned calories. A woman's body is a work in progress, with fat at one end (failure) and thin – no, skinny; no, fleshless – at the other (success), and it didn't seem possible that I had found a man who didn't care about any of it.

Raphael merely said, putting on an accent from the American South, 'Need some meat on the bones, honey!'

He freed me from the tyranny of that age-old female anxiety 'Does my bum look big in this?' because, as far as he was concerned, if the answer was yes, then that was great. I listened in wonder, slowly learning to accept myself because Raphael accepted me. He healed old traumas with a joke, and helped me to lay down burdens that I had been carrying for too long.

He was also that astounding creature, a loyal guy. He was attractive and flirty, but I wasn't worried about him cheating on me. I knew those men – in fact, like most women, after bitter experience I could spot them at fifty paces and sensed them even before they rounded the corner. Raphael wasn't one of them. Another blessing. In fact, frankly, a miracle.

But despite being loyal and trustworthy himself, to my surprise, Raphael didn't trust me. He was jealous, something I hadn't experienced before. A harsh expression settled on his face. *That guy was looking at you, that guy was smiling at you* … Even the guy delivering dog food was suspect. One morning, I returned home from walking Mia, burbling to Raphael about how lucky I was that the Yemin Moshe gardeners had made me coffee. They're lifesavers, I said blithely, unaware of what was coming. I could not believe he was angry that while he slept and I walked our dog I'd been talking to some men who were preparing coffee. There were five of them. It was outdoors. It was not personal. I thought he'd taken leave of his senses. I had recently taught him the expression 'There's no such thing as a free lunch', which he now hurled back at me.

'There's no such thing as a free cup of coffee!' he exclaimed.

'Well, you walk her then! I'll stay here in purdah behind the walls, safe from prying male eyes, and you take Mia out!'

We were both angry and honestly mystified one another. My freedom was important to me, but it wasn't because I wanted to be involved with anyone else. I didn't. What I wanted was to be able to talk freely to whoever I met. It was why I'd become a journalist, after all. I also wanted to be trusted and was hurt that I wasn't. Later, after we'd made up, Raphael told me I should feel flattered, it was because he cared. I never did quite believe that, since I cared about him but didn't put him through a cross-examination about every woman he met.

In the end, I came to accept it as a characteristic of Raphael's, like his abundant hair, or the mole on his shoulder. It was why he was loyal and not a player, and might also be why we had such a strong bond. No one knows what makes love work; it really is a mystery.

15

After months of reporting on the plans for Israel's withdrawal from Gaza, the actual event was upon us. The end had begun for the eight thousand Jewish settlers living in twenty-one difficult-to-defend outposts inside the Gaza Strip. Even Jewish voodoo couldn't save them.

Just days before the withdrawal was due to take place, about twenty religious extremists gathered at midnight in a cemetery to curse Prime Minister Ariel Sharon and to pray for his death. The controversial ritual they carried out was known as a Pulsa Denura, which means 'Pillars of Fire' in Aramaic. Most rabbis dismissed it as superstitious claptrap but a similar ceremony had been held before the murder of Israel's Prime Minister Yitzhak Rabin in 1995. Rabin's killer had come from the same community, a right-wing extremist opposed to plans to divide the land of Israel. The repetition of the ritual was evidence of how marginalised elements in the right wing felt.

It was an ancient rite but these were modern times, so the participants made sure there was a camera on hand. They released the footage in time for the evening news bulletins, giving all of Israel the chance to watch them cavorting in the dark among the graves, muttering deadly incantations in Aramaic. Afterwards, one of the participants, Michael Ben Horin, agreed to be interviewed.

'We prayed for Sharon's death,' he said. 'But it's like a boomerang, if he has more rights than us we will die. It's very dangerous. I almost fainted. You don't do it lightly.'

He paused to let that sink in then continued joyfully, 'We invoked the evil spirits to bring about his death as soon as possible. We didn't invoke him to be killed by a person. He is better defended than Hitler or Stalin, so we knew that wasn't practical. But the evil spirits can end his life in another way.'

The next day, a smiling Sharon told the Israeli public he felt none the worse for wear. He knew how to read his voters. They liked a tough guy.

In August, Meg and Craig and I – and about one thousand other international journalists – headed down to Gaza for the final removal of the Jewish residents. The Israeli army estimated that a hardcore of about fifteen hundred settlers remained, many hiding out in the largest Jewish settlement, the town of Neve Dekalim.

It was hot, stinking hot, and it became more stifling and humid as we neared the border. Couldn't they have done this in winter, we said to each other as we baked in the car. There were journalists, disgruntled settlers and Israeli military vehicles clogging the final part of the road, where it narrowed to two lanes down near Gaza. The route ran through Israeli farm land. Bougainvillea bushes grew wild in the sandy soil, and as we slowed to a crawl my eyes were drawn to the shocks of colour, brilliant clumps of purple, pink and red, against a bleached sky.

When we reached the border the three of us split up so we could report from different areas and share information. The Israeli military, coordinating the entry of the media, provided buses to ferry us in. They dropped us in the town of Neve Dekalim, the Gaza settlers' capital. After that we were on our own. It was well after midnight when we finally boarded the buses, and 3.00am on 18 August 2005, the morning Neve Dekalim was to be evacuated, when we climbed out.

Like everyone else dumped off the bus in the middle of the night, we searched for somewhere to roll out our sleeping bags so that we could grab a couple of hours of sleep, and were joined by a local. A tiny white dog with a sharp face and a curly tail came up to investigate. He seemed lost.

Remembering that Indian tribes set up camp where their dogs halted, we looked to our small friend to decide whether this spot on a lawn just outside the empty Neve Dekalim town council was a good one. He didn't move on, so we took that as a yes and tried to settle down to sleep. There were other journalists in clumps further along. We heard them chatting and giggling before everyone fell silent. The lawns were green and were still being watered, right up to the last minute, as we learned when the sprinklers woke us little more than an hour later, soaking our sleeping bags. What a waste of water! We sat up and looked around grumpily for somewhere dry to move to.

'Bum steer, little dog,' I said to him as we dragged our bags away.

'He's become part of the team!' a Canadian colleague exclaimed more kindly, patting the dog, who appeared even more endearing in the pre-dawn light, one ear up, one down. But he was always looking beyond us for someone else, someone familiar to come back and take him home.

Having been woken at 4.30am we were ready to work soon after dawn. We could see that although the council's sprinklers were still working, the rest of Neve Dekalim appeared to be in decay. Some two thousand five hundred people had lived here, between the main Palestinian town of Khan Yunis and the sea. Their withdrawal had not yet been completed, but their town was already decomposing.

The homes were now mostly empty. The few Jewish settlers who remained had set garbage containers on fire. A cloud of smoke hung over the town, filled with particles of smouldering rubbish and carrying the noxious stink of burning plastic. When I saw Orla later at the house the BBC had rented, we were both hot and filthy, perspiration and burnt trash smeared into our skin. Usually neat as a pin, Orla said she felt like pond scum. I couldn't help smiling. No matter what the situation, she always found the perfect phrase.

The IDF planned to clear Neve Dekalim street by street, removing all families to waiting buses, until every last house was empty. In order to limit violence, it had trained the soldiers to take whatever abuse the settlers hurled at them without responding. This led to remarkable scenes, where twenty-year-old Jewish settlers faced twenty-year-old Jewish soldiers, alternately screaming and begging them to stop this betrayal of their nation, heaping insults on them and comparing them to Nazis removing Jews from their villages in Europe during World War II.

'Don't do this to us, we are all Jews, don't do this to us. A Jew doesn't remove a Jew from his land. You know the last time that this was done to us, you evil Nazis!' one teenager after another shouted, sobbing as they were lifted out.

The comparison was vile, of course. The Jews of Europe were being taken to death camps, and the Gaza settlers only had to move thirty kilometres away, where they had a quarter-of-a-million-dollar resettlement package waiting for them.

In accordance with their training, the Israeli soldiers didn't react. They hugged the crying settlers and moved them onto waiting buses. It was remarkable. In this volatile culture, where conflicts quickly escalate, the IDF had essentially trained its soldiers to turn the other cheek. I watched and wondered whether they shouldn't institute it permanently.

A group of eight Jewish students locked themselves into a basement bomb shelter to avoid being removed. A former New York Police Department hostage negotiator, now a member of the Israeli army, was talking them round. I wandered up at the same time as Aaron Schachter, the American journalist who was my dog buddy, and we both switched on our recorders. The negotiator was calm, the students increasingly shrill and desperate. Everyone had Brooklyn accents.

'Jews are being kicked out of their land. A new Holocaust is about to take place. We are stopping it with our bodies!' one of the students screeched, almost in tears.

'Do you know where the key to the bomb shelter is?' the hostage negotiator kept repeating placidly.

Aaron shut his eyes, grinning as he held up a thumb and mouthed, 'This is so good!' A negotiation like this, in English, was gold dust, sure to make the bulletin.

Many of these remaining settlers had insisted they would only be removed by force, but in fact they believed that God would step in and prevent their removal.

'God's will can occur in the blink of an eye,' they explained to me earnestly at the next street to be cleared, while the soldiers prepared to evacuate them.

Some pinned yellow stars of David to their children's clothes and made them walk out of their homes with their hands up. It was an echo of Nazi Germany that the children were too young to understand but that offended many Israelis. I watched parents walking towards the buses and handing their children to the soldiers, saying theatrically, 'Here – you take them!' as if they really had to give them away to prevent them being killed. I was standing near a bus, recording, when one angry mother pushed her baby out the window, dangling him as if she planned to drop him. The baby began to cry, then to howl in distress.

'Take him, take him!' she screamed, and I instinctively reached up, microphone in one hand, camera in the other, to catch her crying infant. She shook him again as if he were a sack before a soldier appeared and managed to persuade her to pull the baby back inside.

I was shocked. I feared that child would always know on some level that his mother had been prepared to treat him like that to make a political point. Or perhaps she really had been prepared to let him go. She'd certainly convinced me.

When the scenes were broadcast on the news in Israel, there were calls for these parents to be prosecuted for abusing their children. Eran Sternberg, the former spokesman for the Gaza settlement bloc, defended them. His answer was an example of the twisted logic that applied here in the parallel universe of Gaza.

'I am satisfied with everything that these parents decided for their children,' he said. 'I know those people and I don't think there are more responsible parents in all of Israel. It is the state which is criminal and crazy, throwing people into the street after three generations in their homes.'

I walked up to the next tranche of houses to be cleared. Although I had charged my batteries the previous night, they already seemed to be running low. Annoyed, I remembered that I had left my spares in my bag under Orla's desk back at the BBC house. I wandered along a back street of small cottages surrounded by greenery. Inside one house, with vines trailing prettily over it, I found a family waiting to be evacuated. Their electricity was still working and they let me plug my recorder into their wall socket to charge.

Both parents in this helpful family were in their thirties and very attractive. They were from a Yemenite background, and the father, Avram, had begun his life as a secular Jew and served in the Israeli army. Afterwards he became ultra-Orthodox, growing long curly earlocks and spending his days studying holy texts. He and his wife had three children. The youngest was a boy who had long ringlets hanging down over his shoulders. In their tradition, boys only have their first haircut when they are three years old. With his almond-shaped black eyes, he looked like a beautiful girl. His older sisters played with him while their father talked to me.

'This is our land ...' Avram explained, leafing through the Old Testament for the appropriate verse to read out to me. It never ceased to surprise me how much of the discourse here was conducted on the basis of biblical sources. Still, I'd heard this argument more than once and knew the response.

'But even in biblical times, the children of Israel never held Gaza.'

'Yes, that was our mistake. Samson didn't follow God's instructions. You see, here it is,' he said, triumphantly turning the pages of his book to the right verse.

While my battery charged, he read to me from the Old Testament. Nothing in his house had been packed – not one tea cup, nor one holy book. When the soldiers came, he stood to lose all these possessions. He denied this was irresponsible.

'God's will can occur,' he began, and I finished off the local hymn, which I now knew by heart, 'In the blink of an eye. Yes, yes, I know.'

In the end that's what this story was all about. Faith. You either have it or you don't, and since my batteries were now charged I, who didn't have it, could leave this kind family who were awaiting their departure like an execution and expecting to be spared from it by God's grace. I said goodbye and wished them well. I went back out to see that most of Neve Dekalim had now been cleared and that they were next in line.

At the back of this Jewish town, Palestinians were clearing out the settlers' possessions on an almost industrial scale. Just as had happened at the smaller settlement of Ganei Tal the previous month, the settlers had sold some goods and dumped the rest. Enterprising locals were there with their donkeys and carts to take them. Everybody was making money somehow. Some would repair the goods and use or sell them, others were charging a fee for the removal. Only the long-suffering donkeys weren't in on the game. My neighbour in Jerusalem, the Spanish journalist Josefina de la Cruz, saw one donkey ferry so many loads that it collapsed and died in harness in front of her.

After the final sobbing family of settlers had been removed from their home there was one remaining area to be cleared: the main synagogue. About one thousand Jewish teenagers had infiltrated illegally into the Gaza Strip over the past few weeks. They were here instead of going to summer camp and they had taken refuge in the synagogue. It was a white building, on two levels, with a large concourse in front of it, surrounded by trees and shrubs.

The teenagers had lived here for days now without adult supervision. They were wearing red and orange T-shirts, like protesters in Ukraine's recent Orange Revolution, the boys in jeans, the girls in denim skirts. They were smelly and dirty – well, that wasn't hard, so was I – but they were clapping their hands with jerky actions and singing songs hoarsely and wildly, in fits and starts, now starting their own song, now joining someone else's. By the time I saw them, it felt as if they were fraying, falling apart. They were all singing, spitting, sweating, shrieking, crooning and cursing. Probably, beneath the bravado, they were also frightened.

I watched them shouting and pointing dramatically at Israeli soldiers, tears alternating with curses. I'd wander away and come back, and they'd still be at it. I felt I'd stumbled into some Gaza version of *The Crucible* and almost expected to hear one of the teenagers jump up and exclaim, 'I saw Sarah Good with the Devil!' before they collapsed crying and could be carted away. Still, there was one place where it was even crazier: Shirat Hayam.

Shirat Hayam, Hebrew for 'Song of the Sea', was a tiny settlement right on the beach across the road from Neve Dekalim. It was only four years old, and about fifteen families lived there, either in trailers or in abandoned buildings that had been Egyptian army officers' barracks from the period before 1967, when Egypt controlled the Gaza Strip. Over the past three months, the settlers had been renovating the Egyptian barracks as a signal to their government that they were not planning to move.

The beach was closed to Palestinians, of course, and the settlement sat behind barbed wire, with a row of breeze-block walls inside that, and a watchtower. The residents had fenced themselves in, like all the Gaza settlers, but the size and the location made their efforts appear more extreme, as if they had created their very own boutique beach prison camp. The older boys were surfers, their hair bleached blond under their skullcaps. But it wasn't all hippies. Israeli military historian Aryeh Yitzhaki was a resident. Four days ago, after finally accepting that his government was going to carry out the withdrawal, he'd proclaimed independence for Shirat Hayam and renamed it the 'Independent Jewish Authority in Gaza Beach'. He'd named himself temporary leader until elections could be held next week and sent an appeal for recognition of his new country to the UN and the Red Cross.

Another resident was Omri Ron-Tal, the son of the head of Israel's armed forces, Major General Iftah Ron-Tal. While the top officer was in another part of Gaza clearing out the remaining settlers, his son, daughter-in-law and grandson were sitting in Shirat Hayam, waiting to be moved out themselves.

The settlers at Shirat Hayam prayed outside on the sand, the teenage surfers barefoot with their prayer shawls over their heads. They had placed a barricade of junk outside the barbed-wire fence at the entrance to the settlement – old vehicles and industrial waste, with rolls of razor wire slung across the top. When I arrived, it had been set alight, as if the day wasn't hot and frantic enough.

Israeli soldiers surrounded the settlement. They stopped near the breeze-block wall, where a group of settlers confronted them. I watched the stand-off. The combatants were framed by razor wire, and the heat from the burning barricades licked at us all. I looked up to see that a small child had climbed onto one of the breeze blocks above them and was crouched on his haunches on this narrow ledge, gazing down with his head in his hands. In so many ways the image of that child alone in that dangerous spot – out there on the edge removed from the rest of the population which he was regarding uncomprehendingly – summed up the Gaza settlements for me.

When the soldiers prepared to move in, the young people climbed onto the roof of a building in the centre of Shirat Hayam. They had put a fence around it on which they'd hung handwritten signs: 'I was born here' and 'I have no other country'. Their 'leader', Aryeh Yitzhaki, climbed onto another roof, armed with a machine gun, and told the soldiers gathered below that the house was booby-trapped and that he would shoot if anyone came up. Five settlers swam out to sea to avoid capture. The IDF picked up three on a raft, one swam back, and one succumbed to the waves and had to be rescued by a soldier, who pulled her from the water unconscious.

Somehow, in the end, the overall pattern repeated itself here too. Yitzhaki was talked down without firing a shot. He emerged wrapped in an Israeli flag and said, 'I could have launched the second Masada in Shirat Hayam, but I decided to negotiate, so as to avoid loss of life.'

The sun was low in the sky as the last women and bleached-blond children were removed from their trailers. Waves pounded the beach. Shirat Hayam was finally empty.

I left during the fast-descending Mediterranean twilight. I had done a number of live interviews throughout the day and had to go and edit all the material I had gathered into a package for the evening bulletins. I returned to Neve Dekalim to collect my laptop and sleeping bag from under Orla's desk. The air was still moist and heavy with smouldering trash. I was squatting with other journalists in an abandoned house, which we were thrilled to find had electricity. As I set to work my eyes were burning, and after so little sleep I felt weak, filthy and exhausted. 'Pond scum' didn't come close.

At the end of that long hot week, I reflected that the Gaza withdrawal had worked out differently to how we'd anticipated. There was rebellion but no real violence. In fact, it took place almost without any weapons being fired. In that sense the Israeli military strategy was highly effective.

The Palestinians watched at a distance from behind the fences which had kept them out of these areas for decades. Fatah police held Hamas gunmen back so they wouldn't interrupt the withdrawal with any 'symbolic' military action. Hamas announced that this was only the first step in the liberation of every inch of Palestine, and indeed they claimed it as their victory. It was not a negotiated departure, an exchange of land for peace. The Israelis were 'running away' and Hamas said exultantly it was the result of their policy of military resistance.

During the previous year, Palestinian authorities hadn't really believed the withdrawal would take place, but they had requested that if Israel did depart, it should destroy all the buildings it had constructed. 'This style of building doesn't suit us. We have to plan for eighty thousand or eight hundred thousand, not eight thousand. We need high-rise and we want to construct our own cities and towns and not be limited by the buildings the Israelis have put up,' the governor of Khan Yunis had told me a week earlier, standing in front of architectural drawings in his office.

On the final day, Israeli bulldozers destroyed buildings which the Israeli government had constructed at huge cost. They razed everything they'd built there, including synagogues. It was a strange, painful sight, given Jewish history in Europe, to watch Jews destroying synagogues. Next, they unearthed the graves of Jews buried in the Gaza Strip. Nothing was to remain.

'The Jewish settlement of Gaza was a historic mistake,' veteran Israeli politician Shimon Peres said bluntly. These images confirmed that, and underscored the futility of such an enterprise.

I have covered far more dangerous stories but rarely have I been exposed to so much festering religious madness. As we drove back to Jerusalem I felt shell-shocked, as if something inside me had cracked in the heat and hysteria. In a tired haze, I wondered whether the Israeli withdrawal from Gaza had left me with some form of post traumatic stress disorder. But there was no time for PTSD, or even relaxation, post-Gaza, because when I got back home Mia went into heat.

She was eight months old, still a puppy herself, but nature deemed that she was ready to be a mother. I disagreed, and certainly couldn't have coped with any more puppies right then, so I set out to protect her from her suitors.

The ten-metre lead was a thing of the past. I held Mia on a tight leash at all times now. For safety's sake, we abandoned the park and I took to walking her at night, short walks at a brisk pace on streets where we were less likely to see other dogs. In case we did meet anyone, I learned to say painstakingly in Hebrew, 'My dog is in heat. Has your dog been neutered?' But I inevitably got it wrong, asking instead: 'Has your dog been fumigated?'

I tried not to leave Mia at home by herself much either. I took her to visit Raphael at his parents' home in Jerusalem, where she was generally well behaved. On one occasion she needed to go outside and we met her favorite local dog, Rocky, the handsome white Samoyed from across the road. I held Mia as I tried to explain to his owner why I had to keep her away. 'Has Rocky been fumigated?'

Meg and Craig's was also a refuge, one of the few homes with a dog where we were safe, since Chucho *had* been neutered. And probably fumigated, too. I sank down into Meg's sofa, one day, with a cup of coffee and a pile of the latest American magazines, which her newspaper had Fed Ex-ed into Jerusalem. After the religious hysteria of Gaza, I revelled in the glossy escapism of *Vanity Fair*. A long article about Jennifer Aniston's split from Brad Pitt was just what the doctor ordered. It let me dive right into a different world.

Demi Moore had married Ashton Kutcher since we'd come back from Gaza, and there was also an article on the popularity of the porn star memoir – 'Debbie Does Barnes & Noble' – but before I'd done more than point out the clever title to Meg we realised that something was wrong with the dogs. Their chasing was more desperate than usual. Chucho was frenzied and Mia snapped and growled at him as if he were just another lout from the park. Then it went one romp too far and we heard a terrible howl from the next room.

'I think we better separate Romeo and Juliet,' said Meg as we pulled the dogs apart.

Back at home, Mia jumped onto the coffee table, and stood there, shaking uncontrollably.

'Poor little thing,' I murmured as I patted her, 'this won't last much longer.'

I hoped I was telling her the truth.

Our front door was now firmly closed and Mia was no longer at the gate, head poking through like a mermaid, to lure males to their ruin. But even so, more dogs than usual were stopping by. One of the newcomers to the doorstep was a large, ungainly brown dog, about a year old. Actually he wasn't just ungainly; he was downright ugly. Even a mother couldn't love him. I didn't worry too much about him, sure he would move on like the others. Then I was closing window after window – slam, slam, slam – as Mia hopped ahead of me to get nearer to him, like a scene in a slapstick comedy. Oh no! Out of all her suitors, he was The One. Mia had fallen for the ugly dog. With no money or breeding or family.

I found myself actually saying out loud, 'But, Mia – why him? You could do so much better!'

Dogs show you an unpleasant side of yourself.

The next time Mia and I visited Raphael at his parents' place, pushing two male dogs away to get indoors, his oldest sister was over too, with her children. When she asked how things were going, I didn't tell her about Gaza, since by some unwritten agreement we didn't discuss politics. Instead I told her that life was currently dominated by my dog being in heat. That put Raphael in a bad mood.

'You said Mia was *your* dog, you didn't say she was *our* dog!'

Those hormones were making everyone sensitive. I tried to distract him by telling him about Ashton Kutcher and Demi Moore, but that didn't work since it turned out that Raphael was a huge Bruce Willis fan.

'Can you believe she would do that to Bruce Willis? *To Bruce Willis?*' he repeated, aggrieved.

I told him what I'd read yesterday, which was that they were already divorced when Demi Moore met her new young husband. Also, Willis attended the wedding and said he liked Kutcher.

Raphael was not convinced. 'He has to say that and pretend he doesn't care or he will seem weak, and he can't do that because he's an action hero. But it's not what he really feels,' he said darkly. Raphael seemed to be taking the betrayal of Bruce Willis personally.

Mia distracted us by stretching and going to sit by the door, a sign she needed to go out. Raphael's nephews and nieces said they wanted to come too. On this excursion, I would be in charge of a ten-year-old girl, a six-year-old boy and a radioactive eight-month-old dog. We opened the door and there on the doorstep was Rocky from across the road. I'd never seen him loose before, and he seemed less well groomed and more aggressive than in the past, jumping onto Mia right there on the steps.

I pushed Rocky off while Raphael's nephew and niece stood behind me squealing. Great; an incident and we hadn't even left the house. To calm the children I told them that we could quickly take Rocky home and then go on our walk undisturbed. I dragged Mia ahead of him, but she was like an electronic rabbit leading a greyhound. We rounded the corner and climbed the stairs into Rocky's back yard to see ... Rocky, tied up in his usual place. For a moment I thought it was an optical illusion, but, no, there were two Samoyeds. I gazed from one to the other, from Rocky One to Rocky Two, in dismay.

There was a moment of silence as we all took each other in before everyone let loose. Rocky One – the real Rocky – couldn't believe that we had brought around his sweetheart with a rival male in tow. He started barking and flinging himself to the length of his chain. Rocky Two ran towards him, a frontal assault which had the benefit of freedom, while Raphael's nephew and niece stood shrieking, making as much noise as the dogs, only higher pitched. I pushed Rocky Two away and hustled my little brood back to the house. The femme fatale could pee another time.

Raphael said that maybe we should let Mia have one litter of puppies before we had her spayed, but once I'd seen Brown Dog I knew there was no point. No one would take puppies sired by him. We wouldn't be able to give them away. Raphael and Meg disagreed. They said I was exaggerating and that Brown Dog had his good points.

No one could deny that determination was one of them. Brown Dog sat on our doorstep for four days, without eating or drinking. I stepped over him each time I left the house, locking poor quivering Mia in behind me. Orla was right to describe me as an abbess at a nunnery. On the second day, when I returned home during a rare autumn downpour, Brown Dog was shivering on the step, as wet as a fish. Through the window I could see Mia lying on the sofa, her head on a pillow. The princess was warm and dry, while her devoted admirer suffered outside.

I tried not to feel sorry for him because he was keeping us prisoner. There was only one entrance to the apartment and he was there 24/7. I decided that to avoid stress, I'd simply drive her away from him to a park in the next suburb. I hurried her past him to the car. He watched us in disbelief, his expression of betrayal almost comical. I turned on the ignition, let off the handbrake and headed down the driveway. It felt good to get away.

But when I looked in the rear-view mirror there he was, running down the driveway and into the street. I turned right onto a four-lane road and stopped at a traffic light. He was there behind us. I took another turn, hoping to lose him, but as we pulled up at the park I could hear his paws drumming on the road. I decided to keep going. Surely I could drive faster than a dog?

The answer, in the short term, was no. A driver has to stop at traffic lights. A dog doesn't. The next time we stopped on a busy street he actually overtook us, but realising something was wrong, he turned his head and wove his way back through the traffic, trotting purposefully towards the car. When he reached us he stood up on his hind legs, put his paws on the door closest to Mia and gazed at her. She was on the back seat straining towards him, whimpering. I felt like I had exited reality, had moved into a film, a human extra on the set of a canine romantic comedy.

'And you didn't let them do it?' a soft-hearted Australian friend asked in disbelief. 'How could you be so cruel? No *man* has ever exhibited half as much devotion to me!'

When we returned home I leaned out the window to snap a picture of the tenacious Brown Dog. I sent it out to friends, the email slugged 'Siege of nunnery continues for 5th day'. Nabil the money changer emailed back: 'What do you mean? The dog is very cute. Let's have a wedding!'

As with every romance, it's all about timing. Her suitor's passions didn't subside, but Mia's did once her window for conceiving closed. On the fifth evening, Brown Dog's owner turned up. A plump Israeli woman walked past our house and yelped, 'Ushkush! I've been so worried about you!'

She looked at Mia and me accusingly, 'Has he been here ALL this time?', and knelt down beside him. 'You poor silly dog,' she crooned, stroking him, which is more or less what I said to Mia.

'Once you reach forty …' I started the sentence then froze, not even certain what point I had been going to make, for the vital thing to remember was that I was talking to Raphael, who didn't know that I was forty. It wasn't the first time I'd done it, so obviously I was a bad liar, or perhaps it didn't take Sigmund Freud to see that I actually wanted to tell him the truth about my age.

Still it was a shock when Raphael asked me outright late one night: 'So, how old *are* you?'

Early one morning, to be more precise, for once again it was 3.00am and my sweet Vampyr was wide awake. I was lying in the crook of his arm, almost asleep, because most people who get up early to walk a dog are tired by the wee hours of the following day, and I hadn't been sleeping well while I'd been on guard duty with Mia. As the question hung in the air, almost achieving a material form, I tried to compute what I'd told him my age was when we'd first met and how long ago that was now.

I said I was thirty-five, but it was just before our birthdays, so was I thirty-six, and what do I have to add – no, subtract … My thoughts were so muddled that I realised I simply couldn't do it. I needed a pen and paper to be able to tell him how old I was. So instead I told him the truth.

'You can't possibly expect me to know the answer to that question.'

We both began giggling, a chuckle that developed into a rolling laugh that went on and on as we re-infected each other. It was an acknowledgement that I wasn't telling him the truth and that we both knew it. I looked at Raphael in the semi-darkness and promised him that I would tell him soon, when I was not so tired. I didn't have the energy for that conversation right then. It still frightened me. He kissed my cheek and told me to go to sleep. As I shut my eyes I wondered when I would ever be less tired, and if it would make a difference to him once he knew.

Mia was becoming fat and sluggish. She no longer raced up the Yemin Moshe steps ahead of me, turning corners and disappearing around them. Instead, she shuffled companionably by my side. I never had to go looking for her any more, because she was always by me, walking slowly and contentedly. In fact, she tired quickly and sometimes had to sit to regain her breath. She became more affectionate but also uncharacteristically jealous, snapping and snarling if I patted another dog.

I tried to hide the extent of these disturbing changes from myself, though I did ask Raphael if he'd noticed anything. Loyally, he said no; Mia was perfect. A chance remark when we were out on our morning walk shook me out of my denial. A Palestinian worker, who was painting some guttering on one of the stone houses, looked down from his ladder as Mia waddled up the stairs and said, 'That dog's pregnant!'

So that's *it!* I thought. *That explains why she's so different.*

Out loud, I said dismissively, 'No, that's impossible. How could she be pregnant?'

The worker leaned on his ladder and looked down at me pityingly.

I decided not to try to explain in my bad Arabic that I did understand how a dog gets pregnant, but I was not sure how *this dog* could be pregnant since I'd worked so hard to guard her from all incoming males. But I asked everyone we met that morning what they thought: the guard at our favourite cafe; Moshko the deli owner who kept salami offcuts for Mia; even the clients waiting at the salon for Rikki my beautician. When I held Mia so they could get a side view, the women all agreed that she seemed quite plump under all that fur, and could very well be pregnant. Rikki poked her head over the top of the railing from the waxing room upstairs, honey-coloured curls tumbling over her shoulders, and agreed that from her angle it looked quite likely.

'But how could it be?' I wailed.

They all looked at me pityingly.

It was time to go to the vet. I was tense while he examined Mia, until he gave his diagnosis: she wasn't pregnant; she merely thought she was. It was a phantom pregnancy.

'*A what?*' I asked in disbelief.

That was something I'd only heard of in humans, in fact sixteenth-century Spanish queens who had the misfortune to be married to Henry VIII.

'No, it's very common,' the vet assured me. 'The dogs show all the signs of a real pregnancy, including tiredness, weight gain, and by the end they even lactate and produce milk. But then it all goes back to normal.'

He explained that the condition was understood to have originated long ago, when dogs were wild and lived in packs like wolves. At that time only the alpha female had puppies. The other females developed a phantom pregnancy in order to be attuned to her so they'd be ready to lactate when she did and could help to feed the babies, the future of their pack. *It takes a village …*

16

Israel's withdrawal had failed to make the population in Gaza more secure. Instead, it had intensified the turf war between Fatah and Hamas, the two main Palestinian groups competing to control the Gaza Strip. Other armed gangs were also taking to the streets. Kidnappings and assassinations were becoming more common. Gaza appeared to be descending into lawlessness.

On an autumn morning, sweltering like mid summer, I woke to news of another assassination. This time the victim was one of the most powerful men in Gaza. Fatah strongman Moussa Arafat had been Yasser Arafat's nephew, and the chief of the security forces. Now he was dead.

A convoy of twenty vehicles had driven up to his seaside home in the early hours of the morning, and militants armed with assault rifles and anti-tank missiles had pulled him into the street and killed him there. They had taken out someone widely despised as corrupt, but the message to the public was clear. If it can happen to Moussa Arafat, it can happen to anyone. The gangs rule Gaza now, not Fatah.

I recorded some interviews by phone and filed a story from Jerusalem. By the time I'd completed the job and was ready to walk Mia, it was after 10.00am. We headed out into the relentless heat. I enjoyed the feel of the sun on my skin, but it was different for dogs – creatures that didn't sweat and wore fur coats. Really we should have been walking at 6.30am, I chastised myself.

We headed down the sandstone steps to the closest park, the one where the gardeners often prepared coffee for us. It was way too late for that service. We rounded the corner to see an unusual sight in a dry land. The sprinklers were on at full pelt, creating arcs of water which shimmered in the sun. Small children were running through them squealing – an enchanting sound. Apparently, the sprinklers had needed maintenance work and the Yemin Moshe kindergarten was reaping the benefit. Mia trotted down confidently to a circle of tiny children, tail wagging. She rolled over onto her back, paws over her eyes, waiting to be adored. The kindergarten teacher was thrilled.

'Who is this sweet dog?'

I told them her name. They yelled out 'Mia! Mia!' as they patted her tummy. When everyone in the little group had had their go, Mia sat up. The teacher threw her arms around Mia's neck. 'This is how you should say hello to a dog!' she instructed the children, burying her face in Mia's fur and loudly kissing her. 'Mwa, mwa, MWA!!'

The children followed suit, hugging and kissing Mia's caramel coat, their small hands clenched in her fur. If it hurt her she gave no indication. Soon there were almost no children running through the sprinklers. Instead, they were gathered in a knot around my fluffy canine magnet. Mia moved into the shade of an olive tree and the children moved with her. More children joined in and I could barely see her; but I could see them, climbing on top of the tree's knobbly roots to reach her, playing with her ears and tail, screeching with happiness. They tumbled over her and each other, almost puppies themselves, one darting out of the pack every so often to tell me about dogs they had at home.

Her profound love of children was one of Mia's most endearing qualities. I thought of her as a UN goodwill ambassador whose job it was to teach children that 'dogs are your friends'. Last week, she'd streaked across the park at top speed. I thought she'd seen a cat. No, just a baby.

It was a burning love.

She was always on the lookout for kids – in the park, in the cafe, at the supermarket – and she had an MO. Once she spotted a family, she ran up like a bullet then slowed down ten metres away, approaching almost on her belly, tail wagging, to show she was not a threat.

She put a lot of time into it, sitting patiently until small, terrified children dared to walk up and pat her gingerly, and then more confidently, their doubting faces wreathed in smiles. When she turned to lick them – the aim of the operation from her point of view – they often jumped back in fear and we'd start all over again. Mia would wait patiently through this phase too, while I coaxed the children back. By the end, she was licking them and, on a good day, they were feeding her any treats they had on them. Mission accomplished.

That morning at the sprinklers, Mia refused to leave until the last wet child had wriggled into dry clothes and had had a chance to play.

'Say goodbye to Mia now, children!' The teachers shepherded the last reluctant dog lovers out of the park.

No child from that kindergarten – 'Mwa, mwa, MWA!!!'– would ever be scared of dogs, unlike other terrified children we often met. Religious Jews and Muslims both regarded dogs as unclean. The more faith you had the less tolerant you were of dogs, and many other things, it seemed.

Mia could clear a hillside of Palestinian children just by appearing on the horizon. They would run off, some crying. Once I grabbed her, they would come back, looking nervous as the tears dried on their cheeks. But as soon as they had patted her tentatively, a horrible turnaround would take place. They would begin hitting her, kicking her and throwing stones. I learned the Arabic phrases for 'Don't be afraid!', 'Come back' and 'Leave her alone! Stop that!', and almost without fail had to use them in quick succession. Children model the behaviour they're taught. It's terrible to imagine what treatment they'd seen being meted out to dogs.

One hot morning, autumn still shimmering like summer, a group of ultra-Orthodox Jewish boys were in the park ahead of us. They looked like tiny adults, dressed in black suits, white shirts and black fedora hats. Mia ran up and they scattered, two of them screaming in fear, when they saw her. Anticipating a game, Mia ran after them. I caught her but, taking pity on the terrified boys wearing those unsuitable clothes winter and summer alike, I told them they should act against their instincts next time and stand still.

'Just let the dog go by. Running encourages a dog to chase you; they think you want to play with them,' I explained. 'I know it's hard, but if you can manage to just stand still you will usually be fine.'

Most of them kept running but the oldest boy stopped and responded, 'Ah, like with a snake?'

'Yes, just the same,' I said, glad he understood the principle so quickly. It seemed for these boys there was no difference between a snake and a domestic pet.

The boy nodded wisely and, one hand holding the hat on his head, he called to the smaller boys to stop running. They returned slowly, still unsure, but I was holding Mia and she sat calmly to be admired and petted. Seven boys in wide-brimmed hats inched forward. They kept their distance but their focus was total, as if they were a band of (small) white men in Africa advancing on their first lion.

'What big teeth she has,' said one.

'What a big tail she has,' said another.

I wondered if they knew 'Red Riding Hood', or if this was their natural speech. Mia tipped over onto her back, paws over her eyes. A third boy asked, 'Is she a girl?'

When I said yes, the youngest child asked the killer question.

'How can you tell?'

I looked desperately at the seven small faces under the brims of their hats, all turned towards me curiously, and felt myself growing pale. *How can I tell she's a girl? How can I tell she's a girl?* I muttered to myself, wondering why it was down to me to give sex education to young fundamentalists so early in the day, before I'd ingested any caffeine. My mind was a blank. I looked at the ringleader, the one who'd understood about the snake, and the best I could come up with was, 'You tell them.'

Later Raphael said that the proper answer to that question was, 'Just like you do with people.'

The olive tree is the symbol of this land. Extending an olive branch has been a sign of peace since biblical times, when Noah sent out a dove from his Ark and it returned with an olive branch to indicate that the flood waters were receding. An olive tree takes so long to nurture that if you extend an olive branch you are also showing that you have had enough of war and want to go back to tending your trees and producing your oil.

Yet there was little peace when the time came for the olive harvest in the West Bank. Palestinians reported that some Jewish settlers had prevented them from harvesting their olives or, even worse, burned or cut down their trees so they would never be able to harvest olives from them again. Palestinian farmers also reported a campaign of harassment, which included killing their sheep and goats, poisoning their wells and often attacking them physically too. Sometimes, it was only the presence of international and Israeli volunteers that enabled the Palestinians to bring in their crop.

I decided to return to Yanun, a village I'd gone to three years ago, when I'd first arrived. Home to only one hundred and fifty Palestinians, mostly farmers, it was located in the north of the West Bank, five kilometres south of the town of Nablus and, most significantly, in a valley directly below the Jewish settlement of Itamar. From 1967, Israeli policy in the West Bank had been to send settlers to 'grab the hilltops'.

Itamar was established in the 1980s on the hilltop above Yanun. The settlement now had more than one thousand residents and it had staked claims to all the hilltops in the area, spawning five 'illegal outposts' which had Yanun surrounded. The Palestinian villagers were frightened to venture into their own fields because ideological young settlers from Itamar patrolled the ridges above. Known as the 'hilltop youth', they were rapidly turning into the militant wing of the settler movement.

Due to the potential for violence, any Palestinian harvest had to be coordinated with the Israeli military. On that first visit, I had joined a group of international and Israeli volunteers who were going to help the Palestinians harvest their crops. My translator, Nuha, said she would meet us there. A group of about two dozen volunteers gathered, with Israeli military consent, to assist about an equal number of Palestinian villagers. No one was armed.

We set out. The villagers hadn't dared go out to their fields for months, due to threats from the Jewish settlers. Now the paths to the fields were blocked with large rocks. They spent half an hour removing the rocks and then marched into the fields to work. They laid plastic sheets beneath the trees and began beating the branches with sticks so that the olives fell onto the sheets and could be gathered up. Everyone had their set tasks, and there were companionable exchanges in many languages as the work settled into a rhythm. I interviewed the Palestinian villagers and then, because I was working for Irish radio that day, I also interviewed Robbie Kelly, a volunteer from Ireland who had been spending his annual holiday there, helping with the olive harvest.

The sun was shining. There were no machines. The only sounds we heard were sticks hitting branches and fruit falling. The air was filled with dust and a sharp green scent, a little like eucalyptus. It was how olives had been harvested for thousands of years. It was Good Labour, man working with Nature, not against her, and it reminded me of Tolstoy's descriptions of Russian peasants harvesting wheat fields in the 1800s. Then someone stepped into the twenty-first century and listened to the radio. An Israeli volunteer warned that he'd heard a news report about a Palestinian suicide bombing in the large Jewish settlement town of Ariel, in the centre of the West Bank. The villagers decided to pack up.

I remember feeling disappointed, for they'd barely been there two hours and hadn't achieved much yet. But although they'd had nothing to do with the attack in Ariel, they feared vigilante reprisals. It turned out they were right. I left the fields ahead of the group, ringing Nuha and trying to arrange another set of interviews because there was no point her coming out here now. As the Palestinians walked out carrying the morning's harvest, a group of settlers came running down the hill from Itamar. There were eight or nine young men carrying sticks and batons. Some also had guns. They gave the impression of being completely wild, a gang of home-schooled, drugged-out religious hippies. They shouted, 'Terrorists!' and threw stones and then punches. Robbie Kelly, in the front, was among the first to be hit.

'We approached them with our hands out front to show that we were coming in peace. I was frightened but more for the Palestinians. We were in a certain amount of danger but it was much more serious for them.'

It also turned out to be dangerous for other volunteers, who were on the outside of the group. James Delaplaine, an American in his seventies, had been walking more slowly at the back of the group and found that his age did not protect him. 'One settler hit me with a rifle butt, breaking my glasses. He kept repeating, "Do you want to be dead?" I'm seventy-four years old but I don't want to be dead, however.'

The whole incident had lasted barely ten minutes but it left eight people injured. By the time the IDF arrived, the settlers had disappeared. This incident had followed a month of violence in the area. From there, I went to meet Nuha at the Palestinian village of Akrabeh where a farmer had been seriously injured days before. Adel

Ghaleb had been in the fields when a group set upon him. They broke his legs with rocks and hit him on the head with a rifle butt, causing him to lose his sight in one eye.

When we entered Ghaleb's house, he was lying on his side on a single bed in the main room. A rough bandage around his head had covered his eye. He appeared weak and in pain, and was not been able sit up. I interviewed him where he was. He was certain his assailants were Jewish settlers.

'They broke my bones with the rifle butt, hitting me in the ribs as well as in the eye.' His voice was feeble. 'Then they broke my mobile phone so that I couldn't call for help. In what way did I annoy them? I was only tending my olives.'

The next day the Akrabeh farmers went out into their fields surrounded by other Palestinians from their village. For one of them, 24-year-old Hani ben Yemini, that act of courage proved fatal. He was shot in the back and killed. His mother, Shalah, told me that her last words to him were to be careful.

'I told him to look after his nineteen-year-old brother, who also went with him, and he said, "Don't worry, there will be hundreds of us; maybe the settlers will be afraid to attack when they see so many of us."'

The assailant had not been seen, but Hani's father, Mustafa, blamed the settlers. 'This year is worse than last year. Last year they harassed us and they killed our sheep, but we could still collect our olives. This year it is really dangerous, without the peace groups and the Israeli volunteers, we could not pick any olives at all.'

At the time, Israeli police said they were investigating that murder. However, the majority of these incidents remain unsolved. After I'd returned from Akrabeh, I called the police spokesman. He said that the police were involved in fighting a 'terror war', and his officers could not guarantee the safety of Palestinian citizens in the West Bank any more than they could guarantee the safety of Jewish citizens inside Israel.

Over the following months, the attacks in Yanun had become so bad that the villagers had taken a vote and decided to temporarily abandon their homes and seek refuge in safer villages. They had left behind only two old people who refused to accept the collective decision to go. This year, with the support of Western volunteers, the villagers had returned to Yanun. I decided to go back there to do a story on their first olive harvest.

In many ways, it was a reprise of my initial visit. A beautiful day, the sun warm, the air cool. A group of Palestinians, Israelis and Western volunteers marching through the olive groves. They put down the plastic sheets and commenced again to beat the olive trees, which released dust, along with their spicy scent, into the air. But it no longer had the innocence of Good Labour, or of Tolstoy's epic harvest scenes. I knew how quickly it could become dangerous, and was on edge the whole time.

I recorded my interviews and the lovely rhythmic sound of the olive trees being beaten. They succeeded in working for longer that day, putting in five productive hours. But then someone thought they saw young men on the ridges above. They called the IDF, who advised them to call it a day. And so they did, everyone trooping back out, carrying their olives in plastic sacks taken from Israeli building sites. The villagers were pleased because, relatively speaking, five hours was a good result, but it was extraordinary to me that the harvest had to stop and start when the Israeli military said so. Palestinian farmers now needed police protection to harvest their crops and even to walk onto their own fields, a further restriction in their increasingly constrained lives.

When the autumn finally cooled, my Russian neighbour Damira invited herself over for tea.

Damira lived simply, often without a job, a TV or even a phone. She barely had the money to feed herself, but was always looking after abandoned kittens, puppies and birds. She was full of Russian superstitions and folk wisdom. She showed a coin to the new moon so that she would have a prosperous month. Although she didn't own a house herself, she was studying feng shui. There was a large mansion between our two small apartments. It had had a succession of wealthy owners, who had each immediately begun noisy, expensive and, it seemed, endless renovations. A swimming pool was dug. Then it was filled in. Mosaic floors were laid. Then they were ripped up. But after all that, no one ever moved in.

'You see, a house can have bad luck and be abandoned, just like a person.' Damira paused. 'Over there, the front entrance is in the wrong place. It's to the side, so no positive energies can get in. It is here in your apartment too,' she said, pointing at my gate, 'but don't worry, I've checked and the good energies aren't blocked.'

Damira had said she had an announcement to make, and I was wondering if that was it when she put down her tea cup and said she was planning to leave Israel. 'I am moving to France,' she declared. She'd made the decision after a holiday in Paris, where she'd 'felt like a woman again'. I guess a religious town like Jerusalem is not much good for that. I hoped Paris would treat her well. She didn't have family there either, and it's hard to start over twice. I liked Damira; she was kind and had a calming presence, and I enjoyed hearing all her firmly held superstitions. I was sorry that she was leaving. She didn't say she was going to a lover, but I sensed that she might be and hoped she wouldn't have her heart broken. She gave up her job running room service at a hotel around the corner, sold her few possessions, and said her farewells. She left, a lonely figure, with one small suitcase. I think she was sadder to part from Mia than any of us.

Israel's Prime Minister Ariel Sharon was leaving the right-wing Likud party, twenty-five years after he had helped to found it. Following the withdrawal from Gaza, he had plans for further unilateral

231

withdrawals from territory in the West Bank, but the Likud party did not support him. Sharon decided that if he couldn't carry the party on this issue, he would simply found a new one.

I worked late on that political story and walked Mia, as I often did, following my midnight deadline. Yemin Moshe was dark, cold and a little eerie, many of its familiar buildings changed by the lonely night-time shadows. I was always reassured when I saw Mustafa the Palestinian carpenter, another night-time walker, with stubby, adoring Steve padding faithfully by his side. Mia might not be much of a guard dog, but Steve was an animal you could rely on to protect you. Tonight Mustafa was climbing the stairs with a new dog by his side.

'Hello there! Where's Steve?' I asked.

Mustafa looked down and said sadly, 'Steve is dead.'

'*Dead?!* How did he die?'

'Somebody put down poison and he ate it.'

He said no more but stood in front of me with his head bowed, a portrait of suffering. To help him get over the loss of Steve, a friend in the Old City had given him this new dog. She had Alsatian colouring and was taller and prettier than Steve was – not that that would be hard – but Mustafa had named her Taali, Arabic for 'Come Here!', so I could see she hadn't really touched his heart.

'So, we see how it goes,' Mustafa said.

Taali appeared to know she was on trial, the rebound relationship after the true love ended. She was slight and modest, almost meek. As soon as Mia spotted her, she attacked.

'No it is alright, let her,' Mustafa said serenely. 'It is because we are near her house. That is why Mia is protective.'

But Mia was so fierce and loud that eventually even a dog whisperer couldn't bear it any more. Mustafa separated the two females and we all walked up the stairs, Mia on a leash, looking wild and pleased with herself, Taali, without a leash or even a collar, climbing timidly by Mustafa's side.

The next late night when we saw Mustafa, a month had passed and he looked happier. So did Taali. She had filled out and appeared more confident, as if she wasn't on probation any longer. Walking with them was a huge Rottweiler, so large he was more like a calf than a dog.

'I am minding this big one for a friend. He doesn't know how to deal with him and so he asked me to help him. His name is Sambo,' Mustafa explained, 'but I call him … Steve.'

I tried not to smile. He'd really loved that animal.

Neither of his dogs was on a leash and Mustafa said he tended to walk late at night now because the huge Rottweiler frightened people. Looking at his vast dark head and firm jaws, I could understand why. He even frightened Mia, who backed away from him; it was the first time I'd seen her scared of another dog. Still, he had friendly eyes, so I decided to try to stay relaxed.

Although the new Steve had only been with Mustafa for a week, he already seemed obedient. He walked behind us, coming when he was called, leaving – reluctantly – when Mustafa told him to go off on his own. We sat on a bench in the park, the Old City of Jerusalem spread out beneath us. Lights twinkled in the distance beyond the walls, which were lit by pale orange floodlights. When I looked around to check on the animals, I saw that without being told to Mustafa's dogs were lying near our bench. They were not too close – they didn't want our attention – but not too far away either. They just wanted to be in Mustafa's orbit. Mia, afraid of the Rottweiler, stayed close to me.

Mustafa looked at the dogs and said, 'With the face of this one and the body of that one, it is almost like I have my old Steve back.'

It wasn't true; they looked nothing like Steve. But there was no point saying anything. Some dogs, like some people, get under your skin. A stranger walked by, a young man on his own late at night, and Mustafa's dogs suddenly swooped to sit close beside us, one on each side. I realised with awe that they were guarding us. The stranger walked on. Though he hadn't called the dogs to him, Mustafa now told them to go. They fanned out down the hill, and Mia finally felt safe enough to go sniffing too.

We sat in companionable silence, watching the dark shapes of the dogs against the grass. Finally Mustafa spoke, jolting me out of a reverie about why the computer had worked so slowly tonight and whether I needed to get a technician in to look at it, and all those 'de-processing' thoughts that crowd in at the end of a long day.

'You see, that one is running there, he is thinking it is good to have some freedom, I will run now. And Taali, she is running in the opposite direction, she is following her nose, she is relaxed. But your dog, she is still not sure about Steve, so she is thinking about staying closer to us.'

I looked at him. So this was what being a dog whisperer was. He was actually inside the dogs' heads. He knew what they were thinking!

Mustafa spoke softly to the Rottweiler and he padded up, a massive dark presence with a docile gaze. Mustafa clipped a leash to his collar and held him, liberating the females to play. Mia and Taali danced towards one another, throwing themselves down on their front paws, a friendly gesture, before they sprang up and chased each other around in circles.

'You see, that was what they wanted,' Mustafa said with satisfaction. 'I knew it.'

When they finished, Mustafa called Taali over. He removed Steve's leash and headed back to the Old City, his animals pacing obediently behind him. I was amazed by the whole experience but when I described it later at the dog park, some Israelis could hardly bear to listen. They were appalled that I would walk on my own at night with 'an Arab' without any form of protection.

'He's not an Arab; he's a person, whom I know. His name is Mustafa and I don't need any protection from him. If he'd wanted to, those dogs could have pinned me down a long time ago. In fact, *he's* my protection against dangerous strangers.'

That argument failed to convince them. After decades of conflict, people here were suspicious of each other, and these feelings were only becoming stronger. At the creation of the state of Israel in 1948, there had been much more contact between Arabs and Israelis than there was today. With each passing year, attitudes were hardening and relationships of all kinds – between employers, neighbours or friends – were becoming fewer.

Lovers were the rarest of all.

Raphael and I came across one of the last Arab–Israeli love stories at a Jerusalem cafe. Nocturno was a small, dark cafe in the centre of town, which Raphael had introduced me to. It had wicker furniture that didn't match, and service that was erratic, giving it a lazy, bohemian feel. You could drink coffee or alcohol, and we often took Mia, who had by now turned into an exemplary cafe dog. The waiters brought her water without being asked and she uncomplainingly settled beneath the table and fell asleep.

The maitre d' at Nocturno was a woman called Jasmine, a warm, pretty blonde with a thick ponytail and an infectious smile. She had an unusual quality, a mixture of authority and vulnerability, which made her a magnet at the bar. She was also a classically trained dancer who was doing this job while playing the lead in a real life version of *Romeo and Juliet*. Jasmine Avissar was a Jewish Israeli who had fallen in love with a Muslim Palestinian.

The man she loved, Osama Zatar, was a sculptor from Ramallah. He was tall with long dark hair, which he tied back, like a more gentle-looking Antonio Banderas. Jasmine called him Assi, and they'd met three years ago when they were both working at the Atarot dog pound, the same one where I'd gone with Meg and Craig to choose their dog, Chucho. In 2003 Jasmine and Assi were doing the night shift together. There, in those unpromising surroundings, trying to make a difference for abandoned animals, the beautiful dancer and the handsome sculptor fell in love.

It was an unusual story for many reasons. First, there were not that many places left where Israelis and Palestinians *could* meet. It is a crime for Israelis to enter the towns in what is designated Area A of the West Bank – the areas under full Palestinian control; and Palestinians are forbidden to enter any part of Israel without a permit. This separation has been reinforced by the wall Israel is building across the West Bank. After the Second Intifada began in the year 2000, Israeli employment policy changed and many Palestinians from the West Bank and Gaza who'd worked in Israel were no longer given permits. Too many suicide bombers had slipped in with them. The Atarot dog pound was an anomaly, a loophole, one of the few places where two people from opposite sides of the conflict could still work together legally.

For Jasmine and Assi, their troubles began once they fell in love. It wasn't their families, for unlike Shakespeare's warring clans, the Montagues and the Capulets, Jasmine and Assi's parents were not the obstacle. In this modern-day story of 'star cross'd lovers', the problem was the state. Neither side smiled on a love like this. Their troubles multiplied when they wanted to get married. Where could they marry? Which state? Which religion?

By early 2004 they'd found a Muslim sheikh in East Jerusalem who was prepared to marry them. But they still needed a place.

'We couldn't bring the sheikh to the dog pound,' Jasmine said.

They told their story to a taxi driver from East Jerusalem who sometimes brought strays to the pound. He'd arrived with a dog just when they were trying to figure out what to do. Touched by their plight, he offered them his home. He said he was doubly honoured when this sheikh turned out to be the one who'd conducted the weddings in his own family, officiating at both his and his brother's marriage ceremonies. That night Jasmine and Osama fed the animals, went to the taxi driver's home to be married and then returned to the pound. The next morning they told their bosses. There were no congratulations. Instead, they were both fired.

They didn't have salaries and suddenly they didn't have anywhere they could be together. Assi was not granted a permit to move to Israel. For a while Jasmine went to and from Ramallah, but the Israeli army would not give her permission to live there permanently. The couple hired lawyers to challenge these rulings. Jasmine's father wrote a letter to Israel's Interior Minister.

'In my whole life I never imagined that I would have to request an elementary right to life and love,' he wrote, 'for the sake of my daughter, Jasmine, who chose for herself a fine young man from Ramallah by the name of Osama, with whom she worked together at the Society for the Prevention of Cruelty to Animals. And now I am busy with cruelty to parents and cruelty to children.'

While this bureaucracy dragged on, the only place the two could legally meet was at the main checkpoint at Ramallah. A picture of the two of them hugging each other there was front page of an Israeli weekend magazine. They were an unusual couple in that dismal setting – handsome, well dressed, somehow golden, a husband and wife forced to see each other for snatched periods beside a five-metre-high concrete wall, piles of rubbish rotting at their feet.

That was when Jasmine began working at the Nocturno cafe. Raphael and I were there one winter's evening, drinking hot chocolate, Mia huddled at our feet, when a Chinese journalist was at the bar, gathering material for a story about the divided lovers. He interviewed Raphael, as a typical Israeli, to see what he thought of the couple's predicament. To my surprise, Raphael said he was sad that Jasmine hadn't married a Jewish man and stayed with her people.

He paused then added, 'But she will always be an angel.'

17

'The heart has its reasons which reason knows nothing of,' wrote French philosopher and mathematician Blaise Pascal in the 1600s, and it's still as true of dogs – and humans – as it was then.

Very unfairly, it always seemed to me, Mia loved Raphael the most. He was lazy about day-to-day dog care and didn't strain himself to buy her food or to take her for walks or to the vet. But she didn't mind about any of that, or that it was me who fed her, brushed her and pulled ticks out of her fur, always making sure to do the icky job of crushing them between my fingernails before throwing them away so that they wouldn't simply hop back on at another spot. It seemed the main lesson about loyalty Mia had absorbed was that it was Raphael who had saved her way back at the start, and she simply adored him.

But Raphael and I were starting to adore each other less. The end of the affair is hard to write about, almost as hard as it is to live through, watching love die slowly by inches. All the positive qualities that made it so easy for us to be with each other – humour, interest, goodwill and generosity, or some largeness of spirit – seemed to be diminishing and now we were more often impatient, angry and unwilling to make an effort. We both felt taken for granted and seemed to be sniping at each other rather than talking. An English friend says that relationships fail when people can no longer give each other the benefit of the doubt. I remembered that when, after one particularly grim, loveless exchange, Raphael and I agreed to separate.

Even though I knew it was for the best, once we were apart I missed him terribly. In that strange way 'that reason knows nothing of' I no longer remembered the Raphael with whom I had been getting on badly. Instead it was as if a camera operator had pulled focus while filming and crystal clear in the front of frame was the sweet person I loved, who loved me. The one I laughed with. He was the one I missed. Can you ever get that one back?

A week after we parted, Raphael called. He said he missed Mia and wanted to take her for a while. Oh, he missed *Mia.* Just when I thought things couldn't get any worse … I couldn't cope with a custody battle so I suggested that maybe we should take her in turns, like in a real divorce. Thankfully, he agreed that I could have the first go.

After I put down the phone I went to look for Mia and found her curled up in a neat ball in her favourite spot on her carpet near my bed. I smiled and knelt to pat her. One of the many things I hadn't thought through when we found her was that we could one day be fighting over her. She opened her eyes and then languidly arched her back, exposing her tummy so that I could scratch it. She closed her eyes again with a mixture of pleasure and drowsiness. As I rubbed her soft fur, I wondered if she would always tie me to Raphael.

My days felt empty. Breaking up with Raphael seemed to have changed the nature of time. It was now dense and weighty, like the heavy water physicists use in nuclear bombs. What were all those urgent things I always needed to do? I made a list and discovered they were still there, but seemed to demand more energy than I could muster. Instead, I went for coffee with Meg and Orla. We sat outside, under a brazier, at a restaurant Orla liked in the centre of town. She insisted that we order the hot chocolate cake, which arrived baked on the outside but still warm and runny in the centre. It was great to spend time in their loving company. They walked that fine line that girlfriends always have to, sympathising but not saying too much in case it wasn't really over and you got back together.

'At least I never told him how old I was!'

We all laughed.

'If you're no longer happy with someone, you don't have to stay with them. There's no point,' Orla encouraged me as we left. 'Just remember, it's important to stay busy.'

I knew that, but I didn't have the strength for any of my work, which was how I usually kept busy. It all seemed too serious or too sad. Then I remembered there was one story I'd been working on in fits and starts that I might be able to face tackling. Fortune-tellers. I went back to my files to look up the numbers.

For locals in the know, there's magic everywhere. I was surprised to find how much the women I interviewed look to the stars to explain their fates. Palestinian and Israeli women don't just go to fortune-tellers, they rely on them, and like a Roman emperor, each has her favourite soothsayer. Often it's a priest.

Jews and Muslims both believe that magic resides in the hands of holy men, and there are rabbis and imams who do a brisk side business in telling fortunes. The Samaritans also cash in. They are a tiny sect who broke off from Judaism long before the time of Jesus. In the New Testament, Jesus told the parable of the Good Samaritan, entrenching them as a byword for kindness and helping your neighbour. Today there are less than one thousand Samaritans left, making it possibly the smallest religion in the world. Like the gypsies in Europe, they are a group of outsiders who've become famous for their magical powers. Their tiny community is split in two, with one part in the Palestinian territories and the other in Israel. A few months ago, I had gone up to see the group living in the West Bank, near their main holy site, Mount Gerizim, just outside Nablus, where they celebrate Passover by killing sheep in a huge dawn sacrifice.

The first thing that had struck me was that their religious service was a fascinating fusion of Judaism and Islam. They call their house of worship a 'synagogue', though the one I was in looked more like

240

a mosque. It contained a large, empty carpeted room, where men knelt and touched their foreheads on the floor. Everyone who entered removed their shoes, and the priest and the worshippers wore long white robes, with red fezzes on their heads. The Samaritans share the Jews' holy book, the Torah, but believe only in the Five Books of Moses and dismiss anything written after that. They keep their Torah in an ark, taking it out and holding it up, every so often, just like in a Jewish service. The service lasted for over three hours that Saturday and was conducted in Aramaic, the language Jesus spoke. Afterwards, the priest, splendid in his vestments, told me he had an office in town where he told fortunes and I was welcome to come for an interview, but it would have to be in Arabic.

Later that week, I trooped back up to Nablus with my translator, Nuha, and an Australian journalist, Toni O'Loughlin, a close friend who was also writing about local mysticism. The office was on a nondescript street, a small drab shopfront opposite a garage. The priest was no longer in his robes. The grey suit he wore instead made him look like an insurance salesman. The mechanics across the street played their music loud and it floated into the office as the priest went through his files, preparing for the day ahead. Some clients wanted their futures told. Others needed him to recover stolen money. Most needed help with family problems: infertility, children who weren't getting married, a second wife appearing on the horizon. He said the most demanding part of his work was lifting curses.

'I'll put a spell on you!' is taken literally here. Curses – placing them and lifting them – are big business. Muslims believe that angels and djinns, good spirits and bad, lie in wait by the side of the road or under your house to help you or trip you up or take you over, so that your home and even your body is no longer your own. They don't do this of their own accord, though; the bad djinns are 'owned' by certain fortune-tellers and can be conjured up by them, on behalf of a business rival, say, or your wife if you are thinking of a second marriage.

The Samaritan priest said he saw curse-lifting as fighting the forces of darkness. His weapon of choice was an amulet in which he placed protective words from the Old Testament.

'The worst case I've ever seen was of a young child taken over by a djinn. She was talking to this djinn all the time, and lost touch with reality. I made a special amulet for her – a *hijab al Yussifi*, an amulet of Joseph – and she managed to get out of this disaster.'

He said he wouldn't himself curse someone, of course, no matter how much money he was offered. That would be going over to the dark side. When I asked if he told people the truth, even when he foresaw bad things in their future, he said that he did. He talked the talk, but there was something about him I didn't trust. Toni and I agreed that, even more than most people in this particular service industry, he seemed to be saying what he thought we wanted to hear. Or perhaps he was just too grey. You want your conman to have some charm.

After we returned from Nablus, Nuha rang in great excitement and said that her aunt's gardener's wife had been possessed by an evil spirit and he had agreed to talk to us.

The gardener, Abu Hikmet, lived in Bethany, a Palestinian village known from the New Testament. One of Jesus's disciples, Lazarus, lived there with his sisters. Jesus often visited and performed a famous miracle there, raising Lazarus from the dead. Palestinians call Bethany Al-Azarieh, from the Arabic for Lazarus, in tribute to this story. The village is five kilometres from the Mount of Olives and has for centuries been regarded as part of greater Jerusalem, but it is now cut off by the barrier Israel is building in the West Bank. When we discussed where to meet, Abu Hikmet offered to come over to us, on the Israeli side.

'It will save you time,' he said, and he was right. Simple journeys which had once taken ten minutes could now take hours, as you drove around the barrier or waited at checkpoints to cross it.

We drove past the eight-metre-high grey concrete wall up to the Al-Azarieh checkpoint. Someone had painted 'Control + Alt + Delete' in huge blue letters. I had to explain the joke to Nuha, who was not very technical. Protest graffiti had become a feature since the barrier – a wall in some parts and a fence in others – had begun snaking through more than seven hundred kilometres of the West Bank. Palestinians called it the Apartheid Wall, and said it was also a land grab, since more than ten per cent of the West Bank would end up on the Israeli side once it was completed. Israelis said the route was determined by security considerations.

When we arrived at the checkpoint gate, a thin man in his late forties was standing outside. Abu Hikmet had a pinched face with a small moustache and troubled brown eyes. Neatly dressed and plain speaking, he did not smile when we said hello, and often drew his eyebrows together in a worried frown. I decided to get down to business and do the interview right there. We perched on a couple of rocks at the end of an open-air car park, looking out over the stony fields on the Israeli side of the wall, and Abu Hikmet told us his sad tale. He spoke in Arabic and Nuha translated.

Six weeks earlier, he said, his wife started having headaches and soon found her limbs moving without her control. Then she began speaking in strange voices. I asked if he'd considered taking her to a doctor but he dismissed that out of hand.

'No, there's no point, she's not sick with a normal disease.'

He paused.

'We know it's a djinn because when she opens her mouth she sounds like a horse. The djinn can take over her body and her head for days at a time. She feels one in her breast, one in her abdomen, one in her leg.'

I said that he seemed to be implying she was aware of her condition.

'Of course she knows, because she starts screaming when she's not screaming; she starts crying when she's not crying; they scream and they cry.'

This was all the result of a curse, obviously, and Abu Hikmet said he could identify the family responsible, 'because we have no other enemies'. A boy from the village had fallen in love with his eldest daughter when he saw her walking to school. He had proposed marriage, but Abu Hikmet's wife had refused, first because their daughter was only seventeen, but also because this young man was not from a good family and was not the right match. So the boy's family had cursed Abu Hikmet's wife. He sighed.

He seemed such an ordinary Palestinian working man, apparently reliable, not flaky or hysterical, and yet he was so earnest about this. I asked if I could see his wife, but he said no, it wasn't suitable; she was too ill to see strangers. He wanted the curse lifted, and had made the long drive north to the Samaritan priest in Nablus, but, like me, he hadn't taken to him and he was going to see a Muslim imam next.

'The djinn disappears when we read to her from the Koran.'

As Abu Hikmet prepared to cross back to his village on the other side of the barrier, which had towered over our interview, on impulse I asked him which was worse, the wall or the djinns.

'The djinns,' he answered solemnly. 'They can travel anywhere and will not be stopped by any wall, no matter how high.'

After interviewing the Samaritan priest, I had begun looking for a secular fortune-teller as well, to complete the story, but I'd been distracted by breaking news and had put it on the back burner. Now, bruised myself, it was time to resume the search.

Across the Middle East, the medium the mediums like best is coffee. They prepare it, you drink it, then they tip out the grounds and read the patterns that are left behind in the dregs. In both Hebrew and Arabic it is called 'opening' the cup, and a Christian Arab woman named Margo was reputed to be the best coffee opener in Jerusalem. She had Israeli and Arab clients, and people travelled from overseas for her insights, amulets and potions.

It was a cool winter afternoon when I went to see her, the light fading early from the sky. At the last moment I'd decided to take Mia with me, I am not sure why, and as I tried to find the apartment in an old working-class neighbourhood in Jerusalem, it was a decision I began to regret. After a few wrong turns, tugging at each other we climbed up a dark, narrow stairwell.

I knocked on the door. Standing in the dark, holding my impatient dog, I wasn't sure what I was doing there, and had to fight a sudden urge to leave. The door opened and light spilled out onto us.

'Margo?' I asked, as a plump, careworn woman with shiny hair and sad eyes invited us to come in. My first impression was of intense ordinariness. No gypsy bangles and scarf, no crystal ball, just tracksuit bottoms, a white T-shirt and a constantly ringing mobile phone. They liked their magicians understated here. Margo led me into her small super-clean apartment.

'I do the floors every day; I can't go to bed if I haven't,' she said.

The washing machine was running and the air smelled of suds. Apparently cleanliness, like spirituality, was genetic. Margo had inherited both from her immaculate coffee-reading grandmother, though the 'second sight' had skipped her mother and all her sisters. Margo said she was currently teaching coffee reading to one of her neighbours, a Jewish woman who, she could see, also had the gift. I was mesmerised by what a great story those two women would make: Arab and Israeli reaching across the political divide to meet in the spirit world and share their secrets.

I sat down in Margo's spotless lounge room, holding Mia close. Margo's five-year-old son wanted to play with her but he was a little frightened. She soon had him under her spell. Margo said she didn't mind that I'd brought Mia, she liked dogs; but she did ask twice if she was clean.

While Margo smoked, she told me a little of her life story. She had grown up in the Old City of Jerusalem, where her mother still lived.

When she was twenty-one she had fallen in love with a Muslim and had married him over the opposition of her Christian family. Such marriages were rare, for even though both were Palestinian Arabs, neither religion accepted them. One party had to convert and lose their family, for they were almost inevitably ex-communicated. That was what had happened to Margo.

She had endured years of suffering since her marriage. After her family had cut her off, Margo had had to bring up her children more or less by herself.

'I didn't even know how to cook! I had to teach myself and try to remember my mother's recipes.'

It turned out that her true love was not a good father and not a good husband either, as she discovered when she caught him cheating on her. By the time Mia and I arrived on her doorstep, they were in the process of separating. 'Second sight' didn't protect you from making the wrong decisions in your own life, it seemed.

Later, when I told Rikki the Jewish beautician about this visit, she said that mediums always had difficult personal lives. It was the price they paid for their extra sensitivity about everyone else. Or perhaps it's just always easier to be wiser for someone else than yourself.

Margo went to her kitchen to brew up some sweet black coffee. She served it in a traditional Arab coffee cup made of engraved china, small and bell-shaped, with no handle. She brought it out with a plate of biscuits, which she had baked. It was very sociable. We both drank coffee and Margo emptied the dregs from my cup and looked at the pattern in the remaining powder drying there.

The first thing she said was, 'Oh no! Why did you wait so long to come?'

Not an auspicious beginning. I had actually tried to come three months ago, straight after I'd interviewed the Samaritan priest, but I'd been told that Margo was going through a hard time and that I shouldn't bother her right then. Obviously the cup said different.

Margo was concerned at the time I had taken because, as she announced dramatically, 'You have a curse!'

I felt relief coursing through me – So *that's* what it is! – and instantly comprehended why people come back to their fortune-tellers over and over. They wanted this simple explanation of their suffering. They hadn't done anything wrong; it wasn't life dealing them a bad hand; instead, a terrible external force was responsible. Not God, not Fate. *Someone* had put a curse on them and it could be lifted!

'*Aindek il ayin*. You have the eye,' she said, meaning the evil eye. 'People are jealous and so they have put a curse on you. This one is very bad and it goes back fourteen years. Who did you know fourteen years ago who would do this to you?'

I tried to remember where I was fourteen years ago. Even what city I was living in eluded me for a moment. When I figured out that I had been in London working at BBC-TV, I started laughing. Putting curses on people was not a British way to go on. It's true that TV Centre at White City was full of competitive types who hated each other, but finding a fortune-teller in W8 and forking over hard-earned cash to curse a rival seemed extreme, even by BBC standards. The fortune-teller was already working her magic. I hadn't laughed like that for days. When I tried to explain all this to Margo, she didn't understand what I was talking about.

'You are lucky you have come to me so that I can remove it,' she said severely. 'But in the future, you have to be more careful of people's jealousy.'

Margo spoke to me in a mixture of all the languages she knew – Arabic, English and Hebrew – and this somehow made the whole experience more enjoyable and mysterious.

'*Fhimti alay?* Do you understand me?' she asked in Arabic, and I found that amazingly I did understand; I understood everything, because she pitched it at just the right level.

Life, she explained earnestly, was a constant battle between the forces of good and evil. Fortune-tellers, those with the third eye and a link to the spirit world, were ranged in between, mediating. Sometimes the witchcraft Margo fought was so strong that she herself was laid low, and she had once been almost killed in the battle. But so far she had always triumphed. Margo knew how to curse people, of course, but she would never do that. Clients frequently asked her to, and even offered her large sums of money, but she always refused, although she was not wealthy, because she only used her power for good, not evil. I had never before heard someone say that sentence in all seriousness.

When I thought back, it wasn't so different to the Samaritan priest's spiel. I guess I liked Margo more, so I was prepared to believe her, though when the priest had said it, it sounded phoney. Margo promised that she would lift my curse. If it didn't work immediately, she warned, she might have to come to my house to check whether someone had done some witchcraft there. If they had, she would provide me with an amulet to hang in the doorway in order to fight it. But I wasn't to worry any more. All would be well.

Looking down at the coffee cup, she said she could see that a lover whose name began with R was unhappy and that a book I was writing would do well. Twirling the cup in her hand for the last time, she asked quizzically, 'And you were thinking of giving the dog away, weren't you?'

I looked at this plump, ordinary-seeming woman, whom people crossed continents to see. Surely I couldn't take any of this seriously, could I? When I'd gone to the Samaritan priest, I hadn't asked him to tell my fortune. It had been more of an interview. This was different. I'd come here vulnerable, without a translator, asking about myself as much as seeking information for a story. Perhaps her own hard life made me more open to Margo with her Caped Crusader fight against evil spirits, and her insight into my feelings about Mia and a boyfriend whose name started with R.

Most importantly, she put me in a much better mood. I paid and found myself agreeing to return for a curse-lifting ceremony. It transpired that this was how you entered into an ongoing relationship with your fortune-teller, or as we would call them in the West, your therapist.

It's hard to come home to an empty house. The particular hollow sound the key makes in the lock when you are returning to a dark, empty dwelling dampens your spirits, even if you are in a good mood. It can be devastating if you come home tired or feeling sorry for yourself. The clang of the door in a foreign city where you don't know many people is even more resounding. Another good reason to have a pet. No matter what kind of mood I was in, Mia was there to greet me, trotting briskly from the bedroom where she'd been sleeping or already at the door shimmying around on her back legs, front paws in the air.

She also helped me fight that other hazard of living alone: becoming self-centred and set in your ways. Sometimes an empty home can feel like an echo chamber, feeding all your negative thoughts back to you. But with Mia there, I was not really alone. In fact I was being minutely observed. She had become like a small canine professor whose specialty subject was me. She knew when I changed my shoes that I would leave the house, and would go to sit by the door. She knew when I sniffed her neck in a concerned way that a bath would likely follow, and would run away to hide under the bed. She knew when my mobile phone rang that I usually answered it, and if I didn't do it quickly enough, she looked from me to the phone and motioned her head towards it, as if to say, 'Hurry up and get that!'

Raphael had loved that so much he would stop me from answering a call so he could watch Mia 'telling' me to get it. Laughing with pleasure, he'd said we should train her to take messages as well. That memory made me sad for a moment, and I buried my face in Mia's fur, much like I used to do with Alfie, the Old English Sheepdog, when I was fourteen and felt that same wordless consolation.

'Pets fill in lots of gaps,' Meg said in her best Dr Dog voice, and she was right.

Dogs see us when we think we are alone – without makeup, stepping out of the shower, sleeping, sad, quiet, suddenly happy and dancing for no reason in the middle of the lounge room. They don't care if our hair's going grey, or if we're balding or getting fatter. Or how badly we dance. They see everything and like everything they see. They offer us the gift of acceptance, and that non-judgmental gaze creates great intimacy.

There is nothing insincere about dogs. They are all instinct, no inhibition and no pretence. They greet us trustingly, exposing their vulnerable tummies, paws in the air, to say hello. They thump their tails with happiness when we enter a room. They want our attention and then break off as we pat them to lick their private parts or to chase a fly buzzing nearby, snapping their teeth to catch it. They exist in the moment, in fact only in the moment, without planning or conniving or brooding on the past.

Like small children dogs wake up energetic and happy. But unlike children they don't answer back. Dogs will never grow up and tell you they hate you and that your taste in music is putrid and, by the way, so is your new boyfriend. They will never push you away and say, 'Not in front of other people, it's not cool!' and roll over to hide their mid-sections. And as a tough American friend jokes, unlike with your children, when your dog gets pregnant and you've had enough, you can sell the babies.

It's a tactile relationship. They lick your ankles and sometimes your toes. You brush their fur and scratch their ears. That's an experience dogs relish that only a human can provide them. It's odd, almost a design flaw, that dogs can't scratch each other's ears. Maybe it's a sign that we are meant for each other after all.

A British politician who has left politics and now writes about dogs – a far better use of his time – says the fact that they live such short lives is proof that God doesn't exist. For if there was a God, He'd have created dogs that lived for the same length of time as humans, and we wouldn't have to be parted early from our best friends.

On a cold winter night, Raphael came over to pick up the things he'd left behind. A guitar. A video recorder. Some clothes. We sat awkwardly on the sofa, side by side and far apart, like strangers at a bus stop, looking ahead at his forlorn pile of possessions. Actually, we were worse than strangers, an uncomfortable silence spreading between us. I stole a glance at his beautiful face, so familiar and dear to me, and wondered – once more with feeling – where love goes.

All these nuances were lost on Mia. She'd been as happy as it was possible for an animal to be from the moment Raphael walked in, jumping all over him and rolling onto her back in one fluid movement, paws over her eyes, inviting him to scratch her tummy. But she couldn't actually lie still long enough to allow him to do that, jumping back up and repeating the whole motion all over again, like an acrobat. Then she raced in circles round the room.

Like most children of divorced parents, it was clear where her hopes lay. To make sure we understood the full extent of her emotion, Mia did something she'd never done before. Seeing us on the sofa in that constrained, uncomfortable silence, she hopped up into the gap between us, wriggling round to face the same direction we were looking. Now there were three of us sitting looking ahead. But Mia had changed the atmosphere. She sat turning her head from one of us to the other, grinning her happy foxy grin. I almost expected her to put a paw up on each of our shoulders and say, 'See, kids, isn't this better?'

We looked at each other and laughed. The ice was broken. Our hands met on her fur. Mia stayed there between us, a bundle of canine joy, while we talked. Then we pushed her off and held each other close, Raphael tucking my hair behind my ears as he smiled at me. 'I missed you so much,' we both said at once. We promised to be kinder to each other, and to give it another chance.

In December Israel's Prime Minister, Ariel Sharon, had a brain haemorrhage and collapsed into a coma, from which he didn't wake.

As I reported on it, I recalled the voodoo ceremony to end his life, which had been held only six months back. Sharon wasn't dead but he might as well have been. He was in what doctors called a 'permanent vegetative state', suspended between life and death and hooked up to machines that performed all his vital functions, including breathing. I wondered what the participants in that Pulsa Denura ceremony were thinking. I didn't have to wait long to find out. From then on, many in the religious right claimed openly that Sharon's condition was his punishment for withdrawing from Gaza and seeking to divide the Land of Israel.

Once again Mia provided perspective. None of that bad news concerned her. She was turning one and experiencing her first Jerusalem winter. The air was sharp and cold. She grew a downy undercoat and fluffed up, to help protect her against the elements, which this year included snow. It fell on the tropical plants, and the palm fronds and bougainvillea appeared indignant in their white coats. Israelis came from the rest of the country where it didn't snow to build snowmen and to throw snowballs, and to marvel at this strange visitation from another continent.

The dusting of white rarely lasted for long, but before this snowfall had melted, Mia found a new friend. Yogi was the real deal: a pure Canaanite dog, undiluted by any other breed, auburn-coloured, sharp-faced, slender and muscly. They were evenly matched, and fell for each other from the first moment. Hours of impassioned running and chasing followed. They tore around each other and the trees, first in circles then ovals and parabolas, one excited pattern after another. Then they changed direction. You got a workout just watching as they slid by on the snow, and strangers stopped, spellbound.

'It makes you happy to be alive just seeing them,' cried a plump, bejewelled American tourist, whose running days were behind her.

Yogi's owner was Micah, a tall, slow-talking Israeli, who looked like an Easter Island statue. He worked as a bodyguard for the American ambassador and spoke English with an accent I'd never heard before except in 1950s Hollywood movies.

He laughed when I asked, 'Would you take a bullet for the ambassador?'

There was steel deep down in that laugh, so I guess the answer was yes. Sounding like he'd stepped out of *On the Waterfront*, he told me the story of how he found Yogi. Three years earlier Micah had been walking in this park when he'd heard an animal crying. He'd followed the sound until he saw a puppy, about six months old, lying beneath some bushes with a badly broken leg. Micah crawled in, lifted the small injured animal onto his jacket and carried it to the vet. When he walked in, clutching his miserable bundle, the vet said, 'I know that dog!'

Earlier in the week another family had brought the same dog to the same clinic. It had been injured in a car accident. When the vet quoted them the price of the series of operations necessary to save Yogi's life, the family said they wanted a second opinion. They took Yogi home and called the vet back to say they'd found a cheaper option. Then they'd dumped him in the bushes to die a lonely, painful death. Now almost a week after he'd been injured, Yogi was back in the same surgery being given a second chance.

Yogi's good fortune was that it was Micah who found him and was prepared to bear the cost and time involved in nursing him back to health. But Micah believed that the luck was his, because he got to keep Yogi, who was a great dog. Micah was right, Yogi was a fantastic dog, but I think they were both lucky – and that was the marvel of opening your heart to a dog.

I loved this tale because fate had stepped in to save the dog, and also to deposit him back at the same vet, so that Micah would know the story. It had been revealed. They were meant for each other. Like meeting someone in the same cafe twice.

Maybe I was just happy to be back with Raphael.

'It's good to see the roses in your cheeks,' Orla remarked, the next time she saw me, adding that three weeks apart didn't count as a real break-up.

Our suburb was becoming dangerous. A man, often armed with a stick, was touching women up in public. It had begun as a few unpleasant incidents occurring here and there, but was rapidly evolving into something darker and more violent. He was now breaking into the homes of single women and assaulting them. We didn't know if it was the same man or if there were two crazies out there, but we did know the attacks were escalating. The latest victim, from a street near mine, was left naked on the floor of her house, covered in blood. The tempo was also increasing, so that for a period of two weeks there was an attack every other day. The tension of waiting to become the next victim affected every woman living in the area.

My neighbours instructed me not to walk my dog 'at night'. It was pitch dark by 5.00pm at that time of year, so that didn't leave much time to take Mia out. In the end I compromised, going out with her – and even walking from the car to the house – while I was on the phone to Raphael, just in case.

It was frightening to live through a crime wave and also strange because, while I had been exposed to a lot of violence living here, it had all been related to the conflict. This was different. It could have been a man stalking women in Jakarta or Johannesburg – it just happened to be Jerusalem. It was not political, it was criminal and it was personal. The police were involved and had organised residents to patrol the neighbourhood in the evenings, but if this man was not caught soon I was afraid that he would rape and possibly even kill someone. My fears turned out to be well founded.

On Valentine's Day, he broke into the house of Sarah the English doctor. She was talking on the phone to her friend Aviva that evening when she heard an unexpected noise. Sarah interrupted Aviva and said, 'Wait, it sounds like there's someone in here.'

At that moment the attacker grabbed the phone from her hand and pulled the cable out of the wall. Sarah found herself staring up at a strong man in his twenties, wearing a brown leather jacket, jeans and a blue T-shirt. He had not covered his face. He told her his name was Walid and then he pulled out a knife and forced her into her bedroom. Sarah was aware that her nine-year-old son was asleep in the next room, so she struggled but didn't scream. The attacker punched her in the face. Then he raped her.

When the phone line had gone dead, Sarah's friend Aviva had frozen in terror before racing to organise help. She called people she knew who lived in our suburb. Ten minutes later a neighbour ran to Sarah's house and called out from downstairs, 'Sarah, are you alright?'

Despite the knife at her throat, she shouted back, 'No. I'm not alright!'

The man on top of her punched her in the face again. Sarah thought he was probably also angry because he couldn't maintain his erection, which the police later told us was a common feature with serial rapists. Only when the rapist heard the front gate being opened and footsteps on the stairs did he finally run, springing down to the street from the second floor.

'Don't worry about me, go catch him,' Sarah shouted with characteristic cool down the stairs. 'He's jumped off the balcony!'

The neighbour chased the rapist but failed to catch him. In the meantime, Sarah called the police. They came and removed all the forensic evidence. In addition to bodily fluids the man left his knife and a shoe behind. Calm, despite her battered face and two black eyes, Sarah gave police a precise and detailed description of her attacker.

She credited the Dalai Lama with saving her life.

'I was talking to Aviva because the Dalai Lama said he would come to our centre on his next visit to Israel. And if I hadn't been on the phone, who knows what that creep would have done to me ...'

I took Mia over to visit Sarah. There are times when a touch says more than words, and others when there's no substitute for burying your face in a friendly animal's fur. Sarah sat holding Mia close for a long time.

'She is such a lovely dog,' she said, bright-eyed. It was the most emotional I would see her during the entire episode.

Sarah suspected that her attacker was likely to be from the Old City, though she could never explain why. She had worked there for many years as a children's doctor, and believed that she would recognise him if she saw him. She wanted to go and look for him and asked me to accompany her. I was apprehensive – what would we do if we found him? – but finally agreed on condition that if she did see someone she recognised, we wouldn't have to catch him ourselves. I didn't think that outcome was actually likely, but my hope was that the search would do Sarah good in some way.

I took Mia home and Sarah and I set off, marching briskly, both of us tense. The CBC news desk called at that moment and I said I wasn't in the office and wouldn't be back for another two hours. I must have sounded sharp because they didn't ask any more questions and just told me to call when I could.

It proved a very strange experience to walk through the crowded alleyways of the Old City, ignoring the scents of incense and perfume and rank meat, and the eye-catching fabrics and glowing gemstones, to look for a young man wearing a tan leather jacket whom I had never seen before. I spent most of my time watching Sarah.

She was well known there due to her work as a doctor and also because it was where she did most of her shopping. That made it more surreal, for while we walked and scoped out young Arab men, older Arab men who knew Sarah almost jumped out of their skin when they saw her bruised face. They ran out to ask what had happened. Standing first by a sweet stall, then a pizzeria and finally a shoe shop, she described being raped to one concerned Palestinian man after another and asked them to keep an eye out, and to let her know if they saw or heard anything.

I saw the shock in their eyes and couldn't keep the admiration out of my own. I couldn't imagine many Palestinian women being so frank after a sexual assault. Sarah put the shame right back where it belonged, on the perpetrator. She was not the one besmirched by this, and as I stood watching her I felt that was perhaps the most remarkable thing of the past twenty-four hours.

We didn't find him that afternoon, but it turned out that we didn't need to. In a way Sarah had already caught him. The description she had given to the police was so precise they'd made a sketch that was almost like a photograph. When they fed it into their computer, it spat out the attacker's details. His name was not Walid, but he was a 23-year-old unemployed Palestinian from the village of Ras Al-Amoud, in East Jerusalem. He was currently on house arrest for a series of burglaries he'd committed twelve months ago – here in Yemin Moshe. The police raced over to arrest him. He confessed straight away.

In such circumstances, Israeli police procedure is to take the suspect back to the crime scene and to film him re-enacting the crime and repeating his confession on camera. That's why, thirty-six hours after the assault, the police rang Sarah and asked her to leave her house so that they could bring the rapist back there. It felt like a double violation to me but they explained that they couldn't risk Sarah seeing him before they'd held an ID parade. A meeting at that stage would render any identification she made in a line-up worthless.

Sarah and her son, Uri, left their house. The attacker showed the police on camera where he'd climbed in and how he'd jumped out. He'd also confessed to attacks on other women in the area and was so talkative he told police about crimes they hadn't connected him to yet. When they took him for a walk around Yemin Moshe so that he could point out the places where he'd carried out his attacks, he stopped at my front gate. He said he'd been trying to break in here too, but had been surprised by someone walking up the path and had run off.

The next day two cops came by to tell me the news, and to examine the gate for any signs of an attempted break-in. Mia jumped up on them and I had to hold her back while they checked the gate. They showed me scratched markings on the lock, which gave me a nasty cold feeling. When I was at home, my front door was usually open, so he would only have had a chance to work on the gate when we were asleep or when I wasn't there and Mia was most likely inside. I wondered what she would have done if he'd made it in. Probably welcomed him. I couldn't imagine that someone who was prepared to beat and rape women would hesitate to throttle an animal. If he hadn't been interrupted, I could have come home to find Mia dead and him there waiting for me.

After the police left, I held Mia close, laying my cheek against her soft ears. 'You don't know what we've escaped from, my sweet dog.'

My time with the police was over, but Sarah's was just beginning. Her next ordeal was the ID parade. Brought up on American TV cop shows, I expected two-way mirrors and anonymity. But no; here in the Land of the Long Revenge a victim had to walk along the line of men, stand in front of her attacker and put her hand on his shoulder. A police photographer went 'snap' and captured the moment for posterity, and only then could the victim remove her hand.

I couldn't believe it. Sarah was more sanguine. She said she picked out her attacker the moment she saw him, but walked along the line

258

twice to be sure, and then coolly put her hand on his shoulder. What a woman.

I asked her afterwards how she was able to describe him in such minute detail, since I was certain I would struggle to provide a useful description. She said it was easy, and reminded me that she was the daughter of a cartoonist. For more than sixty years, her father, Ralph Sallon, had drawn some of the most eminent people in the world, brilliant depictions, full of character and depth. As a result, she said, 'I'm good with faces.'

Sarah confessed that when she saw her attacker again in the line-up she'd become aware of two things. The first was that he looked stronger than she remembered. 'So it's just as well that I didn't try to resist him. I didn't do anything because Uri was sleeping in the next room, but it may actually have saved my life.'

The other thing was that when she'd described him to the police illustrator, she hadn't done such a good job.

'I didn't get his ears right.'

I stared at her in disbelief.

I reminded her that this man had attacked nine women before her and none of them had identified him or enabled police to capture him and that she had ended his reign of terror. But she wasn't listening. Eccentric heroine that she was, Sarah was still grumbling about the ears. She really was Ralph Sallon's daughter.

18

For lo, the winter is past, the rain is over and gone; the flowers
appear on the earth; the time of the singing of birds is come,
and the voice of the turtledove is heard ... Arise my love,
my fair one, and come away!

Song of Solomon

Spring was here. The almond trees blossomed, glowing pink and white. Wildflowers carpeted the deserts and forests, and your heart sang at the sight, all the more precious for being short-lived. In a matter of weeks, these flowers withered away, burnt by the sun which beat down fiercely once more.

The weather was changeable. Cold, blustery mornings when blossoms were blown off trees were followed by hot, dusty afternoons when the air felt thick with sand.

'It's dusty fog!' Raphael explained, using a purpose-built word in Hebrew that we don't have in English. The dusty fog was mostly sand that had been blown all the way from the deserts of Saudi Arabia. That seemed very romantic to me, and I didn't mind the strange hot haze, as I was grateful simply to be able to walk outside once more without fear of being attacked.

Dusty fog usually heralds the arrival of Easter, a pagan spring festival which had been absorbed and refashioned by Christianity. In Jerusalem, it meant Good Friday in the Old City. Tens of thousands of Christian pilgrims from all over the world came to walk in Christ's footsteps along the Via Dolorosa, the Way of Sorrows, where He had carried His Cross. The pilgrimage ended at the Church of the Holy Sepulchre, where I'd gone on my first cold, lonely Christmas, when the Intifada had kept most visitors away. They were back now in force, and this year would be even more crowded than usual, for all the Christian denominations were coming at once.

Easter usually fell on a different date for the Orthodox churches, but on the rare years when the dates coincided, everyone crowded into the narrow Old City lanes together – Copts, Greek Orthodox, Russian Orthodox, Assyrians, Maronites and Ethiopian Orthodox, along with Catholics, Presbyterians, Methodists, Lutherans, Anglicans, Evangelicals – and that was just for starters. In addition there were Muslims going to Friday prayers, plus Jewish worshippers preparing for their Sabbath and Passover.

The pilgrims, like the girl guides, came prepared, but the one vital piece of gear they couldn't cart through Israeli customs was a cross. They could make it through with a gold crucifix round their neck, of course, but if they wanted to carry a proper wooden cross, the size of a man, for their walk along the Via Dolorosa, they had to hire it. In the Old City of Jerusalem, the supplier of this key commodity was a Palestinian Muslim.

'Yes, I'm the one who brings the crosses to the pilgrims,' Arafat Aboutin told me when I called.

We agreed to meet so that I could record a first interview before Good Friday. He suggested a cafe I didn't recognise and then gave me the following directions: 'Via Dolorosa, Fifth Station of the Cross.' That made me laugh out loud. It also made me aware I'd been in Jerusalem a long time, because I knew where to go.

The cafe was pleasantly smoky and noisy. Men were playing cards and backgammon and smoking water pipes, small cups of aromatic black coffee at their elbows. The most popular tobacco for the water pipes was *tufahteen* – two apples – and its sweet scent filled the room. Arafat Aboutin arrived late. He was a tall, clean-shaven, bad-tempered man in his thirties. Years of exposure to pilgrims had failed to fill him with goodwill to all men. He sat down and explained his business model. He didn't charge for the crosses, but for photos he took of the pilgrims carrying them. He wasn't sure he was in the right job, but it was a family business so he kept it going.

'About eighty years ago my grandfather worked with an Armenian guide who taught him the business. He took black-and-white photos and developed them himself.'

Aboutin had a warehouse not far from the cafe where he stored his collection of forty crosses of various heights and weights.

'Some people ask for the heavy crosses, the young mans. But the old mans, no. And sometimes four or five people will carry it together and switch.'

I asked if he liked the pilgrims, and he said yes, but I could see he didn't mean it. I asked again. The pilgrims were alright generally, but too many forgot to return the crosses at the end of the procession, he said darkly. I left, amused by that Chaucerian image of thieving pilgrims, who took the crosses and ran.

On the morning of Good Friday, I walked from my house to the Old City. The crush began outside the walls, where thousands of pilgrims had gathered to walk the fourteen Stations of the Cross, from the Lions' Gate to the Church of the Holy Sepulchre. It was a truly international festival and people of all colours, nationalities and accents spoke into my microphone, as we slowly inched forward down the crowded lanes. I interviewed pilgrims from Africa and Australia, Poland and Patagonia, each radiating joy and a deep sense of purpose. They said that walking in Christ's footsteps on the day He won salvation for all men was the dream of a lifetime. The sun was shining, the air smelled of baking bread and incense, and everyone was smiling. Spring is the right time for a festival of renewal.

Despite Aboutin's grumpiness, his family business was testament to how entwined the main religions are here. A Christian pilgrim could have a Jewish tour guide and hire his cross from a Muslim. When I asked the pilgrims about this, they seemed to like these small shoots of religious co-existence.

'How can you explain that, except that God works in mysterious ways?' a Nigerian pilgrim responded. He was a huge man with a deep bass laugh, a delicious rolling sound which lasted longer than the answer he'd given.

As she lifted her cross, a Czech pilgrim agreed. 'This city is a funny city and that shows you how wonderful God is. You cannot really understand what's happening in Jerusalem … all you understand is that God is love.'

Buoyed by their spirit, I went along my way. Well, crawled along my way. Hundreds of Israeli police had been deployed to control the crowd, adding to the crush. At the corner of the Via Dolorosa, just after the Fourth Station, where a sorrowful Mary saw her bleeding and battered Son, it became so crowded that police stopped the procession. We were at a standstill, squashed behind barriers. The pilgrims sang psalms in various languages, Arabic mingling with Chinese, Swahili with Latin. Most were patient, but I recorded some of them fighting with police. After half an hour, we inched slowly forward, all still pressed together. Then, at a spot where two lanes met, police halted us again.

'Stop! Stop them!' one cop shouted across the lane to the others standing near me. 'I have Muslims here. They have to cross!'

A Jewish policeman forced a space and ushered the Muslim worshippers across the Christian crowd so they could go to the Al-Aqsa Mosque for their Friday prayers. Only in Jerusalem …

After that, the throng moved slowly forward again. One group stood out. They were dressed in historic costumes and were re-enacting the passion of Christ. Though this was accepted in countries like the Philippines, it was controversial here and local Christians did not endorse it. I hung back till they caught up with me. A pilgrim dressed as one of Jesus's followers told me they were Catholic charismatics from California.

'We are from the Christ in You the Hope of Glory International Ministry. For the first time this year we've joined forces with a group of Protestants from South Korea,' she said.

They'd brought their own blood and crown of thorns, but their cross came from Arafat Aboutin. Their Jesus was Korean. He walked bare-chested, his body smeared with fake blood, dragging the cross. He'd been working out at the gym in preparation for the role. The Roman centurions, wearing purple skirts, gold breastplates, and helmets with tall red plumes, were from California. Bob Paton was the chief centurion. A tall, sandy-haired man in his fifties, he said he'd come for the past three years.

'Yep, every year, because Jesus Christ gave His life on Calvary so we could enjoy eternal life.'

It was also his third year as a centurion, and I couldn't help asking if he ever yearned to play Jesus rather than a Roman. His answer was very practical.

'No. At my age it would be pretty tiring to carry that thing,' he replied, gesturing at the wooden cross, before rushing back to join the walk to Calvary.

The pilgrims were shouting, 'Jesus – help Him, Veronica!' and then just calling out imploringly, 'Jesus! JESUS!!' while Bob the centurion told them meanly to move on.

They didn't have permission to enter the Church of the Holy Sepulchre to perform their crucifixion, so they enacted it in a lane nearby instead. The centurions tied Jesus to the Cross and raised him. It was startling to see a cross with a human being covered in blood here at this spot. Although up to this point their play-acting had often seemed closer to farce, that moment had real power. I stood in contemplation before this image of endurance and suffering then asked Bob to point out their leader.

'It's Momma Joanne. She's down at the pizza place; she's wearing a blond wig and she's in charge of this group.'

Joanne Petronella – or, as everyone called her, Momma Joanne – was also from California. She was sitting in a wheelchair and was indeed wearing a blond wig, a huge teased white-blond number, Dolly Parton style. We were back to farce.

'I'm just a woman who loves the Lord and has been called on by God for a ministry of teaching the Word and healing, and wherever we go we take medicines, Bibles and toys.'

When I asked about whether this re-enactment was controversial with the local churches, she proved she could also be tough.

'Well, if it is, they've never said anything to us, and if they did, to each his own.'

Momma Joanne had injured her hip, so she couldn't walk the route this year, but said she'd be back next year, after surgery.

'I'll be marching and you know it!'

Off to one side, Bob the centurion was washing the blood off his hands. He couldn't get over the crowds, which he described as 'heart crushing' and much worse than in previous years. But he agreed it was a good experience.

'It's always a good experience, especially when it's over,' Bob said sourly. He was about as cheerful as Arafat Aboutin, the cross Cross Guy.

I came home exhausted but had to finish my story quickly because Meg was having an Easter party. She'd asked if she could leave her dog Chucho at my place for the evening. She thought he wouldn't be able to cope with all the people and would bark himself into a frenzy and upset everyone.

I was a bit flustered, since I'd tried minding Chucho when Meg and Craig went on holiday not long after we brought him home from the pound. They were only away for five days, but it was a scarring experience because Chucho barely ate and refused to let me attach a leash to him or take him outside. He looked so devastated each time I arrived home that I began to dread entering the apartment. They say dogs have no sense of time – if you're gone for a day it's the same as if you're gone for a month – but I swear Chucho was counting the hours. On the third day, when he heard my key in the lock, he looked up expectantly, saw that it was me, put his head in his paws and howled. It was a wail of utter anguish and I stood frozen to the spot. It was very hard to steel myself to return home after that.

Even now, eighteen months on, he had still never let me pat him, so I wasn't sure how it would work out. Meg said confidently it would be fine. She brought him down that afternoon and left quickly. Craig was making margaritas and it was her job to squeeze limes. As soon as the door closed and Chucho understood he'd been left behind, he became very agitated. Even Mia couldn't distract him. He paced nervously from room to room, like a caged lion. I decided it might be best to ignore him for a while and went back to what I needed to do, which was to find my favourite pink party frock. Once I was dressed, I checked on Chucho, saw he was still pacing and went to apply my makeup.

After about two minutes, the house suddenly felt quiet, too quiet. I came out holding my mascara, brush in one hand, container in the other, to see the gate and the front door open and both dogs gone. For a moment I couldn't take in the evidence of my own eyes.

I always lock that gate. How did the dogs manage to unlock it?

Then my brain caught up with reality and I realised that I must not have locked the gate, and that someone else had been inside. The house was long and narrow, one room leading to the other, so I could see at a glance that no one was still here, but I couldn't believe that a thief had gotten into a house with *two* dogs, and that neither of them had made the slightest sound, including Barkmeister Chucho.

I was so worried about losing Chucho that I didn't even check to see if anything had been stolen. I ran straight outside. Mia was there, close by. Phew. That meant the intruder had just left or Mia would have scarpered by now. Chucho was nowhere to be seen. I knew that even if I found him, he wouldn't let me catch him, so I had no option but to call Meg and tell her the bad news.

She said calmly that she'd be right over. I grabbed two leashes, put on running shoes and headed out the door. I met Meg in the park, the only other woman wearing a party frock and running shoes – *snap!* – and we soon found Chucho, contentedly sniffing spring flowers. He was happy to see Meg and, to my relief, easy to lead back home. It was only when we were all safely inside that I noticed that the thief had made off with my wallet and my laptop. *MY LAPTOP.*

Lost credit cards, driver's licence and cash were an irritation, but my computer was my life. Everything I had was on that laptop, including my personal archive, my stories and my editing programs. To make matters worse, I hadn't done a back-up in months. It was a blow straight to the solar plexus.

I left the dogs and went up to Meg's to cancel my credit cards and to drink too many margaritas. When I called Raphael, he said I was welcome at his place in Tel Aviv, but I couldn't move. Craig went down to my apartment and brought both dogs back up so that we could all sleep over at their place.

'We'll make you breakfast,' Meg said consolingly.

The next morning I called the Israeli police but they said the chances of catching the thief were almost nil. They would send out a fingerprint guy if I insisted, but I shouldn't hold out any hopes. I felt battered. A week later I was sitting at the dog park, recounting my experience to the other owners while our dogs romped happily nearby. I'd just reached the part where the thief came in and neither dog made a sound, even bark-a-minute Chucho, when my mobile phone rang.

'Hello, is that Irris Makler?' asked a voice I didn't recognise. 'I have your laptop. Want to buy it back from me?'

Blow number two to the solar plexus.

The man on the line called himself Mohammed. He said he lived in Ramallah and insisted he wasn't the thief, but said he'd bought my laptop from the thief at a cheap price. Nevertheless he wanted to charge me $2000 to buy it back, which was more than the cost of a new laptop.

He said creepily that he knew all about me, since he'd been reading everything on my computer. By the end of the call, I wasn't sure if he was a thief or a stalker. I snapped into journalist mode and set up to record our next conversation, then contacted the police in both Ramallah and Jerusalem so that the calls could be traced. Mia helped by barking each time he rang. *Too late now, Mia. Where were you when we needed you?*

The conversations were friendly, way too friendly, even cloying, and they made me uncomfortable. But I kept going and passed on Mohammed's details, including his phone numbers and email address – the disturbing iloveyou4ever@fortygigs.com – to police in both cities. They said to keep him talking and that they would see what they could do. In the meantime, I had to decide if I should pay up. Raphael said no, it was way too dangerous and had the potential to go wrong.

'A week ago you thought your laptop was gone and you'd begun to accept it. You should continue with that process and pretend this never happened. It's a dream and not a good one,' he said.

Common sense told me that Raphael was right. What if things went wrong and instead of an exchange, Mohammed made off with my money as well as my laptop? But his offer was like seeing a loved one come back from the dead. I wanted my old laptop back, and here it was, being dangled in front of me. After it had been stolen, I'd checked my back-up and found that the disk had become corrupted.

Who knew that could happen? In future I will back up everything twice, I promise, but right now this meant I had very little of my material. I was so torn that I called the Israeli police again. They encouraged me to set up a meeting.

'Make it tomorrow night. We'll catch him in the act!'

'I'll meet you at nine o'clock tonight. No, let's make it ten, on the main street outside the Shuafat refugee camp,' Mohammed offered. 'I can't wait to see you in real life.'

I didn't want to meet him on the street, especially so late at night, so I suggested a safer location up the road.

'How about tomorrow night at the Hyatt Hotel?'

But Mohammed was getting nervous.

'Why not today? Why are you taking so long? Maybe it is too late. My brother is a policeman and he says it is dangerous for me to hold on to stolen property.'

That made me catch my breath. 'Yes, I know it's stolen, because it's been stolen from me, you may recall, Mohammed.'

'Don't be angry with me, I thought we were friends,' he whined.

We agreed on nine o'clock the next night, a time that suited the Israeli police and the reluctant Mohammed. After I put the phone down, I remembered that it didn't suit me quite as well because the BBC was recording its annual Reith Lecture in Jerusalem that night. Every year since 1948, a leading figure has lectured on contemporary issues in a series broadcast on BBC-Radio and TV. This year's lecturer was the internationally renowned pianist and conductor Daniel Barenboim. A thoughtful, brilliant, charming musical genius, he was also a vocal Jewish supporter of the Palestinians. Tickets were hard to come by but my Australian friend Toni O'Loughlin had wangled one for me. I was having doubts about going, but she dismissed them.

'Don't let that laptop overshadow everything else in your life. The lecture will finish by 8.00, and that will leave you an hour to get to your rendezvous with the thief and the police at 9.00,' Toni said in a practical voice.

Seeing how nervous I was, she suggested that her Israeli translator, who also spoke Arabic, should come with me to do the swap. I gave Mohammed's contact numbers to the translator before trooping into the lecture hall. It was a sparkling affair. An invited audience of the great and the good of East and West Jerusalem had come to hear Barenboim. But I became increasingly nervous when the lecture didn't start on time, because we couldn't just enter and leave as we pleased. The BBC locked us in so the recording wouldn't be disrupted.

Coordinating where and when I would meet the Israeli police was also proving difficult. They kept asking me to call them back, and I had to creep out of my seat and stand behind heavy red curtains at the back of the hall to talk to them. The contrast was absurd, the grand speech, the polite laughter and clapping, and me whispering behind a dusty curtain about a stolen laptop. I called the translator. He said not to worry; in his opinion it would work more smoothly without me there. I felt a surge of relief. I didn't want to be involved in this high-anxiety cops-and-robbers routine. After my third call to the police, I realised that they were simply not going to turn up, although they had told me to set up this meeting, and specified the day and time that suited them

In the end, no one showed. Neither Mohammed nor the Israeli police made an appearance. The translator said he'd gone out to have a look, but by now I didn't know if I should believe him either. This was one of those instances that brought home to me how much I was an outsider and didn't understand the rules here. I couldn't decide who I was angriest with – the cops, the thief or myself for being taken in by them. I did contact Mohammed one more time, to see why he hadn't come. He said it had all been taking too long, so he'd sold my laptop to someone else.

'They've probably already wiped your hard disk,' he added offhandedly.

I slammed the phone down. On top of being angry, I felt foolish. If I had simply said no when Mohammed had called me, I would have saved myself all this stress. At one stage, I had actually laid my hands on the money for him, though I hadn't told Raphael about that. When I told him now, he didn't say I told you so but, in his positive way, said it was all for the best.

'He probably did want a second go and was planning to steal your money as well as your laptop. This way, nothing bad happened to you. You should just say thank you for that and put this episode behind you. And don't keep brooding on it.'

That was easier said than done. I took Mia on a route march around the Yemin Moshe parks, on a short leash at double pace. It failed to calm me down. If I'd had that thief in front of me, I honestly think I'd have killed him. When I went to bed that night, my sleep was fitful and filled with strange dreams. Mia donned her Superdog costume, a red cape and a blue vest with 'S' on the front, and flew to Ramallah. Like George Reeves in the 1950s TV series of *Superman* she had her front paws out, but otherwise seemed quite static. Like Reeves, she also seemed relaxed. Although she could obviously fly cross-country, she followed the route I usually took when I drove, via the turn-off near the Atarot dog pound. When she reached Ramallah, she used her advanced super-canine hearing and sight to locate Mohammed's house.

She saw my laptop, which Mohammed hadn't sold to anyone else – *I knew it!* – and flew down to retrieve it. On the ground, her Superdog costume melted away. Now she just looked like an ordinary dog, and no one would suspect her at all. She ran in through the back door, ignored the food in the kitchen and headed straight for Mohammed's room. She fetched the laptop and a picture of Mohammed so that I'd be able to recognise him when I saw him, and ran out with both in her mouth. In one bound of her powerful hind legs she was back in the sky, outlined against a full moon, cape streaming behind her, paws stretched forward.

And that's when I fell into a deep sleep. Before the revenge scene …

When I told Sarah the English doctor about this vision, she recommended a holiday.

'I can't pay for a holiday,' I replied. 'I'm still waiting for my replacement credit cards to arrive.'

Sarah said she was going to a kibbutz in the Negev Desert, where her friend lived, to celebrate Passover. She invited me along.

'Come with us to visit Elaine. Her kibbutz is in the southern desert; it's hot and dry and it will distract you. You can bring Mia. It will be great fun,' Sarah offered kindly.

Raphael was committed to celebrating Passover with his family and said he wouldn't come with us to the kibbutz. He invited me to his parents', but I decided that Sarah was right and a change would do me good. Raphael and I agreed that when I came back we would have a special celebration for our first anniversary with Mia. Had it already been a year? In the relative way of time, it seemed both much shorter and much longer, and sometimes I couldn't remember when she hadn't been with us.

I packed clothes, books and dog food, picked up Sarah and Uri, and we set off on the drive south. Sarah's facial bruising was healing well. If the attack had a serious effect on her spirits, I never saw it. She seemed to have no long-lasting psychological scars, simply resuming life as she had lived it before, with her mixture of confidence and commitment. As we drove out of Jerusalem, she was telling me about how various men reacted to hearing of the sexual assault. Nabi, a Palestinian carpenter she had known for years, had been very distressed, but after the rapist was caught he put his own spin on things.

'Was he really twenty-three years old? No; how can that be? What would he want with you? You're an old woman. He was obviously sick or mad, that's the only explanation,' Nabi told Sarah.

Sarah recounted this, laughing and exasperated at once.

She and Uri were soon asleep, but Mia stood supervising throughout the long, hot drive. I enjoyed the calming barrenness of the desert. Kibbutz Ketura, when it finally appeared, was a small scrap of green, reclaimed from the stony wasteland.

The kibbutz, the Israeli experiment in socialism, was mostly disappearing now. While the ideals were inspiring – from each according to his ability, to each according to his need, the strong carrying the weak – it seemed no one anywhere in the world could live for the benefit of the collective with no reward for effort. Not over the long haul. It appeared to be beyond human nature, whether it was enforced, as it had been in Russia, or voluntary, as it was on the kibbutz. Today most had 'privatised' themselves, splitting their assets and charging for things that used to be free, like laundry and food.

We drove into Kibbutz Ketura, past a collection of low concrete bungalows, home to three hundred people who lived surrounded by fields of palm trees and the sturdy desert plants being grown by Sarah's friend Elaine.

Elaine Solowey was an environmental scientist. She specialised in cultivating plants suited to the desert and 'marginal land', a description that covers more than half of the land in both Israel and Australia. Elaine had grown up as a Christian in the United Sates. In her twenties she'd discovered that her mother was Jewish. This led her to come to Israel to explore her own Jewishness. She married, had five sons and stayed. Kibbutz Ketura had been her home for more than twenty-five years.

Elaine showed us to a small two-room house that the kibbutz reserved for guests. She used the trees to instruct me on how to get back to her home – turn left when you see the big chestnut tree, keep going straight from there till you reach the fig, take a diagonal where you see a clump of pomegranate trees – till I was forced to admit that I couldn't tell a beech from a birch. I could identify a eucalyptus and that was about it. Elaine laughed and gave me other signposts as well.

The next morning I successfully found my way to her house, navigating the paths between the bungalows and the trees she had planted. While Sarah and Uri went to the kibbutz swimming pool, Elaine showed me around. The residential area was lovely: small homes were surrounded by desert plants and shaded by large trees. It felt rustic and inviting. Some people had strung hammocks between the trees and dragged sofas out, and they were sitting there, hair still spiky with sleep, having their first coffee of the morning. They patted Mia when she ran up to say hello. A farm, a factory and an environmental science academy, where Elaine also taught, were further out, away from the homes, on the edges of the village. The tawny desert hills rose up behind the kibbutz.

It was only the start of spring but the sun was already beating down. Barely an inch of rain fell here each year. It seemed as if the residents were clawing an existence out of the wilderness and that if they let their guard down for an instant, the desert would creep back and bury them. 'The price of liberty is eternal vigilance' was the inscription on an RSL monument near the municipal sports field we'd used when I was in high school. That's how I felt it was here. Elaine smiled when I told her that, because it led neatly to her favourite subject.

'To survive today we need a different kind of vigilance,' she said. 'How did we ever think we could grow crops like rice and cotton in a dry country like this? It's insane. We haven't got enough water. Even banana and citrus trees are too thirsty for this climate. We have to grow trees that need less water and suit the terrain.'

We reached her greenhouses, small rickety buildings with dark, humid interiors, a relief from the bright sun outside. They were filled

274

with the scent of compost and aromatic herbs. Elaine was Sarah's partner in her project to test the medicinal properties of plants from the Bible. The first problem they'd had to overcome was that most of the plants – including frankincense and myrrh, which the Three Wise Men brought as gifts for the infant Jesus – no longer grew in Israel. In the land of the Bible, these plants had become extinct.

In order for Sarah to test them back in her lab, the plants had to be returned here, to their native habitat. That presented another difficulty, because the plants now grew mostly in Arab and African countries that didn't have diplomatic ties with Israel. It had not been easy for Elaine to source them and then to cultivate them in her desert greenhouses in the quantities which were needed for scientific testing. In fact, that process took the better part of ten years, but Elaine said you learned to take the long view when you grew trees. And she'd done it. Her biblical garden now contained frankincense, myrrh, lalob and the poetically named balm of gilead.

'This project is about revival,' Elaine said proudly.

She pulled a leaf off the balm of gilead and handed it to me, instructing me to rub it between my fingers. The scent was fresh, a cross between spearmint and rosemary, and so strong it was almost overpowering. I closed my eyes, already able to smell the shampoo they could produce. And market! Elaine said that these plants had been used to make incense for the Jewish Temple in Jerusalem.

'On the floor of the synagogue in Ein Gedi there is a mosaic which says, "Cursed be he who reveals the secret of our community". Their secret was that they knew how to make perfume from these trees, and because of this skill the community in Ein Gedi was still in place well after the Romans had driven out or enslaved everyone else.' She paused. 'This is a community that was saved by its trees.'

When the Romans defeated the Jews, forty years after the death of Christ, they pulled up all their trees and orchards as a final sign of conquest. The savannah where these plants had once grown freely, which had stretched from the Dead Sea south of Jerusalem down to the southern Negev, where we were standing, had slowly turned into a desert. Two thousand years later it was still barren.

We walked out of the first greenhouse back into the bright sunlight, and Elaine told me about her part in another project she was involved in with Sarah. In a world first, they were attempting to revive a plant that had been extinct for two thousand years.

The ancient Judean date had been on the coins of the kingdom of Judea, and had been important economically as well as being used medicinally and in Jewish religious ceremonies, but it had died out after the Romans burned down all the orchards.

The dates being grown across the region today were from Iraqi date palms. The only relics of the Judean date were some ancient seeds dug up by archaeologists in the 1960s at the desert fortress of Masada near the Dead Sea. The story of Masada, where a small group of less than one thousand Jews made a final stand against the Romans, has been woven into the Israeli psyche. The Jews were protected by their location, high up on a desert mountain. The Romans laid siege to the fortress and built a ramp for their assault, but when they broke through after three months they found everyone dead. The Jews of Masada had committed suicide to avoid being taken alive, and they'd left a storehouse of food to show that they hadn't killed themselves because of hunger. Or at least that was the story told by the Jewish historian of the time, Josephus. Israeli archaeologists in the 1960s said that much of his account was borne out by their dig.

The last remaining Judean date seeds were preserved for centuries with other food scraps in the hot, dry sand beneath Masada. Unearthed by Israeli archaeologists, they sat in a drawer at the Hebrew University for another forty years, until Sarah conceived the idea of trying to revive them. You couldn't complain that Sarah aimed low. Her inspiration came from her deep connection to the history of that period. Sometimes when I was with her, it seemed that the Essenes and other groups from the time of Jesus were more vivid to her than the people who actually surrounded her in the present.

'Yes, of course they are!' Sarah admitted cheerily. 'Has it taken you all this time to figure that out?'

The Hebrew University was responsible for the Masada relics, and it turned down Sarah's request for date seeds. Then she applied to one of the original archaeologists on the Masada team, and he agreed that she could take three seeds. Elaine had planted them, each in its own pot here in her greenhouse. Seven weeks later, to her complete surprise, one sprouted. It wasn't the usual dark green of a healthy date plant, but it was still a shoot! She did a double take.

'I just didn't think a seed that old could sprout!' Elaine said, still astonished. 'It was very, very pale, a weird light green with sort of white mottling on it, and for a while, I wasn't sure it was going to live.'

The young plant confounded her expectations. By the time of my visit, one year on, it was standing thirty centimetres tall and had grown healthy emerald leaves. Sarah and Elaine had named it Methuselah, after the oldest person in the Bible. I stood looking at it in wonder.

'I move it around, so that no one will know where it is. It's a big responsibility,' Elaine said as she locked the greenhouse and we walked back to her home.

There was one more hitch. Date plants come in two types, male and female. Only female plants reproduce. For Methuselah to be able to bear fruit, it – or she – would have to be female. And the team wouldn't know *that* for another five years.

We ate the Passover meal at Elaine's home. As they sang the holiday hymns, I discovered that Sarah had a beautiful voice. One prayer is always recited by the youngest person at the table. Sarah's son, Uri, said it loudly and confidently, and she beamed with pride. She persuaded me that while I was at the kibbutz, I should do a report on her world-beating date seed. It turned out to be the most popular story I have done in my entire time in the Middle East.

The kibbutz lay to the south of the wilderness described in the New Testament, where Jesus spent his forty days and nights fighting the temptations of the Devil. I wanted to see the rock formations and experience that windy, stony silence so that I would hopefully gain some perspective on life. And laptop thieves. And letting go of anger.

The first day after the Passover meal it was simply too hot for climbing. By 8.00am it was already more than thirty degrees Celsius.

'There is a trail through our palm forest where joggers go and that's nice and shady!' Elaine offered.

But I was holding out for the desert experience. The next morning it was cooler. I took lots of water, and Mia and I set out before 7.00am. We passed through the back gate of the kibbutz and headed into the hills. The desert started immediately. It was not sandy, just stony, and the colours varied. There were swathes of brown, blond and pink stones. Mia was perfectly camouflaged, so I clipped the leash to her collar.

When we began climbing, I felt exhilarated. We both drank frequently; there was a breeze and it didn't seem to be as hot as yesterday. But I couldn't help noticing that my adventurous dog was not happy. She kept looking longingly back over her shoulder at the kibbutz, a neat green patch beneath us, getting steadily smaller. As we scrambled up over the steep rocks, Mia sat down every moment she could. The path was much steeper than I'd expected, and I began to wonder whether perhaps it was the kind of walk you should do the first time with someone experienced. At our next water stop, another sheer rocky precipice above us, I figured that if we fell, they'd need to chopper us out, and regretfully decided to turn back.

I'd found the deep silence and the caramel rocks enticing, but Mia ran as fast as she could down the steep, slippery slope, pulling me behind her. I had to yank her back for my own protection.

'Mia, stop, it's dangerous!'

Once we were on the flat again, heading back across the plain of pink stones to the kibbutz, I remembered the jogging track through the palm trees which Elaine had suggested. Perhaps we could give that a go, after all. But when we walked back through the kibbutz gate, Mia ran up to the first building she saw, plonked herself down in the shade and then keeled over on her side. She lay there panting, her eyes glassy.

I gave her water but she couldn't drink. She just lay panting loudly. I was terrified that I'd killed her. I patted her and whispered to her and told her to keep breathing. After a short time, I tried the water again. This time she did drink a little, but still couldn't get up. When she finally sat up, it took some time before she could walk slowly back to our room, stopping in shady spots along the way for water. When we arrived, she collapsed again. To my great relief, Sarah was in the room. It's always a good idea to travel with your own doctor.

'I'm also good with animals. On all the treks I did in Nepal I looked after the donkeys. I was the de facto vet, you know,' Sarah said brightly. 'You're in good hands.'

She prescribed water with salt and sugar mixed in it in equal parts to replace Mia's lost body fluids, and pronounced that, with luck, the patient would live. There was a twinkle in her eye as she looked at me, but I was mortified.

I couldn't imagine Raphael's reaction if I'd killed our dog, especially after all my lectures to him about caring responsibly for animals. I simply hadn't understood how dry this area was or how quickly dogs overheat, and what that weight of fur means out in the desert. Mia was very sensibly lying on her side on the cold stone floor, which she might well be doing at this time of day even if she hadn't collapsed. I lay down next to her, appreciating what a compact dog she was. I'd initially been disappointed that she hadn't grown bigger but now, curled into me, she seemed the perfect size. I stroked her head, and promised that I would never do that to her again. She opened her eyes and looked at me without any hint of blame. She lifted her head and licked my shoulder, and then lay back and closed her eyes again.

I was aware that I hadn't thought about my laptop all morning and suddenly it didn't matter so much. There were things that were more valuable than material possessions. How could I have forgotten to be grateful for them?

19

When we returned to Jerusalem, there was a knock at the door. I saw the familiar silhouette of my old neighbour Damira through the glass. Surprised, I opened the door, and almost blurted out, 'I thought you were in Paris!' but once I saw her face I knew that that would be the wrong thing to do.

She looked sad and a little more defeated, and said simply that it hadn't worked out for her there and she was back for good. She had even fewer possessions than before, but she had returned from Paris with a new Russian tea set.

'When I find an apartment, I will make you tea,' she said brightly.

We didn't discuss what went wrong. Instead, we went for a walk. Mia greeted her excitedly, jumping up on her and eliciting the only smile I saw on Damira's face for weeks.

We headed out of the park and down to the main road, the beautiful avenue of grand sandstone houses where Raphael and I had gone for our birthday dinner when we first met, and where Craig had been ordering pizza when a suicide bomber blew up the cafe next door. It had the haunting name Emek Refaim, 'Valley of Ghosts' in Hebrew. The Old Testament book of Prophets described a place called Emek Refaim, where a legendary race of giants lived. If it's the same location, the giants disappeared long ago. Their only possible legacy was the super high property prices. The suicide bombings had not stopped the steady climb in the value of land here, and as prices rose, developers moved in.

They were planning high-rise for both sides of the street, which would change its character entirely and spoil it, of course. Residents fighting these plans found they also had to fight corruption on the city council. Some things are the same the world over. But until the good guys lost, which is how I suspected the story would end, the street remained magical and slightly old-worldy. Even an increase in traffic and kosher burger bars hadn't diminished its charm. As we walked, I saw new handwritten signs on the ornate old buildings: 'No high rise in the German Colony' and 'Emek Refaim is a one-storey street'. We passed cars banked up at a standstill. They honked loudly, impatiently and, of course, fruitlessly. Whenever I complained to Raphael about this, he said there was no point. Noisy, futile aggression was an expression of the national soul.

'I will help with Mia, if you need me to,' Damira offered at my gate, when we returned home.

As it happened, I did need her, for 2006 turned out to be a very busy news year. It started with the Palestinian elections. Less than a month after Ariel Sharon's collapse, the Islamist group Hamas swept to power in a landslide election in the Palestinian Authority, the administration which ran the Palestinian territories of Gaza and the West Bank. Hamas routed Fatah, the party of Yasser Arafat, a surprise result that confounded both the pollsters and the parties themselves. From the time Arafat had first joined the Palestinian Liberation Organisation in the early 1960s, it had described itself as 'the sole legitimate representative of the Palestinian people'. Now it was out of power.

From the interviews I'd conducted during the elections, it seemed to be a vote for change, but one against Fatah corruption rather than in favour of Islamic militancy. Still, there was no doubt it shifted the political kaleidoscope. There was now a hard-line Islamic government which didn't recognise the state of Israel right on Israel's border.

Rocket fire from the Gaza Strip into Israel increased. In the south Israeli civilians, their existence now ruled by air-raid sirens, were constantly rushing backwards and forwards to bomb shelters. This kept casualties low, but it brought ordinary life to a halt. Israel fired tank shells back into Gaza in an attempt to deter the militants. They often hit civilians, and many more Palestinians than Israelis died in these exchanges, leading an Israeli-born historian who opposed his government's policies to describe this as the strategy of 'an eye for an eyelash'.

One hot afternoon in mid June, Israeli tanks fired shells onto a crowded Gaza beach where Palestinian families were picnicking. Seven members of one family died. A Palestinian cameraman arrived just as one of the children, who had been spared, ran along the beach shrieking and sobbing. She was wearing a blue T-shirt and her hair was flying out behind her, her dress and her location a contrast with the terrible reality. She threw herself down beside her dead father. The image and even more the sound were absolutely heart-rending. Twelve-year-old Huda Ghalia stumbling along the blood-soaked sand at Beit Lahiya and crying out to a family who were already dead seemed to epitomise Palestinian suffering.

The impact of those images and her keening cry, which seemed to sear your soul, attracted international condemnation. The Israeli military investigated immediately. It found the Israeli tanks had fired six shells onto the beach at Beit Lahiya that afternoon. They could show where five of them landed, but even though they didn't know where the sixth went, they concluded it couldn't have killed the Ghalia family because the timing was wrong. According to their calculations, that shell had only been fired after the family was hit. The military inquiry exonerated its troops.

I interviewed doctors at the hospital in Beit Lahiya, who disputed the Israeli military's timings, and also a munitions expert for Human Rights Watch who happened to be in Gaza on another investigation at the time. He said the pattern of injuries was more consistent with a tank shell (the Palestinian argument) than with the Ghalia family stepping on a bomb that had been left under the sand (the Israeli argument). In the end, I became convinced that the simplest explanation was the most likely and that it was an Israeli tank shell that killed the Ghalia family. Either way, whoever was right, in the end Huda Ghalia and her badly injured sisters and brothers had to build new lives without their father and six other family members.

Two weeks later, Hamas militants carried out a raid from Gaza into southern Israel. They dug a tunnel under the border, emerging on the Israeli side. There they killed two Israeli soldiers and wounded four more. They took one of the wounded, nineteen-year-old Corporal Gilad Shalit, back through the tunnel into Gaza. He was now a Hamas hostage. Shalit was the first Israeli soldier to be taken captive by Palestinians in twelve years. I handed my dog and my keys over to Damira. I told her I was going back to Gaza and didn't know exactly when I would return, but I'd just got in a new sack of dog food so we were good for a month.

On my last visit I had stayed near Beit Lahiya, the poor area in the north of the Gaza Strip where the Ghalia family lived and had been picnicking when Israeli troops shelled the beach. This time, I went further south, down to hot, crowded Gaza City, where high-rise buildings towered above sandy streets. It was looking meaner and more neglected than it had only a few months ago.

There were still bakeries and falafel stands, crowded streets and noisy daytime traffic. The clothes shops still had dummies standing in a row outside, dressed in long, modest women's coats of various dark shades: Gaza chic. But the people seemed thinner and angrier. All the women wore headscarves now. There was rubbish everywhere and the streets emptied at sunset. There was little of the vibrant nightlife common across the Arab world. Following the election of Hamas Islamists, a drab joylessness was taking hold.

There were groups of armed men, another new feature, and I was starting to hear about abductions. 'High-value' Israeli soldiers weren't the only targets; so were journalists and, increasingly, ordinary Palestinians too.

I was told that a Palestinian friend, Nadia, had been one of those kidnapped, and lucky enough to be released, so I went to see her. Nadia was a Mediterranean beauty. A smart, sensual, artistic policewoman, she had moved to Gaza City two years earlier, when her husband got a job working in the Gaza office of Palestinian President Mahmoud Abbas. Since then, she had begun wearing the hijab, choosing to cover her hair for the first time as a woman in her thirties when she was already a mother of two children.

'Why should I show off my beauty when there is so much suffering in Gaza at this time? It's not pressing for me. You see blood wherever you go, you see sad women, who've lost their husbands and children. I don't want to show off, to look like I don't care. I want to show I am a member of this society.'

She and her husband had been abducted when they were driving to work. The kidnappers believed that Nadia's husband had information about Moussa Arafat, the security chief who had been assassinated this past autumn. Since then, Gaza had been awash with rumours about Moussa Arafat's secret stashes of money and weapons. The rumours were enticing enough to spark kidnappings, even 'on spec'.

However Nadia's husband had no information about Moussa Arafat's bank accounts, nor anything else that could help them. Nor did Nadia. She was pregnant and terrified. The kidnappers handcuffed her, blindfolded her and when they passed an empty stretch of sand, threw her out of the car. They kept her husband so they could take him for interrogation. She begged for her life and that of her unborn child. They performed a mock execution, putting a gun to her head and releasing the catch. She believed she was about to die. Then they sped off and left her there.

'I kept praying to God not to kill me and not to kill my husband, and crying, crying, crying, but no one listened to me. I was in an isolated place on my own and there was no one to hear me, only God.'

A short time later, two men came up and removed her blindfold. Convinced the gunmen had returned to kill her, Nadia began saying the prayer Muslims recite when they are about to die. 'In the name of Allah, the merciful and the compassionate ...'

When they heard that the men said, 'Don't worry, we are police.'

In the end the gang let her husband go too, once he persuaded them he really didn't know anything about Moussa Arafat's money. Nadia now wanted to leave Gaza and move back to the West Bank. She said bitterly that she hated Hamas.

'I feel a very weak woman in this society. Now I know there is no one to protect me, except God.' She paused. 'Look at me. This is what "released unharmed" looks like.'

Gaza City was braced for retaliation by Israel for the kidnapping of its soldier. By night, Israeli jets flew overhead and broke the sound barrier. The sonic boom was as loud as a bomb going off in the next room. It jerked you awake and shattered windows. Gaza's glaziers were kept busy.

By day, the IDF carried out a series of air strikes. Among their targets was Gaza's main power station. Nine missiles hit the station, leaving more than half the Gaza Strip without power. Experts I interviewed assessed that the damage would take months to repair. The impact was felt immediately. Gaza City was mostly high-rise, and when there was no power lifts didn't work. Climbing multiple flights of stairs in that summer heat was not easy. By the time you walked up to an interview in a ninth-floor office, you needed a shower. Everyone kept candles and matches by their front door, but these were no replacement for fans or AC.

Electricity was needed to work the water and sewerage stations, and these vital services were also affected. Gaza was without water for prolonged periods. Shops selling purified bore water did a roaring trade, while at the markets there was a run on generators, fuel and large plastic containers.

'You can't buy a jerry can for love nor money anywhere – the markets have been cleaned out,' one man lining up to buy water complained to me.

While I was out doing an interview about the water shortages, I heard liquid gushing in the street. I went to check the source of this unusual sound and found myself wading through raw sewage. I was working with my Danish friend Allan and we traced the pipe back to the nearest sewerage plant. They showed us their stalled filter pumps, which required electricity to function. Everything was now backing up and sewage was bursting out of pipes. The heat and the stink made my head reel.

Allan went back to Jerusalem that night but I stayed on in Gaza. Not such a smart move, as it turned out, because Israeli authorities closed the border crossing until further notice. No one could enter or leave. That was a hazard of reporting from Gaza, and of course living and working there, but it was a problem for me because I had just learned that I had to be back in Jerusalem in two days' time.

The film Raphael had been working on, *Someone to Run With*, was completed now and had been chosen to open the Jerusalem Film Festival. Raphael and his band would be playing as people walked in. I called the IDF press office to insist that I had to be out of Gaza by Thursday because I had a film premiere to attend. They told me this was the most original 'urgent reason' they'd heard so far for re-opening a border. Next I called Raphael. He was distant, wrapped up in preparations for the concert.

'I've been trying to call you but your phone doesn't work,' he said crossly.

'No, it only works in certain places in Gaza because ...'

'Can you call me back in ten minutes?' he interrupted and hung up.

As it turned out, I couldn't. I didn't seem able to explain to him the constraints of working in Gaza. My Israeli mobile phone only functioned on the roof of the hotel where I was staying. The wireless internet connection functioned on the ground floor. This meant that I was climbing up or down four flights of stairs, carrying my rucksack and laptop whenever I had to feed a story or talk to anyone, which was pretty much all day. The heat was enervating, the smell of sewage hung over everything, and it was so humid I was sweaty by the time I reached the roof. Like the locals, my sleep was broken by the sonic booms. I trudged back upstairs and tried to call Raphael again, reflecting that my inability to explain any of this to him was part of the impermeable curtain that had fallen between Israelis and Palestinians. They couldn't see each other and had no interest in imagining each other's lives.

Naturally, I couldn't get through to Jerusalem. When the line finally connected half an hour later, Raphael was not answering his phone. I tried the IDF press office again to see if the Gaza border crossing was open. It wasn't. As I headed back downstairs to try to feed my story on the power shortage, I wondered what this relationship was about.

The border crossing remained closed and I stayed the next night too. It was the final of the soccer World Cup and there was mayhem at my hotel. Up till the seventies, the Marna guesthouse was where all the journalists stayed. Then more modern hotels were built on the beachfront, with better phone lines and restaurants, and the journalists moved there. But I liked the old-fashioned charm of the Marna. In the morning they served a special marmalade, thick, dark and bitter-sweet, cooked to the recipe of some long-departed British matron, and they had a library of hard-cover English books, including nineteenth-century bodice rippers.

Most of all I liked its new owner, who ensured that prices were modest and service good. His name was Basel, and a hotelier more different from Basil Fawlty would be hard to imagine. He was a most unusual man: independent, competent, relaxed and secular. He was slowly remodelling the Marna, planning a garden cafe with a cappuccino machine and French cakes prepared daily by a specially trained chef. He had imported both the man and the machine from Egypt. For Gaza, these were visionary steps. Who needed journalists? He would build a local clientele. His marketing strategy was proving itself during this World Cup.

He brought in twenty television sets so that everyone who could fit into his garden bar could watch the final. Hundreds of young men arrived. If there was a power cut, no one would have to miss a moment, because Basel had a generator and enough fuel to power it for a week.

'As soon as I heard that an Israeli soldier was kidnapped I went to the markets and I bought up all the generator fuel they had.'

'*Zizou! Ya Zizou!*' On the night of the final, the young men cheered on the French captain Zinedine Zidane. The star, of Algerian descent, was a favourite here, and his fans told me darkly that any break in the satellite transmission was planned interference by Israeli aircraft. The men were in their twenties and thirties and football mad, but they were all drinking tea. Hamas militants had burned down restaurants that sold alcohol, and since Hamas politicians had come to power, alcohol was now forbidden in Islamic Gaza. Basel made his money on the ice-cream and cake the men ate, and the hookah pipes they smoked.

I included the World Cup match in a longer feature I was doing for Irish radio about how Gaza was enduring the power cuts, and went to bed exhausted. I hadn't spoken to Raphael and still didn't know if I would make it back to Jerusalem in time for his film the following night.

In the morning the IDF called and said it was opening the crossing, 'but only for a short time'. The reporters at the Marna checked out and rushed to the border, where we waited in a long line, like journalist refugees. It took hours to cross, and by the time I reached Jerusalem it was evening. Luckily the film festival was taking place close by. It was outside in the Sultan's Pool in the valley below my house. I had time to take a shower and to walk Mia. Raphael still wasn't answering his phone. I popped in on Damira on the way to thank her for looking after Mia. She had found a one-room apartment in a house around the corner. It was scrubbed clean and contained one mattress, one chest of drawers, and a gas ring that could accommodate one pot, which sat near the sink. She travelled so light. She never complained but its bareness made me feel sad.

The night was warm and the familiar paths were scented with lavender and rosemary. Israelis heading to the film festival passed by, talking and laughing, a good humoured, well-dressed crowd, carrying bottles of wine and flavoured vodka. The contrast to Gaza made my head spin. I waited by the gate for Sarah and her son, Uri, as we had agreed to sit together. The sound of Huda Ghalia crying on the beach near her dead father's body started echoing in my head and I couldn't banish it. I began to fear I was going crazy.

Raphael and his band were playing as we walked in. He was staring at me from large screens around the outdoor cinema. The walls of the Old City glowed above us. Dozens of white balloons had been released into the summer sky. They floated above the sandstone walls, light and lovely, suspended for a moment before heading out towards Jordan. This symbol of freedom made me reflect how badly Raphael and I had been getting on. We grated against one another, our differences more pronounced now. Perhaps the white balloons were a sign that I had to let him go.

The crowd enjoyed Raphael's music and the film. I did too, of course, for each scene was full of memories. It was evocative to watch it outdoors on a warm summer night. Raphael's performance was very strong, though there was a strangeness to seeing him as someone else, apart from me, up on a huge screen. He was sitting down the front, but I didn't feel confident enough to go and sit with him, or even to say hello, as we hadn't spoken for days and I wasn't sure how he would react. I was feeling too fragile after Gaza for a cool reception from him, and that distance between us said everything.

Sarah leaned over and said she thought he made a convincing bad guy. 'I liked it when he put his cigarette out on the *mezuzah*,' she giggled, referring to the cylinder containing a prayer that was nailed on door frames in Jewish homes. I couldn't take too much in. Maybe I would have to see it again to be able to tell. Instead, I focused on the dogs, trying to figure out which Golden Retriever was which, when it was Casey and when it was Naana, and had to admit that I couldn't. I picked out the places where I had been on set and remembered Mia with her feet in the Retrievers' water bowl in the street outside the Jerusalem markets, and the night when I'd smuggled her into the hotel where dogs were forbidden, so that we could be with Raphael.

But memories weren't enough. I rang Raphael after the screening and he didn't answer. When we finally spoke he wanted to know why I hadn't come to see him down at the front of the amphitheatre. We had one more impatient misunderstanding, of the 'Why didn't you ...?/But you said ...' variety, and something inside me snapped. We seemed to have lost the ability to talk to each other. Giving each other the benefit of the doubt was long gone.

'We're just not suited; that's all there is to it,' Raphael said, angrily and sadly.

We did finally separate and this time custody didn't seem to be an issue. I got Mia. I was teary and exhausted and desperately in need of a break, but while I was planning one the 2006 Lebanon War began.

In July 2006, a military unit from the Shia Islamist group Hezbollah crossed from Lebanon into Israel, in a similar action to the one on the Gaza border three weeks earlier, when Hamas had captured Gilad Shalit. The Lebanese militants near the border fired anti-tank missiles at two patrolling Israeli armoured vehicles. Their aim was to take Israeli soldiers hostage. As a diversion, Hezbollah also fired long-range rockets into northern Israel. Three Israeli soldiers were killed in the ambush. Two others were wounded – and they were the prize. Hezbollah raced them back to Lebanon. Five more Israeli soldiers died in a failed attempt to rescue them.

Hezbollah filmed the entire operation, including their preparations, showing how they'd played football on their side of the border every day for months to lull the Israeli patrols into a false sense of security. They'd left nothing to chance.

Israel said it regarded the cross-border raid as an act of war. In the parliament, Prime Minister Ehud Olmert announced that Israel would launch an attack against Hezbollah. Olmert listed his war aims, including the return of the two captured Israeli soldiers, as well as the destruction of Hezbollah and Islamic radicalism. Listening to this speech, with these wide-ranging, unachievable aims, gave me a cold feeling. You don't have to be Machiavelli to know that little good can come of a venture where the aims are unattainable from the get-go.

Israel began a massive aerial bombing campaign. Israeli jet fighters struck Hezbollah areas of the Lebanese capital, Beirut, and also civilian targets such as the airport and bridges linking the capital to the south, where Hezbollah had its power base. There was colossal destruction of buildings and infrastructure, as well as huge loss of life. Many of those killed were civilians who were not affiliated with Hezbollah. A ground invasion of southern Lebanon followed.

Hezbollah bombarded Israel with rockets. There was less destruction because the rockets were less sophisticated. But because they were imprecise and no one knew where they would fall, it was difficult to protect against them. Once again it was civilians who paid the price. The first Israeli casualty was Monica Seidman, a woman who had emigrated from Argentina three years ago. She was killed by a direct strike while having coffee on her balcony in the town of Nahariya.

Craig went to Lebanon, and Meg and I headed north. As we were driving there, eight employees of the Haifa Railways were killed when a rocket hit their depot. We did a detour to visit the site. Haifa was the third largest city in Israel, and the Israeli government had not expected major rocket attacks that far south. Haifa's main hospital was the treatment centre for all casualties in the north of the country – which meant every civilian who was injured in this war – and yet the hospital itself was not fortified to withstand rocket fire. The hospital had to re-locate its Emergency department and its operating theatres down to underground bomb shelters.

The longer range rockets being fired by Hezbollah led thousands of Israelis to stream south. Those who remained in the Israeli towns close to the border with Lebanon were the old, the poor and the sick, mostly migrants who didn't have anywhere to go and didn't know anyone further south who could help.

'We survive because we are living under the ground like rats,' an old woman told me in Russian.

The IDF put me on to its beeper service and sent me a message every time a rocket landed. My mobile phone made a delightful burble of sound, like the one that signalled the arrival of the fairy on children's TV shows. That sound used to set my pulses racing because it meant a message from Raphael. Now there were Katyusha rockets instead of kisses … Yet I was like one of Pavlov's dogs: I couldn't stop myself expecting to hear something happy from him.

I wanted to talk to Meg about Raphael, but there was little opportunity and my personal sorrows were dwarfed by the story we were reporting. She and I were standing outside a Haifa apartment block which had taken a direct hit. The incoming Hezbollah rocket had torn a hole in the side of the building, and we gazed in at someone's furniture and possessions, nothing where they had left it when they went to work that morning. There was a tangle of noisy reporters cramming around the shocked owner of the apartment. She was late finding out about the rocket attack because she had just returned from her mother's funeral.

After we had enough material, we gave two other journalists a lift back to the hotel, where we were all returning to file. In the car I could see Meg watching me.

'Chin up,' she said softly. 'You'll be fine.'

I tried for a light tone. 'I didn't know I looked that bad.'

'No, you don't,' she said, taking me seriously. 'But just hang in there. You're doing the right thing. Don't forget that. You can't stay with someone who doesn't make you happy. When things are over, you get out.'

I kept working – I had no choice. Judging that this was going to be a long conflict, I decided to base myself in Jerusalem and to make periodic trips up north from now on. The next time I went back up it was with Allan, the tall, easy-going Dane. A strange schizophrenia had settled on Israel. It was a state at war in the north, but business as usual further south in the areas which were out of rocket range.

We left the clogged Jerusalem streets during the morning rush hour, battling traffic as always, and when we were halfway up the country, the twilight zone descended. The cars thinned out and soon we were driving along highways that were completely empty. There was no driving, no honking, no braking, just wind and air-raid sirens. Hezbollah aimed their rockets at civilian centres, but once they were fired no knew where they would land.

'We're alright inside a car,' I told Allan as we sped along, the only vehicle for miles. 'The rockets can't hit us while we're moving.'

I believed that even when we heard the sirens again; insistent wails, dull but loud, and as frightening as incoming.

We reached the border unscathed. The next day, when we were back in Jerusalem, a man was killed when a Katyusha rocket landed on his car on precisely that same stretch of road. Allan and I turned around and drove back up again. This time, my illusion of safety punctured, I was more frightened, or perhaps just more realistic. I coped with my fears by telling Allan brightly that we would only die if we were meant to.

'If our time's up, nothing can save us, and otherwise we'll be fine.'

He thought I was going crazy.

I had been brooding about the social worker from Argentina who was killed on the first day of the war. She had returned to Nahariya from holiday that week, almost as if she had an appointment with death. One rocket was fired and killed her instantly. It 'found' her. I told Allan this story to prove my point that you couldn't escape the bullet with your number on it, but he wasn't comforted.

'I prefer the ostrich school of risk-taking,' he said cheerily. 'If I don't look nothing will happen to me.'

I could see that he didn't need these long, morbid discussions, but I couldn't stop myself. I had looked up my favourite Arabian folktale the previous night, after I'd finished working. I needed to unwind before I could sleep and instead of watching trashy TV or doing Sudoku I'd started reading Scheherazade's *1001 Nights*, or *One Thousand Nights and One Night*, as it is romantically called in Arabic, *Alf leyle wa leyle*. The story began in the approved fashion: Once upon a time ... *Fi yom min il ayyam* ...

Once upon a time there was a merchant in Baghdad who sent his servant to the market to buy provisions. The servant returned white and trembling because he had seen Death there. 'He was dressed in black and as pale as the moon that grows thin.'

Death had made a threatening gesture to the servant, who now begged his master for a horse so that he could ride far away from Baghdad to avoid his fate. 'I will go to Samarra and there Death will not find me.'

The master lent the servant his horse, and he galloped off as fast as he could to Samarra. Then the master went down to the marketplace to confront Death, and to ask him why he had made a threatening gesture to his servant.

Death replied, 'That was not a threatening gesture; it was one of surprise. I was astonished to see him in Baghdad, for I have an appointment with him tonight – in Samarra.'

That folktale was the reason I could do this job. And live this strange life. And drive on this road, risking incoming rockets. Now I thought about it, perhaps it was also the reason that I had broken up with Raphael but still kept Mia. She was my fate. My dog from Samarra.

Allan humoured me. He kept driving and listening. When I'd finished retelling Scheherazade's tale, he said, 'We'll be fine then. I've checked. Our numbers aren't up.'

The funeral of Malko Ambao, an Israeli soldier whose family had emigrated from Ethiopia, at first seemed no different from any of the others. I arrived at a small green cemetery in a town on the coast not far from Tel Aviv, and went to stand among the brightly dressed Ethiopian mourners, the best spot for recording. The women were keening in unison, a sad African sound. The Jewish mourner's prayer, the Kaddish, was being intoned over the top, a fusion of the two cultures. The midday sun was beating down on my head. Everyone was crying and gulping and sobbing and sweating, leaking liquid from all their pores. Suddenly, I found myself succumbing to the heat and sorrow, and felt a wail being torn from me too. Once I started crying I couldn't stop. Raphael. Gaza. Lebanon. Exhaustion. Who knew what I was really crying about? Perhaps I was burying my relationship with Raphael in that graveyard, or perhaps it was six months of accumulated stress that had burst out there, but afterwards I felt wrung out and unsure how long I could go on.

The war lasted thirty-four days. When the fighting ended, large swathes of southern Lebanon lay in ruins. More than one thousand Lebanese and more than one hundred and fifty Israelis had been killed. Hezbollah billed it as the 'Divine Victory', but its leader Sheikh Hassan Nasrallah later admitted that if he'd known how Israel would retaliate he would not have authorised the raid that sparked the war.

The conflict failed to free Israel's two abducted soldiers, nor to achieve any of its other grandiose aims; in fact, if anything, it strengthened rather than weakened Hezbollah in Lebanon. The Israeli public was dissatisfied with the way the war was fought, and forced a commission of inquiry into why their politicians had run things so badly. After all that, I was on the verge of collapse. But once again Mia had other plans for me.

20

Mia went into heat; yes, it was already that time again, and while I was now expert at fast-paced late-night walks and keeping male dogs away with sticks, this time round her phantom pregnancy was worse. She became fat and slow much sooner than last time, and was very soon waddling rather than walking. Running was completely out of the question, a forgotten art. She barely made it down the first flight of stairs near our house before stopping. She wouldn't take another step forward and slowly and ponderously climbed back home. She gave me a look that said, *In my condition I can't do any more.* She gained four kilos in a month.

'I could do that!' laughed a plump woman in the dog park.

'Yes, me too,' I replied. 'But we don't weigh sixteen kilos. It's a quarter of her body weight. And she's not actually pregnant!'

Once again, friendly, outgoing Mia turned on any dog that I dared to pat, including launching a suicidal attack on her arch enemy, a tough old German shepherd called Simcha.

Simcha means 'happiness' in Hebrew but, boy, was that a misnomer for this dog. Mia usually gave Simcha a wide berth because she was a biter and had 'form'. But one warm evening not long after the Lebanon War had ended, Simcha and her owner, Miri, walked by our door. I was sitting outside on my front step with Mia, no longer fearful that she would run away. In fact, I'd had a hard time persuading her to leave the sofa and come out this far.

I unthinkingly patted Simcha and all three of us – me, Miri and

Simcha – watched in astonishment as Mia launched herself in fury at the larger dog. Huge, mean, jealous Simcha was thrilled. She could bite her victim *with justification* for once. She threw herself on Mia, growling purposefully. The yipe, yipe, yipe, squeal that Mia emitted was chilling. After we'd separated the dogs and Miri had hauled Simcha away, I realised that Simcha hadn't hurt Mia at all. That terrible racket was pre-emptive. It must be programmed into dogs – a canine early-warning system – for I'd never heard Mia make a sound like it before.

'You silly girl. All that because I patted Simcha?'

As I watched her growing fatter and grouchier, I could see it was time for Mia to be neutered. I admitted to myself that I had been secretly harbouring the idea of letting her have one litter of puppies in case Raphael wanted to take one. That way I would feel that we had drawn a line under the relationship and that Mia really was my dog.

I took a deep breath and called Raphael. He was distant and not very interested. He said he didn't want any of Mia's puppies and as far as he was concerned she could go ahead and have the operation. Well, that was pretty final. The next morning, I took her to a new vet, actually two vets: a husband and wife team. They told me that with her exaggerated symptoms, Mia was a likely candidate for an infected womb.

'When that bursts, it's dangerous and requires emergency surgery. And it's always after midnight. It's better and healthier to have her neutered now,' they advised.

So, with the vets assuring me that she would quickly be fine and restored to herself, and that she would be the same happy, adventurous dog afterwards, Mia went under the knife. She was not yet two years old. She survived the operation but, always one to confound, her reaction was terrible.

She was in a great deal of pain. She'd never slept with me in bed, but on the night after the operation she climbed in and lay next to me, shaking and panting like a train, her little furry chest going up and down, her serene foxy face tormented. She whimpered and then actually started howling. It was a terrible sound, on your own at 2.00am. Raphael was one of the few people always awake at that hour and I phoned him. He was kind and calming, but after we said goodnight I felt even sadder. I looked down at the shaking, miserable dog by my side and felt tears gather in my eyes.

'Oh Mia, please don't infect me with all this sorrow!'

Neither of us slept much as Mia shuddered and cried through the night. The next day she was no better. I took her back to the vets who promised that while it was an unusual reaction she would soon be fine. That night there was still no improvement. She lay next to me crying, almost sobbing, and staring up at me sadly in between howls, as if seeking comfort. I gave her another painkiller, patted her and talked to her softly, but she just moaned and shook. At my wits' end, I called Einav the dog trainer, who was a strong advocate of neutering animals.

'Ohmigod, it's like she's in mourning,' she said.

And that's the best explanation we ever had.

On the third day, Mia finally quietened, but there was one more hurdle to overcome. As soon as she recovered from the surgery, or from her mourning period, whichever it was, Mia started looking for a safe place for her puppies. Apparently, the operation hadn't switched off all her hormones and she still believed she was pregnant.

She dug in the sofa, pulling off the blanket that she'd sat on placidly for months, rearranging all the cushions and constructing a nest there in the hole she'd made. When we were out walking, she disappeared into bushes looking for nesting spots. It broke my heart.

Then a week after the operation, when we were in the top park close to our home, she disappeared into a hole in the ground. If I hadn't actually seen her approach an old water pipe, which barely looked big enough for a guinea pig let alone a dog, and slither inside,

I wouldn't have believed it possible. But that's just what she did, vanishing within seconds.

I lay in the dirt, looking into a pipe which was pointing downwards at a thirty-degree angle, and called down into it. I thought I saw her tail, but it was dark so I wasn't sure. Then I hopped up and tried to look from the top, pulling at the lavender plants growing there; but no luck, the pipe was buried under sandstone. How would she ever get out? Fifteen minutes later she still hadn't emerged and I wasn't sure what to do. Was a dog underground like a cat up a tree? Should I call the fire department? Would we be on the evening news?

It was late autumn and the Yemin Moshe olive trees were heavy with fruit. In Jerusalem, it was an accepted practice for people to harvest the olives in public parks and take them home for their own use. Industrious Arab families had come from the surrounding suburbs to spread plastic sheets under the trees, while young men climbed up and shook the branches. Their mothers and grandmothers, wearing long, dark dresses, stayed below, gathering up the olives which fell. After the nearest family had watched me for a while, one of the teenage boys came over and offered to help. I explained my predicament in bad Arabic – 'Kalbeti taht il ard! My dog is beneath the earth!' – but I could see he didn't believe me. I didn't blame him; I hardly believed it myself. He took my spot in the dirt and gazed down the pipe.

He stood up, clapped his hands to remove the sand and soil, and said he had something we could pull her out with. While he fashioned a noose from a rubber hose, I looked down the pipe and to my astonishment I saw Mia's nose. It was quite far down, but it was her nose, nonetheless. So there had been a turning circle down there after all! After thirty minutes she emerged unharmed and shook herself off, as if she just had to remove a little bit of sand before we continued on our way. I grabbed her and hugged her close.

'Please, get over this soon,' I murmured.

There's no way around it; breaking up is hard to do, and there was a Raphael-shaped hole in my life that I had to fill. Love hadn't been enough. I wasn't sure exactly why, but if I couldn't live with him, it was time to learn to live without him.

Sweet, funny memories constantly intruded, undermining my resolve. How does your mind do that? I would be walking in the park below the house and would suddenly recall with intense clarity Raphael walking Mia in the same place. He'd tied her to the bench beneath the giant, gnarled olive tree so he could play his guitar, and had rung to tell me where to find them. I'd heard the familiar chords before I'd turned the corner. They were sitting in the shade, Raphael singing, Mia at his feet, sunlight falling in shafts on the bleached grass and olive trees behind them. The Old City walls were tawny beyond in the afternoon light. I had stopped for a moment. Everything in that picture had been so beautiful – the location, the music, the man playing, the dog lying nearby listening. I couldn't believe they were waiting for me.

Now they were no longer waiting for me, or at least one of them wasn't. When a memory like that surfaced, it tore at me. I was surprised at the depth of my reaction, for I'd always known this relationship would have to end. But I didn't expect it to end badly. Maybe that was naive and there is no 'good' ending. They all hurt.

My solution was to keep exercising. I decided a new gym would help. Jerusalem is not a city blessed with a wide variety of choice. I tried out a number and didn't really like any of them. The least worst one was located on Mount Scopus, twenty minutes' drive away, too far really, but at least it was open on Saturdays, when most of Jerusalem shut down.

The gym serviced the city's eastern and western halves, so it had a mixed clientele of Arabs and Jews. There, for an hour each day, I had the illusion of co-existence. Israeli women followed the instructions of Walid, the Palestinian trainer, and men from both sides deferred to Arkaday, the Russian Jewish weight-lifter from Novosibirsk, who ruled the weights room. They also helped each other out; two Israelis holding the heavy barbell for a young Palestinian to assist with his repetitions. They counted him to ten, in Hebrew and Arabic, as Arkady supervised nearby, counting in Russian. Then they pushed him to do two more.

'What's wrong, Basam? You're looking tired. It's not that girl again is it? She's not worth losing sleep over! Get rid of her!'

It had its own poetry; men on opposite sides of the line, united against their common enemy – women.

Another plus was that the gym had a steam room, which reminded me of the Russian banya I had loved. The banya came into its own during a Russian winter, when after broiling yourself like a lobster you were doused in freezing water, a fifty-degree drop in temperature that felt like it would stop your heart but somehow revived you instead. Here there was no such contrast, but the enveloping heat made me feel I could sweat all my problems out and emerge cleaner and stronger.

One evening I walked into the change room and heard a song coming from the sauna. Five women were sitting in the jacuzzi, singing together like a choir. They were buxom, with black hair and muscly arms, rolls of fat spilling out over their dark swimsuits, and they were singing traditional Georgian folksongs, wild, poignant tunes that I hadn't heard since Moscow. Steam billowed out of the sauna whenever anyone opened the door, jets of water burbled away beneath them and they harmonised in pure voices that I carried with me all the way home. Some things about living in a foreign place are wonderful.

But the following week, in the same change room, I was standing near my locker, conscious of that good feeling that you have *after* your training session. As I took off my gym gear, I told myself that life wasn't all bad. I would get over this dull ache one day. There was almost a spring in my step until a woman nearby looked me up and down and said, 'You know, you're in good shape, but you could do with losing five kilos.'

I'd never seen her before, even in passing. She wasn't someone I recognised from any of the classes, but she felt she could say that to me! Another reason I was stunned by this example of what passed for making polite conversation with a stranger was that she was one of the fattest women I'd ever seen. I should have said, 'And you, girlfriend, could do with losing another whole person!' But that's the kind of reply you only think up afterwards, driving home or lying in bed at night.

At the time, I just stood there, opening and closing my mouth silently, like a fish. I stomped off to have a shower, and then went home to my dog, who might also have thought I needed to lose weight but mercifully kept her opinions to herself.

Mia didn't seem to miss Raphael or to notice that he was gone. The spaying grief was behind her, and she was once again running about happily in the park, greeting all dogs and humans with delight. She was never as thin again, but she was a much easier dog, for me and I think also for herself.

As if she knew the nights were hard for me, she slept by my side. Night is when you don't remember the bad times, only the good ones. It's some cruel trick of the dark. Sleep was elusive, as I remembered Raphael, and missed him in that bed. I lay awake until I heard the call to prayer from the Al-Aqsa Mosque drifting through the still, cool air.

'Allahu Akbar ...' The hypnotic chant, repeated three times and sung so sweetly, seemed to hang there for a moment before the muezzin continued. It meant it was 4.30am and there was now little chance of sleep. I turned my head and saw Mia's blond foxy face on Raphael's pillow, exactly where he used to lie. It lifted my spirits for a moment. When she deemed I was better, she slept at my feet, or moved back to her rug on the floor.

During our walk one evening, a man caught my attention from across the park. He had dark hair in a ponytail and a guitar slung over his shoulder. He had the same build as Raphael and the same walk. As he strolled over from the other side of the park, smoking, I stood frozen to the spot. When I realised that it wasn't Raphael, I exhaled and looked around for Mia. She had stopped stock-still beside me and was staring too. We both stood like statues, watching a man who wasn't Raphael, till he walked past us. That was when I knew that she missed him too. She just didn't go on about it.

Mia was finally changing from a fox into a dog. If I met a neighbour and stopped to talk, she stood by my side instead of zooming off. She still ran away, of course, but now she also came back. The first time I found her sitting outside the front door waiting for me when I came home I was in such shock that I texted Raphael to tell him.

Once we were inside I sat beside her at the gate, the spot from which she liked to look out and supervise the street. I settled back against the blue iron door and gazed out from dog level at the sandstone path, noticing the feet of people walking by rather than their faces. Mia's head was poking out through the gate, her body in here with me, and as I watched her enjoying the breeze I became aware I'd texted Raphael simply because I missed having someone who cared about her as much as I did. He hadn't answered and he was right not to; it had been a reflex action on my part.

Before I had loved Mia as an extension of him, of us, and now I had to learn to love her for herself.

'We're not three, we're just two,' I told her, really telling myself, as I absentmindedly rubbed her ears.

With no sense of the moment, Mia exploded into high-pitched barking. Another dog had dared to enter the street. She broke off for an instant, drawing her head in to scratch her ear with her hind leg, then poked her head back through the gate to resume her frenzied noise. I smiled to myself. No time for maudlin thoughts. Love either came or it didn't, fretting wouldn't help. Dogs were so no-nonsense.

Sitting on the cool stone floor by my gate, my hand on Mia's fur, watching her watch the street, I understood that by saving this small stray, Raphael had given me a gift which had enriched my life, though things turned out differently to what I expected. Raphael had brought this small, naughty creature into our lives, and now he was gone. I lost the boy but I kept the dog. Her love turned out to be the one that lasted.

For a moment, I wondered if it would have been different if I'd been more sensible in my choice, looking for a husband rather than a boyfriend, for permanence rather than romance. I didn't know the answer but I didn't reproach myself. I didn't regret a single moment with Raphael. Our happy times were among my most joyous memories. I had known myself loved, and it was impossible to regret that.

I did regret not having had a child, but that wasn't down to Raphael. I must not have wanted it enough, for women have babies by themselves if the right man doesn't turn up, and I didn't do that. I've had an exciting and most unusual life. I was true to my talents, rather than sticking with what was expected of me. It had come at a price, and I was not able to have everything. But that's how it goes. I don't know many people who have everything, and especially not many women. As for those few who seem to, perhaps it only appears that way because we are looking in at them from the outside. It's always different inside people's lives; in their hearts.

Some women recover quickly from a love affair and are off dating someone new within weeks. I'm not one of them. Once the sharp ache eased, I found that I still missed Raphael but I was re-adjusting to life alone. I had done it for a long time, it was familiar, and I could be content by myself.

That hard-won contentment was about to be tested further. After more than five years in Jerusalem, Orla was being posted to South Africa. I was happy because her husband was being assigned there too, so they would finally be living together for the first time since they married, but it was very hard to part from her. Jerusalem felt empty without her. Six months later, Meg landed a job at a prestigious American newspaper and was posted to Abu Dhabi in the Gulf. Craig became foreign editor on a new English language paper there. As I walked Mia in the park where she used to play with Chucho, Jerusalem seemed more and more like a 'Valley of Ghosts'.

Work filled my life. Every so often, I'd bump into Raphael, usually outside a cafe in town, strained, sometimes sour encounters that were over in a few moments, but still had the power to upset me. He always asked after Mia, but otherwise we had little to say to each other.

I continued going to the gym, especially after my Australian friend Toni and I fell in love with a class offered at the YMCA gym. The Y was one of Jerusalem's grandest buildings, a sandstone Art Deco gem from the architect who designed the Empire State Building. We walked back from class there, winding our way through the olive trees down to Yemin Moshe, sometimes laughing, sometime troubled – that classic Jerusalem combination. As well as being neighbours and friends, Toni and I had another bond. We were both journalists who wanted to write books, and were encouraging one another to take the plunge and put pen to paper, or at least hand to mouse. We found an English-language writing class, and when we could we walked there, through the sun-dappled streets of Jerusalem's German Colony. One late afternoon after class, Toni and I were heading back down the Bethlehem Road, a broad street lined with oak trees. Toni's hair flared in the sun when we emerged from under the branches.

'Yes, my new hairdresser has gone mad. I'm now officially Russian prostitute blond,' she laughed.

Our silhouettes were far ahead of us on the pavement as we talked about how our books were coming along. I confessed that there was a shadow hanging over my writing. As I dredged up memories about Jerusalem and meeting Raphael and finding Mia, I had to acknowledge that the experiences weren't mine alone. I was beginning to feel that I couldn't continue without contacting Raphael and telling him that I was writing about him.

'No, you don't have to,' Toni said.

'I don't know. I feel that I do,' I replied. 'It's like bad faith otherwise.'

'You don't. Or at least, not yet. Don't worry about it now; just keep going,' Toni advised, with the protective selfishness of the author. 'We often find excuses to stop us writing. Don't let this one be yours.'

Ahead of us was a cafe, which had old overstuffed sofas and armchairs at outdoor tables. I'd always liked it, since they served elaborate salads and mouth-watering pastries, and I glanced over. There, sitting at one of the pavement tables, was Raphael. Blue T-shirt, hair in a ponytail, guitar by his side, cigarettes and phone on the table in front of him. Unmistakably Raphael. How could he have appeared just when we were talking about him? I hadn't seen him in more than a year. It was as if he'd been conjured up by spirits. I pointed him out to Toni, who also did a double take. But she knew a sign from the writing gods when she saw one.

'Guess you will have to tell him after all,' she said out of the side of her mouth as we walked up and said hello.

I introduced them and said to Raphael in a dazed way, 'I was just talking about you.'

After that chance meeting, I called him and we met for coffee, on purpose this time. It was a relief to confess to him that I was writing about us. He made it easier by saying, in his rock star way, that I could write what I liked.

'I trust you.'

He was funny, softer, sweet again, as if some turbulence inside him had calmed. He probably also saw changes in me. Sitting in the cafe where we'd met by chance, twice, where Mia had performed all her tricks in a row to get us to feed her, we each admitted that we hadn't been seeing anyone else.

'What? Really?' We looked at each other in disbelief.

It seemed impossible after more than eighteen months. How could we both still be free?

I am too rational to *really* believe in magic, even though it's true that I did take part in a curse-lifting ceremony with Jerusalem's finest coffee reader. Coincidence is something else again. Serendipity, fate deciding to step in and point you in the right direction, is a level of magic that works for me. Or maybe I'm an opportunist, and it's not in my nature to turn down a chance. The word for opportunity in Arabic, *forsa*, is also the word for holiday, a pairing that I like. This looked like a second chance at love, and we both took it.

Slowly, very slowly, we began to spend time together.

This time round, we are kinder to each other, and also more wary. We know now what great power we have to hurt one another. Whatever it was that poisoned our relationship before seems to have lifted, like mist in the morning. We have fun and laugh and live in a sunny, present moment. We live apart, so we don't fight about cleaning and chores. That might also contribute to our happiness. I don't ever take this contentment for granted; in fact, I'm grateful every day, which is another pleasure of being with Raphael.

Will it last? I don't know. All the old obstacles are still there, including the age gap. I have finally told Raphael how old I am, so at least all the cards are on the table. In his inexplicable way, it's made no difference at all. We spent two happy years together, sometimes forgetting that we had ever been apart, until I was injured in the riot in the Old City.

21

When the ambulance finally took me on a second wild ride to the right hospital – Hadassah, where Sarah the English doctor works – the news wasn't good. My jaw was broken in three places and several of my teeth were knocked out of alignment. My facial nerves had frozen, leaving me with no feeling and a crooked smile, as if I'd had a stroke. The doctors said my frozen face could be temporary – or it could last for the rest of my life. *For the rest of my life!* I let that thought settle as I tried to absorb it.

Doctors stitched my wound and said they would wire my jaw shut when an operating theatre became available. They explained apologetically that we might have to wait twenty-four hours, but I didn't mind because it gave me time to adjust to the idea of six weeks of silence. It seemed unimaginable, forbidding. It's not just that I'm talkative and mediate everything through words; I also talk for a living. I was facing six weeks without work, a long, quiet time to brood about how this had happened to me and what would come next.

I bore no grudges for my injury. People like me who get between two warring sides can't blame the combatants for what happens when we are in the middle. But a permanent defect, like not being able to smile again, was something I wasn't prepared for. I didn't know how to prepare myself for it either.

Doctors wired my jaws shut so the top jaw could act as a splint for the bottom one. When Raphael came to the hospital, it was the first time I ever saw tears in his eyes. My face was bruised and had swollen to twice its size, and when I shook my head the many chins under my jaw wobbled, like those of my first-grade music teacher, whom I suddenly recalled. I felt like a lock-mouthed monster, ugly and repellent, but Raphael didn't care about any of that. He just wanted to hold my hand. After I left hospital, he stayed with me for those six long, silent weeks and never made it seem a burden, even though he was constantly trying to decipher the notes I was scribbling and to interpret for other people not used to my array of squeaks.

I became delightfully, satisfyingly thin, but to my dismay, I found that my psyche was as fragile as my shattered jaw. I was erratic, suddenly furious, or panicked, for no reason. I went from not sweating the small stuff to not being able to identify what small stuff was any more. I'd cry if someone cut in front of me in traffic or over-charged me at a parking station. A small stone hitting my car had me pulling over to the side of the road, sobbing. It was as if I'd lost the membrane that cushions you from the disappointments of everyday life. Throughout all this, Raphael was steadfast and optimistic. He loved me in sickness and in health. My spirits started to heal slowly, knitted back together like bone, by time and his love.

Looking back, I enjoy the fact that it was writing about Mia that played its part in bringing us back together. It has a wonderful symmetry. I sense that she knows what she's done, for she gives me her foxy smile, and I sometimes catch her looking very pleased with herself. If she could speak, I fancy that she would say, 'I had no choice! I had to step in. I couldn't wait for you two to do it by yourselves ...'

Raphael says that if it is fate that brought us back together, then it was organised by a higher power than a dog. He thinks divine intervention is more likely than a canine nudge, while I think it's a bit of both. God, as I remind him, moves in mysterious ways.

I feel that Raphael and Mia are my joy and my fate. I thought I had come here to be a journalist. I could not have predicted that in this burning land it wasn't suffering that was waiting for me, but love. There are days still when I don't believe it, or don't know what I've done to deserve it. But Raphael has taught me that when your prayers are answered you say thank you. This book is my thanks.

ACKNOWLEDGEMENTS

When you write a book while doing your day job, before a publisher comes along, it's hard to keep the faith. I would like to thank my friends all over the world who read the manuscript in its various versions:

Cheryl Bart, who read it in Sydney, more than once; Anyck Beraud, who took it with her on holiday to Paris; Gina Cass-Gottlieb, who took it with her on holiday to Chamonix; Meg Coker, who read it in Abu Dhabi; Margaret Evans, who read it in snowy Edmonton; Elisabeth Grinston, David Mane and Louise Sobel, who read it in Sydney; Lisa Goldman, who read it in Toronto; Jan and Tim McGirk, who read it in Jerusalem and then California; Ruth Macklin and Orley Makler, who read it in Sydney; Liat Silberman, who read it in New York; Wendy Robbins, who read it in London; Annette Young, who read it in Paris; and Delia Rickard, Vida Viliunas and Hannah Webb, who read it in Canberra and persuaded me to change the opening.

I couldn't write, as I couldn't live, without you.

I would also like to thank Fiona Henderson from HarperCollins, who is always there for me in the end.